★ **Blacks and the American Political System**

Blacks and the American Political System

Edited by

Huey L. Perry
and Wayne Parent

University Press of Florida

Gainesville / Tallahassee / Tampa / Boca Raton
Pensacola / Orlando / Miami / Jacksonville

An earlier version of chapter 8, by Michael Combs, was originally published as "The
Supreme Court and African Americans: Personnel and Policy Transformations,"
Howard University Law Journal 36, no. 2 (1993).

00 99 98 97 96 95   6   5   4   3   2   1

Library of Congress Cataloging-in-Publication Data

Blacks and the American political system / edited by Huey L. Perry and Wayne Parent.
   p.   cm.
   Includes bibliographical references (p.   ) and index.
   ISBN 0-8130-1372-0 (cloth : acid-free paper). — ISBN 0-8130-1373-9 (paper : acid-
free paper)
   1. Afro-Americans—Politics and government.   I. Perry, Huey. II. Parent, Wayne,
1955–   .
   E185.615.B5538   1995
   323.1'196073—dc20   95-5917

The University Press of Florida is the scholarly publishing agency for the State
University System of Florida, comprised of Florida A & M University, Florida Atlantic
University, Florida International University, Florida State University, University of
Central Florida, University of Florida, University of North Florida, University of South
Florida, and University of West Florida.

University Press of Florida
15 Northwest 15th Street
Gainesville, FL 32611

This book is dedicated to all our students and our families.

This book is dedicated to all our students and our families.

★ Contents

★ Tables

★ Foreword

Rufus Browning

The United States constitutes one of the world's great historical experiments, testing again and again whether a society in which a system of intensely racialized slavery that endured for two centuries can become a democracy in which the previously enslaved race enjoys social and political equality. As our experience with it attests, this is surely one of the most difficult of all political and social projects.

Africans could be and often were free—that is, not slaves—in the North, where slavery was abolished altogether after the Revolutionary War. Still, a system of intimidation, segregation, and discrimination in every area of life held back the great mass of African Americans in conditions of economic, social, and political subordination.

In the South, legalized bondage of African Americans was overthrown by the Emancipation Proclamation in 1863 and the victory of the North in the Civil War. The post–Civil War amendments to the Constitution placed the transformation from slave to citizen in the law of the land.

Legal slavery was abolished; control of the institutions of society by whites—convinced of their superiority and determined to maintain their power—was not. The passionate moral sympathy that led some whites to campaign for abolition and to work with African Americans in the cause of justice was not sufficient to undo the rigidly racialized structures and beliefs of American society. Yet another story was being written even as discrimination and segregation continued in the North and a caste system was institutionalized in the South to preserve white domination. An African American middle class emerged—not large but sufficiently skilled, stable, autonomous, self-conscious, and organized to lead a broad movement to break down the racial barriers of American society. This movement unfolded into an astonishing variety of political approaches and actions: litigation, legislation, lobbying, electoral mobilization, violent protest, and the great wave of nonviolent protest, led by Martin Luther King, Jr., that was the identifying strategy of the civil rights movement.

The essays in this volume bring into view the recent history and current status of these political efforts at the level of national government and politics. The authors examine political efforts by African Americans and by many groups working together to achieve policy goals espoused by black leaders. They show how these efforts have worked on the institutions, processes, and policies of American national government: the presidency, the executive branch, Congress, and the Supreme Court; elections, political attitudes, and participation; and voting rights, taxation, and spending. They document the issues engaged, the victories, and the defeats.

In addition to documenting the history and status of these efforts, the authors employ elements of the "pluralist" theory of politics to assess them. (See chapters 2 and 11 and chapter summaries throughout.) Pluralist theory was developed to analyze the distribution of power in political systems, in particular, to articulate a test of the claim that power is systematically unequal in communities and states that characterize themselves as "democratic" and to show how the fragmentation of political authority in political systems facilitates group access to at least some points of political power. Pluralist theory is a way of interpreting the democratic aspect of political systems. It does not consider every aspect of democracy, nor does it illuminate every aspect of social and political power. Nevertheless, it permits us to describe and assess real political systems from a democratic perspective.

We know that the resources that groups are able to draw on to influence government are unequally distributed. Some might take the existence of certain social and economic inequalities as conclusive, debate-ending evidence of political inequality, and therefore of the failure of democracy, for which political equality may be seen as a defining characteristic. Pluralist theory takes social and economic inequality as given—indeed, as inevitable—and asks, in effect, how large, diverse societies characterized by inequality might nevertheless realize a kind of democracy.

If it can be shown that resources for political power are systematically and cumulatively unequal and the structures of power are in the hands of one group and systematically closed to others, we are clearly not looking at a democracy. On the other hand, suppose one group in a political system is small, but wealthy; another, not wealthy, but large; a third, neither wealthy nor large, but able to connect its interests persuasively to values widely shared in the society. Here, resources—and potential political influence—are not equal between groups, but they are not systematically and cumulatively unequal, either. Such a society is closer to being democratic than a society in which resources of all kinds are in the hands of one group and other groups are excluded and dominated. Pluralism draws its name from the insight that a diverse society in which many groups have access to many possible points of power is significantly closer to democracy than a society with a sole point of power that one group is able to control.

The editors of this volume conclude that the American political system achieved a degree of pluralism with respect to African Americans in the 1960s. This is not a claim that social, economic, and political equality have been achieved; nor is it a claim that African Americans do not experience many kinds of debilitating discrimination. Nevertheless, many scholars have reached the opposite judgment, so this conclusion is bound to be controversial.

In addition, many observers of racial politics believe that intolerable racism and racial inequality persist in the United States. Obviously, we have not eliminated racism or racially based inequality, and anger over what has not been achieved hinders appreciation of what has been accomplished. The more urgent the need for change, the less relevant the gains of the past and the leadership of the present appear to be. The more determined we are to renew the mobilization of African Americans and their potential allies, the more we must emphasize the minimal nature of current progress for African Americans. If we do so we are likely to find it difficult to respect and acknowledge the effort, leadership, and commitment that it takes to sustain political pressure at the levels and across the broad range of institutions described in this volume. The pursuit of truth requires a balance, holding in mind simultaneously both the great achievements institutionalized in the politics of the present and the moral imperatives of justice that denounce the present. Political action in pursuit of justice requires its own balance, in which justice denied must loom larger than justice already gained.

The opening of the American political system to African Americans—forging a pluralist polity encompassing both blacks and whites—is a creation of historic proportions. The leadership and organized effort that now sustain this great achievement remain necessary and enormously valuable, as the contributions to this volume show. That we may want much more from government should not blind us to the value of existing institutions and leadership. One must hope that they are preserved and strengthened even as the search continues for new forms and strategies of the movement for equality.

★ Preface

This book provides an integrated examination of black politics and American politics at the national level of the political system. The focus of the book is to show the relationship between black politics and American national government and politics. The book examines the character, magnitude, and impact of black politics three decades after the height of the civil rights movement in the mid-1960s and answers several key questions about blacks and the American political process. Are blacks becoming an important part of the institutions of American national government and politics—the executive branch, Congress, the judicial branch, political parties, and the structure of interest groups? What are the current patterns of black political behavior, and do these current patterns differ from earlier post–civil rights patterns of black political activity? What are the implications of the changed relationship between blacks and the Supreme Court for blacks' relationship with Congress and presidents? What are the results of blacks' emphasis on political participation as the primary strategy for group enhancement? What is the impact of black participation in presidential politics? To what extent does pluralist theory, the leading theoretical perspective used in the study of American politics, explain national black politics in the United States?

This book examines black participation and its impact on the American political system at the national level of government and politics. Specifically, the book examines the participation of blacks in national governmental and political institutions and the impact of blacks on the outputs of these institutions. The findings are uneven: Blacks have actively participated in congressional and judicial policy-making and have significantly affected policy outputs of Congress and the Supreme Court. In contrast, blacks have participated less actively in executive policy-making and have had less impact on policy outputs in the executive branch of government. The book's principal contribution to the literature on African American politics is in providing a comprehensive analysis of black politics and its impact on national government and politics. In addition, the book offers findings in this regard to compare and contrast with findings on black politics and its impact on state and local government and politics. The primary audience for this book is upper-level undergraduate students, for which the book should serve well as a required text. The secondary audience for the book is lower-level graduate students, for which the book should serve well as a supplementary text. The book could be also used as supplementary reading for the following courses: seminar on American politics, black politics, civil rights, race and public policy, the presidency, Congress, and the Supreme Court.

This book has undergone a long gestation period. We began formulating plans for the book in the summer of 1984. We experienced the usual delays in producing an edited volume and the usual problems faced by first-time authors of a scholarly book.

We believe that the finished product justifies our persistence. We are grateful to all our contributors. They did all the revisions that we and the reviewers of the book suggested with little complaint. We are also grateful to the reviewers of the manuscript. Their helpful suggestions immeasurably improved the quality of the book. We are extremely grateful to Walda Metcalf, associate director and editor-in-chief of the University Press of Florida. Her professionalism and encouragement were instrumental in the book's completion. The senior editor thanks William E. Moore, vice chancellor for academic affairs, and Marvin L. Yates, chancellor at Southern University-Baton Rouge, for their outstanding support. The senior editor also expresses gratitude to three members of his support staff—Veronica L. Howard, Lorita N. Ford, and Elnora C. Anderson—for their invaluable assistance and to four graduate assistants whose research assistance contributed significantly: Tracey Ambeau, Frederick McBride, Gregory A. Anders, and Katherine

Penn. Ambeau and McBride are coauthors with the senior editor of the chapter on blacks and the executive branch (Chapter 6).

Finally, we thank our families for their support. Their encouragement, in words and actions, sustained us throughout the ten-year period that we worked on this book. While we worked long and hard to produce a worthwhile book, a few aspects probably could benefit from some additional work. However, every published scholarly work reaches a point of closure, and we believe we chose the proper one. We, of course, accept full responsibility for any of the book's shortcomings.

■ *Part I*

Introduction

★ *Chapter 1*

Black Politics in the United States

Huey L. Perry and Wayne Parent

In the span of one generation black politics in the United States has advanced from a primary consideration of acquiring the right to vote for southern blacks to blacks' gaining significant representation in the major institutions of American political life. This transformation of black politics is best characterized as moving from a protest movement primarily outside normal American political channels to established political behavior inside the political system as the predominant mode of political participation. This book analyzes this transformation of African American politics and the challenges it poses for the future of black political life at the national level of the U.S. government. Further, this book argues that this transformation of black politics is fully consistent with pluralist theory, which posits that the American political system is an open, competitive political system and that many different groups can influence the decision-making process of that system.

This book examines in depth black political participation in the federal government of the United States. Most important, it offers an examination of the nexus between black politics and American politics, providing an integrated analysis of both. This chapter describes the development of black political participation in the United States in the twentieth century.

Black Political Participation in the Twentieth Century

Between 1910 and the end of World War II in 1945, black political activity in most of the South was virtually nonexistent. The first four-and-a-half decades of the twentieth century were characterized by quiet legal efforts by southern blacks and their supporters to overcome the obstacles to their participation in the political process instituted by adoption of the new state constitutions by most of the southern states between 1890 and 1910.[1] During this time, no component of the American political system attempted to ameliorate the forced exclusion of southern blacks from the electoral process, except the U.S. Supreme Court; and even Supreme Court rulings favorable to blacks were few and far between during this period. The first Supreme Court ruling favorable to blacks during this period was provided in *Guinn v. United States* in 1915, in which the Supreme Court prohibited the grandfather clause.[2] Because all southern states using the grandfather clause had other devices to prevent blacks from voting, the Court's ruling did little to reenfranchise black voters in the South. Moreover, the purpose of the grandfather clause was less to prevent blacks from voting than to provide a mechanism that would allow southern whites blocked by one or more of the other devices an opportunity to vote. The next Supreme Court ruling favorable to blacks did not come until almost thirty years later, in 1944, when the Court ruled in *Smith v. Allwright* that the white primary was unconstitutional.[3] The Court's ruling in *Smith* outlawing the white primary resulted in a significant increase in the small number of registered black voters in the South.

After *Smith*, the victories came more frequently. Although not directly concerned with political rights for southern blacks, *Brown v. Board of Education of Topeka* in 1954 was a monumental victory for blacks.[4] *Brown* demonstrated to southern blacks that racist legal practices in the South could be successfully challenged. The Supreme Court's decision in *Smith* and especially *Brown* combined with pressure from a growing black civil rights movement created a national environment that prompted the two remaining political branches of the government— Congress and the president—to take action to remove the remaining obstacles to black political participation. Although the 1957 and 1960 Civil Rights Acts, which sought to restore voting rights to southern blacks, were largely symbolic actions, they were important precisely for their symbolism. Congress and the president by their support of these measures signaled to blacks for the first time in the postwar period that they supported the efforts of southern blacks to achieve voting rights.

The principal weakness of the 1957 Civil Rights Act regarding the interests of southern blacks to regain the franchise is that the act allowed suits challenging racial discrimination in matters regarding the right to vote to be filed on a case-by-case basis only. Thus every black individual in the South who felt that he or she had been unfairly denied that right had to file an individual lawsuit contesting such action under the 1957 act. The problems with this arrangement soon became fairly obvious: most blacks denied the opportunity to vote did not have financial resources to pay for a lawsuit. A related problem was the time-consuming nature of this approach. Even if most blacks had the financial wherewithal to pay for a lawsuit, the case-by-case basis required an inordinately long time to pass before appreciable numbers of blacks would be registered to vote.

The 1960 Civil Rights Act sought to address this problem by empowering the U.S. attorney general to file suit on behalf of blacks deemed to have been unfairly denied the right to vote. While this provision represented an improvement over the 1957 act, the fact that lawsuits still had to be filed case by case meant that black voter registration under the 1960 legislation still was awkward and time-consuming. Because of the procedural deficiencies in both measures, very few southern blacks were registered to vote under the 1957 and 1960 Civil Rights Acts.

The watershed period in federal advancement of voting rights in the South was 1964–65. The 1964 Civil Rights Act was a pathbreaking piece of legislation that accorded blacks a substantial measure of rights to public accommodations, higher education, public and private employment, and voting. With respect to the last of these, the act furthered black voting in the South by prohibiting the use of literacy tests to determine qualification and by establishing a sixth-grade education as a proof of literacy. Also in 1964, the states ratified the Twenty-fourth Amendment, which prohibited the use of poll taxes in federal elections.

The most significant action by the federal government in advancing the political rights of southern blacks was the 1965 Voting Rights Act. The act ameliorated all the procedural deficiencies of the 1957 and 1960 laws regarding black voting by authorizing federal marshals to summarily register blacks in states and counties in the South in which less than 50 percent of the voting age population was registered to vote in the presidential election of 1964. The 1965 Voting Rights Act had a dramatic impact on increasing black voter registration in the South: approximately four million new black voters were registered there between 1965 and 1975.

Contemporary Black Political Progress and Problems

While black political participation in the South has increased over the last three decades, it has also increased in the country in general. Increased black political participation has included a substantial rise in the number of black elected and appointed officials. Important examples of this include the 1992 election of the nation's first black female U.S. senator, Carol Moseley Braun (D-Ill.) and the tenure of former U.S. Representative William Gray (D-Pa.). During his last two years of service to Congress, Gray went from being chairman of the Budget Committee to chairman of the House Democratic Caucus to majority whip. Gray was the first black to serve in all three positions. Another significant example is Ronald Brown, the first black to serve as chairman of the Democratic National Committee. He oversaw the extraordinarily successful 1992 Democratic National Convention in New York City and is credited with bringing the party together to engineer Bill Clinton's presidential election in 1992—only the second Democratic presidential victory in twenty-four years.

The seniority system, which plays an important role in leadership selection and which worked against advancing black political interests in the 1960s and 1970s, has begun to benefit blacks, as blacks in Congress have been reelected to office several times from safe seats. Blacks are also beneficiaries of a willingness among white elected officials to appoint blacks to policy-making positions. While black appointments may be closely associated with the degree to which an elected official sees blacks as part of his or her constituency, some blacks are being appointed even by officials who do not see their reelection chances tied to black support. The black appointees of Presidents Ronald Reagan and George Bush are important examples in this regard.

Even though black political progress in the past three decades has been dramatic and some blacks are firmly entrenched in positions of power, black political participation still faces problems. For example, blacks are still elected primarily in majority black districts and jurisdictions. They continue to win few elections in majority white districts and jurisdictions. Although that has been the historical pattern, the 1989, 1990, and 1992 elections suggest some softening in this trend. Of the seven major successful black mayoral candidates in the 1989 elections, four were elected in majority white jurisdictions: David Dinkins in New York City, Norman Rice in Seattle, Washington, Chester Jenkins in Durham, North Carolina, and John Daniels in New Haven, Connecticut. Moreover, Douglas Wilder was elected governor of Virginia, becoming the first black governor since Reconstruction.[5]

Until blacks are better accepted by whites as legitimate candidates for public office, deserving of their support when such support is appropriate, and begin to win significantly more races in majority white districts and jurisdictions, blacks will not become fully integrated into the American political system. One scholar believes that black and American politics will become more integrated in the future in terms of congressional elections. Carol Swain predicts an increase in the number of white members of Congress with sizable numbers of blacks in their districts and more black members of Congress elected from majority white districts.[6]

Another problem confronting black participation in presidential politics, before Bill Clinton's election in 1992, was an increasing marginalization of black influence in presidential elections. In this sphere of politics, it seems incongruous that the increased black political participation since the mid-1960s would be associated with waning black influence in presidential politics. Yet that is precisely what has occurred. A small black electorate was much more influential in presidential elections before 1980 than it has been since then. The black vote was critical to the election of Harry Truman in 1948, John Kennedy in 1960, Jimmy Carter in 1976, and Bill Clinton in 1992. In the face of the Republican party's domination of presidential elections since 1980, the black vote had become increasingly marginalized in presidential elections until Clinton's election in 1992. Katherine Tate's analysis of the strategy and impact of Jesse Jackson's 1984 and 1988 presidential campaigns describes and analyzes the efforts of blacks to reverse their increasing marginalization in presidential politics.[7]

The black vote was critical to Bill Clinton's election in 1992. Approximately one million more blacks voted in 1992 than in 1988, and Clinton received 82 percent of the black vote. The critical electoral support that Clinton received from black voters resulted in unprecedented black cabinet appointments in the Clinton administration, in terms of both the number of black appointments and the substantive nature of the appointments. President Clinton appointed more blacks to his cabinet than any other president in the nation's history. Moreover, he appointed blacks to cabinet positions that no African American had previously held: leadership of the departments of Commerce, Energy, Agriculture, and the Veterans Administration, the first three of which superintend major components of the American economy.

Therefore, the 1992 election of Bill Clinton and its results at least temporarily reversed the marginalization of blacks in presidential politics. This book was completed at the onset of the Clinton administration. The restoration of Democrats and blacks to a position of influence and power in presidential elections may be more telling about the cyclical nature of national political life in the United States than any other aspect of American national politics. At a minimum, it provides an exciting backdrop for the analyses presented here.

The Plan of the Book

Part I consists of this introductory chapter and Chapter 2. In the second chapter, Huey L. Perry provides a theoretical analysis of black politics, examining pluralist theory in terms of its ability to explain black political life in the United States in the twentieth century. This is the lead theoretical chapter—all the others discuss their findings and conclusions in relationship to pluralist theory, indicating the extent to which the pluralist perspective explains or fails to explain their findings and conclusions.

Part II focuses on identifying patterns of black political behavior and participation. In Chapter 3, Wayne Parent and Paul Stekler analyze change and continuity in black political behavior. In Chapter 4, Mfanya D. Tryman examines Jesse Jackson's historic 1984 and 1988 campaigns for the presidential nomination of the Democratic party.

Part III explores black political participation with respect to national political and governmental institutions and how those institutions have affected black political interests. In Chapter 5, Henry Sirgo discusses the interaction between black politics and presidential behavior from Franklin D. Roosevelt to Bill Clinton. In Chapter 6, Huey L. Perry,

Tracey Ambeau, and Frederick McBride examine black participation and influence in the federal executive branch from the administration of Franklin D. Roosevelt through that of Bill Clinton. In Chapter 7, Richard Champagne and Leroy Rieselbach focus on the role of the Congressional Black Caucus in the legislative process and how congressional outputs affect blacks. Michael Combs, in Chapter 8, details the general and historical relationship between blacks and the Supreme Court in the areas of education, voting rights, employment, and housing. Combs concentrates on the impact of Supreme Court decisions on black interests and on Justice Thurgood Marshall's influence on Court rulings.

Part IV examines black efforts to influence the formulation and implementation of selected national public policies and how those public policies have affected black political interests. Dianne Pinderhughes, in Chapter 9, provides an in-depth examination of how the interest articulation activities of civil rights organizations affected the passage of the 1982 Extension of the 1965 Voting Rights Act and how the activities of these organizations, in turn, were affected by the legislation. Lenneal Henderson, Jr., in Chapter 10, analyzes the role blacks played in the formulation of recent major national fiscal policies and the impact of these policies on black interests.

Part V consists of Chapter 11, the concluding chapter. In it Huey L. Perry and Wayne Parent assess the patterns and subpatterns of black political behavior culled from the previous chapters. Perry and Parent also summarize the ability of pluralist theory to explain black political life in the United States in the twentieth century from the perspective of the findings and conclusions presented in chapters 3 through 10. Perry and Parent also suggest some future implications of the present course of national black political activity in the United States as well as some directions for future research on national black politics.

Notes

1. See, for example, J. Morgan Kousser, *The Shaping of Southern Politics: Suffrage Restriction and the Establishment of the One-Party South, 1880–1910* (New Haven: Yale University Press, 1974); V. O. Key, Jr., *Southern Politics in State and Nation, A New Edition* (Knoxville: University of Tennessee Press, 1984); Donald Matthews and James C. Prothro, *Negroes and the New Southern Politics* (New York: Harcourt, Brace and World, 1966); and Steven F. Lawson,

Black Ballots: Voting Rights in the South, 1944–1969 (New York: Columbia University Press, 1976).

2. 238 U.S. 347, 360 (1915). The grandfather clause was a device used by southern states to exempt whites from state poll taxes and literacy laws intended to disenfranchise black voters. It allowed the right to vote to persons who could prove that their grandfather had voted before 1867. This would be impossible for most blacks, since few black people had been granted citizenship before 1867.

3. 321 U.S. 649, 660–61 (1944).

4. 347 U.S. 483 (1954).

5. For a brief analysis of their campaigns and electoral victories, see Huey L. Perry, "Black Electoral Victories in 1989," Symposium, *PS: Political Science and Politics* 23 (June 1990): 141–162. For a fuller analysis, see Huey L. Perry, "Exploring the Meaning and Implications of Deracialization in African American Urban Politics," Minisymposium, *Urban Affairs Quarterly* 27 (December 1991): 181–215.

6. Carol M. Swain, *Black Faces, Black Interests: The Representation of African Americans in Congress* (Cambridge: Harvard University Press, 1993).

7. Katherine Tate, *From Protest to Politics: The New Black Voters in American Elections* (Cambridge: Harvard University Press, 1993).

■ *Chapter 2*

A Theoretical Analysis of National Black Politics in the United States

Huey L. Perry

Although pluralist theory is the leading theoretical perspective employed in the study of American politics,[1] only a few scholarly analyses have examined its capacity to explain black politics in the United States. Most of the few analyses done have found the pluralist perspective unsatisfactory in accounting for the political experiences of blacks.[2] In a theoretical analysis of the social and economic underpinnings of black political life, Marcus Pohlmann, for example, asserts that "the entire concept of black politics is alien to the [pluralist] approach."[3] Dianne Pinderhughes's comparative study of the political experiences of blacks, Italians, and Irish in twentieth-century Chicago also finds the pluralist model unsatisfactory for explaining blacks' political experiences.[4] Similarly, Minion K. C. Morrison asserts that "pluralism is . . . probably the least practical [social science theoretical model] in accounting for the status of blacks in the [political] system."[5]

This chapter examines pluralist theory's explanatory power relative to national black political life in the United States in the twentieth century. A few studies have examined the relevance of pluralist theory for explaining black politics at the state and local levels,[6] and others have examined the relevance of pluralist theory for explaining black politics at the national level.[7] This chapter builds on the latter studies and, in doing so, contributes to establishing a much needed theoretical framework for studying black politics. This chapter enunciates several propositions that constitute the pluralist perspective and analyzes the principal dynamics of twentieth-century national black politics within the context of those propositions.

Major Propositions of Pluralist Theory

Pluralist theory posits that the American political process is driven by competing and conflicting interest groups that attempt to influence the governmental decision-making process so as to advance their interests. These various groups and governmental decision-makers constitute multiple centers of power, and no single center of power is sovereign. Under the pluralist formulation, government decisions and policies are the results of the collective efforts of various interest groups conveying their wants to governmental officials and pressing their claims for favorable action, and the preferences of governmental decision-makers, which may in varying degrees be influenced by interest group activity. This section identifies five major propositions of the pluralist perspective and briefly discusses each in the context of the pluralist literature.

The first proposition posits that although interest groups differ in the amount of resources they use to influence the governmental decision-making process, these differences are dispersed rather than cumulative. For example, one group may have an abundance of resource A but little of resources B and C. Another group may have a huge amount of resource B, a small amount of resource C, but none of resource A. Yet another group may have a substantial amount of resource C and none of resources A and B. If A, B, and C represent the universe of significant political resources, no single group possesses an abundance of all three resources. Rather, the resources are noncumulative or dispersed among the three groups.

The American political system, as Robert Dahl observes, has many different kinds of political resources—"knowledge, information, skill, access to organization, income, wealth, and status, among others"— and they "are unequally distributed among citizens."[8] Therefore, a group that is better off with regard to one resource is not better off than other groups with respect to all or most resources. Two related consequences follow from this noncumulative pattern of political resource allocation. First, many groups have the opportunity to favorably influence the governmental decision-making process; second, it is extremely difficult for any single group to develop ascendant influence on the decision-making process. Thus noncumulative inequalities of political resources help to maintain democracy and constitute the first pluralist proposition, formally stated as follows:

Proposition One (P₁): Political resources among groups are unequal but noncumulative.

The second proposition of pluralist theory, closely related to the first, suggests that the governmental decision-making process is characterized by multiple centers of power, none of which is sovereign. The principal characteristic of Proposition Two is its segmentation of the decision-making process into various policy sectors or issue areas in which various combinations of interest groups and governmental officials exert key influence in making decisions. Competition among the various interest sectors precludes any single sector from becoming ascendant, thereby also helping to maintain democracy. The formal statement of Proposition Two is:

Proposition Two (P₂): The decision-making process is characterized by multiple centers of power without any single center of power being sovereign.

The third pluralist proposition focuses on the constitutional division of the American governmental system and the role that this division plays in promoting interest group access to the decision-making process. Two fundamental constitutional principles underpinning the organization of the American governmental system—federalism and separation of powers—divide the structure of the American governmental system into three levels and each level into three branches respectively. A third fundamental constitutional principle underpinning the structural organization of American government—checks and balances—institutes several ways in which each of the divisions in the American governmental system can influence and, in some cases, thwart the actions of the other divisions in the system. The collective effect of these features is to create several access points where groups can pursue their policy goals. An initial failure need not be the final disposition of a group's efforts to achieve a political goal. Therefore, for example, a group that fails to realize its objective in the executive and legislative branches may successfully press its claim in the courts. Or a group that fails to find relief from a problem at the state and local levels may be able to successfully prosecute its grievance at the national level. Like the first and second propositions, the third proposition also helps to promote democracy. The third proposition is formally stated as follows:

> *Proposition Three* (P₃): The structure of the governmental system provides multiple opportunities for groups to achieve their goals.

The fourth proposition, a logical derivative of the three previous propositions, suggests that public policy formulation is characterized by a process of bargaining and negotiation. Because so many groups and governmental officials attempt to influence the decision-making process and no single group or official enjoys ascendant power and because the principle of checks and balances allows the various structural divisions of government to influence and sometimes block each other's actions, competing groups and governmental officials must engage in negotiation and bargaining in order to produce public policies. The formal statement of Proposition Four is:

> *Proposition Four* (P₄): Public policy formulation is characterized by bargaining and negotiation among interest groups and governmental officials.

The fifth and final pluralist proposition focuses on the outcome of the policy formulation process in relation to the problem being addressed and to previous policy responses to that problem. Logically derived from the fourth proposition, Proposition Five suggests that, given the bargaining and negotiation among interest groups and governmental officials that characterize policy formulation, resultant public policies are usually incremental rather than comprehensive. This means that a particular policy alone does not completely resolve a particular problem; rather, it reflects a minor or moderate adjustment to or improvement on the prior policy solution to the problem. Thus "government policies are an accretion of . . . incremental changes."⁹ The fifth proposition is formally stated as follows:

> *Proposition Five* (P₅): Public policies are usually incremental rather than comprehensive responses to problems.

It is significant that all five propositions are interrelated. The interconnection among the five propositions indicates the presence of a theoretical core in the pluralist perspective. At best, the interconnection indicates that pluralist theory has qualities or properties of theory. At a minimum, the interconnection indicates that pluralist theory is not simply a set of wishful assumptions about how a democratic political system should function. The derivation of these propositions and the discovery of the interconnection among them enhance pluralist theory as a theoretical construct. The above five propositions guide the examination of the extent to which pluralist theory illuminates national black politics in the United States in the twentieth century.

National Black Politics in the Twentieth Century

National black political development in the United States in the twentieth century can be divided into three significant chronological periods. During the first period, 1910–55, black political leaders used federal judicial activism to enlist the aid of the Supreme Court in support of their struggle to restore political and civil rights for blacks in the South. Toward the latter part of this period, blacks attempted to persuade presidents to act in their behalf. The second period, 1955–65, witnessed efforts by southern blacks to achieve political and civil rights during the era of the civil rights movement. The third period, since 1965, saw blacks, after having their voting population expanded by the extension of voting rights to southern blacks during the prior period, rely heavily on electoral politics and bargaining and negotiation to extract favorable policies from the executive and legislative branches of the national government.

Because state and local governments in the South were centrally involved in the de jure oppression of blacks in practically all manifestations of public and private life during the early part of the century and beyond, the only theoretical option blacks had in their effort to enlist governmental support to change the situation in the South was to seek help from the national government. However, during much of the first period, this option also had its limitations, as Congress and presidents demonstrated their unwillingness to support blacks' goals. The unwillingness of Congress and presidents to help meant that blacks' efforts to seek assistance from the national government equaled reliance on litigation in the federal courts as the only practical recourse for pursuing their goals until 1955.

Blacks' Judicial Activism, 1910 to 1955

Between 1880 and 1910, the states of the former Confederacy adopted new constitutions that had the effect of disfranchising the majority of blacks in the South. Procedurally, this was accomplished by incorporating certain devices in their constitutions that restricted the right to vote, including a grandfather clause, a white primary, a poll tax, literacy tests, and character tests.[10] These restrictions were designed to appear racially neutral so as not to openly violate the Fifteenth Amendment.

The early strategy that black leaders developed in their effort to win back the right to vote consisted of testing the constitutionality of these new devices in federal courts. Their first victory came relatively early. In 1915, the Supreme Court ruled in *Guinn v. United States* that the grandfather clause was unconstitutional because it violated the Fifteenth Amendment.[11] However, the Court's ruling was largely a symbolic victory for blacks because the other devices remained in place. The purpose of the grandfather clause had not been to disfranchise blacks per se, but rather to provide a mechanism for exempting poor whites from the other voting impediments directed at blacks.

Almost thirty years passed before blacks received a truly significant victory as a result of litigation in the federal courts: in 1944 the Supreme Court invalidated the white primary in *Smith v. Allwright* on the grounds that it violated the Fifteenth Amendment.[12] *Smith* resulted in a significant increase in black voter registration in the South. The driving force behind this victory, as it had been in *Guinn*, was the National Association for the Advancement of Colored People (NAACP). The NAACP, assisted by some other black organizations, provided the critical leadership by developing the legal strategy employed in the two cases and raising the large sums of money necessary to participate in litigation for these two cases up to the Supreme Court. Regarding the NAACP's role and that of other black organizations in the *Smith* case, Steven Lawson observes: "Mainly through the pressure of the NAACP and independent black organizations, the Supreme Court gradually had formed opinions that eradicated the legal foundation of the white primary."[13]

As significant as blacks' victory was in *Smith*, it paled in comparison to the triumph for blacks ten years later, in 1954, when the Supreme Court ruled in *Brown v. Board of Education*.[14] By ruling unconstitutional de jure racial segregation in public schools on the grounds that it violated the equal protection guarantee of the Fourteenth Amendment, the Court in *Brown*, in effect, dismantled the entire legal foundation of racial segregation in the South. In *Brown*, as it did in *Guinn* and *Smith*, the NAACP provided the critical leadership.[15]

Although litigation in the federal courts dominated blacks' pursuit of political and civil rights in the South between 1910 and 1955, blacks during the 1940s tried to persuade Presidents Franklin Roosevelt and Harry Truman to act in their behalf. Two of these efforts were particularly successful. The first success came in response to pressure by black leaders at the beginning of World War II that Roosevelt facilitate black employment in the war industries. Although the modest-size black vote was a relatively important component of Roosevelt's New Deal coalition, Roosevelt's reluctant decision to create by executive order the Committee on Fair Employment Practices (FEPC) was arrived at more as a means of preventing a threatened march on Washington by blacks rather than as a result of a fear of black electoral punishment.[16]

The principal strategist of the threatened march on Washington was A. Phillip Randolph, president of the Brotherhood of Sleeping Car Porters, the first black labor union in the United States. The success of the strategy was largely attributable to the strong support it received from all major black organizations. The FEPC's goal was to provide equal employment opportunities for blacks in companies that received contracts from the federal government to manufacture products for the war. The FEPC's guidelines were weakly enforced, so its creation turned out to be more a symbolic than a substantive victory for blacks.[17]

The other favorable action that blacks extracted from a president in the 1940s was President Harry Truman's desegregation of the nation's armed forces by executive order in 1948.[18] This decision was also influenced by a threatened protest action by Randolph. This time Randolph threatened to encourage black youths to resist the draft. The major black organizations were centrally involved in the effort to persuade Truman to undertake this action. Truman's decision to desegregate the armed forces, made three months before the presidential election of 1948, reflected his strong interest in improving his electoral prospects.[19] This turned out to have been a shrewd political move as black voters contributed to Truman's narrow margin of victory in an election that many political analysts expected him to lose.

The above discussion supports only one of the five pluralist propositions identified in the previous section. The discussion illustrates the usefulness of the multiple access points proposition (P_3) to blacks' relationship with the governmental system during this period. All access points in the structure of the American governmental system, except that of the federal courts, were closed to blacks for most of this period. Blacks were able to obtain some relief from government-sponsored voting discrimination in the South only from the Supreme Court. Only toward the end of the period were blacks able to extract some support from presidents for other issues on their policy agenda. These accomplishments of blacks are consistent with Samuel Huntington's assessment of the democracy-enhancing aspects of the multiple access feature of American government in the eighteenth and nineteenth centuries:

> The multiplicity of institutions furnished multiple means of access to political power. Those groups unable to influence the national government might be able to dominate state or local governments. Those who could not elect chief executives might still control legislatures or at least legislative committees. Those who were forever weak numerically might find support in judicial bodies anxious to assert their power and to locate a constituency. With rare exceptions most of the significant social and economic groups in American society in the eighteenth and nineteenth centuries could find some way of participating in government and of compounding their influence with governmental authority.[20]

That the above discussion supports only one of the five pluralist propositions indicates that the perspective does not appreciably explain national black politics during this period. It is not surprising that the pluralist perspective would not apply to national black politics during this period. A majority of the black population lived in the South between 1910 and 1955, and during this period southern blacks were virtually excluded from voting. The only basis of traditional political influence that blacks had at their disposal was the relatively small northern black vote. And while the northern black vote occasionally made a difference in presidential elections, as it did in 1948, it did not exert pivotal influence in presidential elections consistently enough and in a large enough number of congressional elections to amass significant and enduring traditional political influence at the national level. Blacks' use of mass protest threats probably contributed as much as, if not more than, their voting toward the creation of the FEPC and the desegregation of the military.

Black Protest and the Civil Rights Years, 1955 to 1965

By the end of the 1950s, with the civil rights movement gearing up and presidents and the Supreme Court having demonstrated the capacity to act in behalf of blacks, Congress entered the civil rights domain in support of blacks. Congress passed the Civil Rights Act of 1957 to provide a measure of civil and political rights to southern blacks. The 1957 legislation turned out to be a largely symbolic act; few blacks were registered under its auspices.[21] The legislation had two principal flaws: the requirement that the attorney general sue for injunction against each county or parish where blacks felt they had been unfairly denied the right to vote and the requirement that the suit contesting the denial be heard by a jury trial.[22] These two requirements made implementation of the act awkward, time-consuming, and expensive. The jury trial requirement was incorporated in the legislation as a result of an amendment in order to appease southern legislators who were opposed to a strong bill.[23] The incorporation of the jury trial provision in the legislation was an effective strategy because at this time in the South's history all-white juries did not convict white officials accused of interfering with blacks' right to vote.

The Civil Rights Act of 1957 was enacted largely because of the intense lobbying efforts by leaders of black and white organizations to persuade President Dwight Eisenhower and Congress to protect blacks' right to vote in the South. The NAACP, the Southern Christian Leadership Conference (SCLC), the Leadership Conference on Civil Rights (LCCR), the Brotherhood of Sleeping Car Porters, other labor organizations, and the American Civil Liberties Union (ACLU) lobbied for the legislation.[24] These organizations and a few others collectively came to be known as the civil rights coalition.

By 1959 it had become clear that the 1957 Civil Rights Act would not guarantee most blacks the right to vote in the South, and civil rights leaders began to push for strengthening legislation. President Eisenhower and Congress responded by enacting the Civil Rights Act of 1960. The 1960 act provided a marginal improvement over the 1957 legislation in its requirement that federal judges appoint referees to supervise the qualifying of blacks for voting registration in those instances where the attorney general could show a pattern of discrimination against blacks. The 1960 act was almost identical to the 1957 act in terms of impact on the problem. It was a largely symbolic act that registered few black voters.[25] Just as it had done with the 1957 legislation, the civil rights coalition actively participated in the bargaining and negotiation that produced the 1960 legislation.

As the ineffectiveness of the 1960 legislation became manifest, civil rights organizations called for additional legislation that would effectively address the problem of continued voting discrimination against blacks in the South. By this time, two new black organizations—the Student Nonviolent Coordinating Committee (SNCC) and the Congress of Racial Equality (CORE)—had emerged as significant actors in the civil rights movement. In 1963 and 1964, the SNCC, CORE, and the SCLC organized massive peaceful protests in the South that brought black protesters into direct confrontation with white public officials who sought to prevent racial change. The object of these demonstrations was to elicit violent responses from public officials and, in the process, publicly dramatize just how far white officials in the South were prepared to go to deny blacks political and civil rights. The ongoing lobbying efforts by representatives of the civil rights coalition combined with the massive protest activities by blacks created a national political environment conducive to ameliorative national legislation. Massive protest activities by blacks in Birmingham, Alabama, in 1963 and Selma, Alabama, in 1964 strongly influenced the passage of the two most significant pieces of civil rights legislation since Reconstruction—the Civil Rights Act of 1964 and the Voting Rights Act of 1965. By the enactment of these two measures, both President Lyndon Johnson and Congress acted boldly on behalf of advancing blacks' rights.

The principal significance of the 1964 legislation lies in the substantive benefits that it provided blacks in the areas of public accommodations, employment, and education. The legislation also incrementally ameliorated blacks' difficulty in voting in the South. It "made a sixth-grade education a presumption of literacy if the question were raised in court, permitted the attorney general to litigate franchise suits before a judicial troika, and prevented registrars from denying the right to vote because of slight errors or omissions by applicants on their registration papers."[26]

Ratification of the Twenty-Fourth Amendment, also in 1964, prohibiting the use of poll taxes in federal elections, also assisted in this effort.

After six governmental actions in fifty years—the *Guinn* and *Smith* Supreme Court rulings in 1915 and 1944, respectively; the 1957, 1960, and 1964 Civil Rights Acts; and the Twenty-Fourth Amendment in 1964—the 1965 Voting Rights Act finally effectively addressed the problem of denying southern blacks the right to vote. The act suspended literacy tests and similar devices in all states or counties and parishes in which less than 50 percent of the voting age population was registered to vote on November 1, 1964; provided for the appointment of federal examiners to register persons in those areas to vote; and authorized the attorney general to file suit in federal court challenging the enforcement of poll taxes as a prerequisite for voting in state and local elections.[27] These provisions and the attorney general's successful suit against poll taxes in state and local elections eliminated all remaining legal impediments to black voting in the South instituted by the new state constitutions between 1880 and 1910.[28] The 1965 Voting Rights Act in effect instituted federal protection of the southern blacks' right to vote and thus increased black voter registration in the South in the late 1960s and early 1970s.

The above discussion strongly supports all five pluralist propositions. This discussion, as did the discussion in the previous section, supports the applicability to black politics of the pluralist proposition regarding the democracy-enhancing aspects of the multiple access feature of American government (P_3). During the civil rights years, while state and local governments in the South continued to be centrally involved in perpetuating legal voting discrimination against blacks, black leaders were able to turn to the national government for a redress of grievances.

The discussion also supports the other pluralist propositions. With regard to the first proposition, support is provided in terms of the differential yet noncumulative nature of resource distribution among the groups comprising the civil rights coalition as well as that among the competing interests arrayed on opposite sides of civil rights issues. The groups constituting the civil rights coalition differed in the kind and magnitude of political resources they employed in the effort to influence governmental decision-makers. The NAACP relied heavily on its influence on the black vote, capacity to raise money, access to nonsouthern public officials, and organization skills; the SCLC, CORE, and the SNCC on protest activities; and labor on its financial resources and access to public officials. Collectively, the most important resources black organizations had during this period were the vote and protest resources.

The organizations in opposition to civil rights measures generally relied on political resources other than those used in their lobbying effort. The principal resources these organizations used were generally ones that the black organizations did not possess in abundance, for example, financial resources, access to public officials, and direct support by southern public officials. The leading interest group opposed to the civil rights movement, basically white southern conservatives, had as their principal political resource direct support by public officials, which was limited in Congress but quite substantial in southern state and local governments. No group or contending interests dominated all political resources that were relevant for influencing public policy in the civil rights domain. Therefore, the various groups involved in the effort to influence government policy in the civil rights domain were characterized by dispersed inequalities in political resources.

The discussion also provides strong and direct support for the second proposition. No single group that attempted to influence decision-making in the civil rights domain enjoyed ascendant power. Black organizations, for example, would not have enjoyed the success they did in achieving some of their policy objectives had it not been for the support their cause received from other organizations in the civil rights coalition. Similarly, southern conservative legislators who largely got their way in the 1957 and 1960 Civil Rights Acts lost out in the 1964 Civil Rights Act and the 1965 Voting Rights Act.

The discussion also supports the fourth proposition. The 1957, 1960, and 1964 Civil Rights Acts and the 1965 Voting Rights Act were also shaped by compromises among the various actors who sought to influence those policies. While the conservative forces exerted greater influence on the two earlier pieces of legislation and the liberal forces exerted greater influence on the two later pieces of legislation, all the statutes were shaped by a negotiation among the contending groups and governmental officials.

The discussion also provides very strong and direct support for the fifth and final pluralist proposition. Including the Supreme Court rulings, six acts of government over a fifty-year period were required before the problem of denying the majority of blacks in the South the right to vote was resolved. The incremental model is applicable here because each of the governmental actions chipped away at the problem until it was gradually resolved. The four pieces of legislation between 1957 and 1965 constitute a classic pattern of incrementalism. Each piece of legislation after the 1957 act built on the previous legislation.

Black Political Incorporation and National Politics

Blacks have been reasonably successful in their efforts to influence the actions of the federal government since 1965, particularly in civil rights policies. This should not be surprising since in the decade before the passage of the 1965 Voting Rights Act, blacks were both more active and more successful at influencing civil rights than they were in any other policy field. By the time the 1965 Voting Rights Act was passed, black organizational leaders had developed a pattern of access to and interaction with the relevant congressional committees and executive departments and offices responsible for policy formulation and implementation in the civil rights domain. With that kind of access to critical policy actors already in place, blacks after 1965 increased their political leverage and thus their influence on the civil rights policy process. As a result, black organizations have favorably influenced the passage of several pieces of civil rights legislation since 1965, including the 1968 Civil Rights Act, and the 1970, 1975, and 1983 extensions of the 1965 Voting Rights Act.

The 1970 and 1983 extensions of the 1965 legislation were enacted during two conservative Republican administrations. The enactment of the 1983 extension is especially representative of the high level of black influence in civil rights. The 1980 Supreme Court ruling in *Mobile v. Bolden* was a major setback in terms of eliminating voting rights discrimination against blacks.[29] Because the original 1965 voting rights legislation was not specific as to whether the intents test or the effects test would be the standard to be satisfied in voting discrimination cases, the Court ruled that until Congress declared otherwise, the intents test rather than the traditionally used effects test would be standard of proof for voting discrimination. The intents test standard requires proof that whites intended to discriminate against blacks when they chose a particular electoral decision rule. The effects test standard simply requires a statistical demonstration of a pattern of racial discrimination. Black organizational leaders successfully lobbied Congress to require the effects test standard in the 1982 legislation. In addition, the 1982 legislation extended federal protection of voting rights for blacks and other minorities for twenty-five years, more than three times longer than the previous, seven-year extension Congress provided in 1975. Although President Ronald Reagan was philosophically opposed to the 1982 legislation, he signed it into law.

President Reagan's approval of the 1982 legislation is an additional indication of the success that blacks enjoy in civil rights policies. The principal demand that blacks have made in civil rights—that is, that they be accorded full political and civil rights—is so fundamental to American democracy that the national government's significant initial commitment to protect southern blacks' right to vote created a national momentum and environment for continued and additional support. President Reagan signed the 1982 extension, despite his disinclination to do so, because to have done otherwise would have given the appearance that he was opposed to blacks' full incorporation into the political process. Such an action would have been an affront to American democratic norms and values.

In other policy areas, blacks have not enjoyed the same measure of success at influencing governmental policy as they have in civil rights. For example, in housing and education, Harold Wolman and Norman Thomas found "an absence of black access and effective black participation at crucial stages in the process."[30] The Wolman and Thomas study is especially relevant here because it is an empirical analysis of the influence that leading black organizations exerted in the two policy areas between 1967 and 1968, and it was conducted for the express purpose of examining the relevance of pluralist theory for black politics in the United States. Wolman and Thomas's assessment in this regard understates the evidence presented in their analysis. A more judicious assessment of their evidence would suggest that blacks' access to policymakers and their participation in the policy process in housing and education were limited during the period of their study, but certainly not absent.

Wolman and Thomas's study contains a few instances in which their assessment belies the evidence presented. In their assessment of the

NAACP's and the Leadership Conference on Civil Rights' influence in housing policy, Wolman and Thomas assert, "Like the NAACP, the Leadership Conference has been almost completely uninvolved in housing legislation."[31] This statement closely follows the authors' inclusion of an observation taken from a *Congressional Quarterly Weekly Report* article that the Leadership Conference and NAACP lobbyist Clarence Mitchell in particular "is credited with playing a major role in the passing of the federal open-housing law in 1967."[32]

Moreover, Wolman and Thomas observe that National Urban League Executive Director Whitney Young "[was] very active personally in the innovation and formulation stage of the housing policy-making process. . . . It seems clear that Young's influence [was] due to his reputation and his personality—and particularly to the high respect that President Johnson held for him—rather than to the resources of the Urban League."[33] Apart from the questionable assumption that Young's influence was personal and thus had no institutional connection to the Urban League, the larger problem is that the authors' assessment of Young's access and influence simply does not square with their prior assessment that blacks lacked "access and effective participation at crucial stages in the [housing and education policy] process."[34]

A similar incongruity exists between the authors' prior assessment noted above and their observation that CORE presented congressional testimony regarding its position on housing policy.[35] Presenting congressional testimony represents some access to policymakers. The authors also made no attempt to evaluate the influence that Robert Weaver, the first secretary of housing and urban development and the first black member of a presidential cabinet, had on housing policy. Although Wolman and Thomas state that their study focuses principally on black organizations, their assessment of black influence in housing and education seems to assess black influence generally (that is, influence inclusive of black organizations and black individuals) in these two policy areas. Therefore, the failure to discuss Weaver's influence in the housing policy process is a significant shortcoming.

Moreover, only thirteen of fifty-nine educational elites interviewed, or 22 percent, felt that the "Negro-urban poor" lacked adequate access to the educational policy process.[36] Apparently, the other 78 percent of the educational policy elites thought that blacks had adequate access to the educational policy process. Similarly, Wolman and Thomas report that of the sixteen interest groups active in housing policy, "the more moderate black organizations, the NAACP and the Urban League, ranked seventh in frequency of the policy-makers' contact while the more militant groups, SNCC and CORE, ranked sixteenth, with many decision-makers almost never communicating with them."[37] Wolman and Thomas seem unappreciative of the rather respectable ranking of the NAACP and the Urban League in terms of the frequency of their contacts with housing policy elites.

Only at the end of Wolman and Thomas's analysis of the influence of the leading black organizations in housing and education do the authors offer an assessment consistent with the evidence presented: "In sum, the responses indicate that black access to the policy-making elites is limited in terms of the reference groups and personal contacts with the influential policy makers and that a sizable, but not substantial, number of those who are influential believe that black people lack adequate access to the process."[38] Therefore, the interview responses in particular and all the evidence generally presented by Wolman and Thomas suggest that black access to policy-makers and their participation in the policy process in the areas of housing and educational policy were either limited or moderate, but not nonexistent as the authors indicate. With respect to the applicability of the pluralist model to black politics, Wolman and Thomas rather modestly conclude, "It appears that the pluralist description of the American political system is not entirely adequate. Our research has shown that black interests and black groups do not, on the whole, possess effective access to the centers of decision making in federal education and housing policy."[39]

As the above discussion indicates, black organizational leaders and lobbyists influenced the passage of the 1968 open-housing legislation, called Title VIII (the fair housing provision) of the Civil Rights Act of 1968. The effort by black organizations to enact Title VIII received support from other organizations such as the American Federation of Labor and Congress of Industrial Organizations (AFL-CIO), the Urban Coalition, and the National Council of Churches, with the strongest support coming from organized labor.[40] After 1965, as during the civil rights years, black organizations needed support from other organizations to pass favorable legislation.

Just as several acts of government led to the 1965 Voting Rights Act, prior governmental actions led to the passage of Title VIII. The federal government's initial action in fair housing was President John Kennedy's issuance of Executive Order 11063 in 1962 "prohibiting discrimination in new housing owned, operated, or subsidized by the federal government."[41] President Kennedy's order was woefully inadequate, as its exemptions applied to "75 percent of new housing and 99 percent of the existing housing stock"; furthermore, the order was weakly enforced.[42] Two years later, Title VI of the 1964 Civil Rights Act, which prohibits discrimination in any program receiving federal financial assistance, provided a rudimentary mechanism for enforcing the fair housing concept. However, Title VI's application as regards fair housing enforcement was limited. Despite continuing protests by CORE and other black organizations, Congress failed to pass open housing legislation in 1966 and 1967.[43]

According to Newman et al., Title VIII of the 1968 Civil Rights Act was enacted because of Martin Luther King, Jr.'s assassination that year and "the masterful legislative lobbying efforts of the NAACP."[44] Newman et al. accord significantly greater credit to the NAACP's role in the passage of Title VIII than do Wolman and Thomas; they support the contention of this chapter that the Wolman and Thomas study understates black organizations' influence over housing policy during the legislative history of Title VIII's enactment. Perhaps Wolman and Thomas's conclusion regarding blacks' lack of access and effective participation in the policy-making process applied to educational policy over the period of their study, but it did not apply to housing policy.

Energy policy is another area that is useful to examine with regard to black participation and influence because it is a scientific and technical policy area, one not generally considered a mainstay of black civil rights interests. This discussion of black participation and influence in energy policy focuses on the administration of President Jimmy Carter because of his efforts to develop the country's first comprehensive national energy policy. Since energy policy affects blacks, as it does all segments of society, one might surmise that black leaders and organizations would be especially interested in trying to fashion a national policy favorable to black interests. Like Wolman and Thomas's study, the present study was conducted with an interest in examining the relevance of pluralist theory for black politics in the United States.[45]

My study concluded with a mixed although generally favorable assessment of black participation and influence in energy policy during the

Carter administration. Blacks had no input "in the initial formulation of national energy policy by the team of Carter energy planners. . . . There was no black representation on the task force of energy planners that formulated the National Energy Plan, the foundation of the nation's energy policy during the Carter years."[46] However, the congressional phase of energy policy-making showed substantial evidence of black input:

> Black organizations and political leaders did quite well in the congressional phase of energy policy-making. Of the three indicators utilized to assess input in that phase of the policy process, black input was rated favorably. Black organizations participated in important congressional energy policy hearings and actively lobbied selected congresspersons active in the area of energy policy. Also, within Congress itself, the Congressional Black Caucus actively participated, and represented black interest, in congressional energy policy-making, even to the point of substantively influencing policy outputs at least on a few occasions.[47]

The findings on black participation in the administrative phase of energy policy-making largely showed minimal input. While black organizations actively lobbied high-level officials in the Department of Energy, blacks were poorly represented as employees in the energy bureaucracy, especially at the policy-making level.[48] While the study does not state a specific conclusion as to whether the evidence presented in the analysis supports or opposes pluralist theory, the evidence suggests moderate support for the pluralist perspective. *Overall,* black participation and influence in energy policy during the Carter years of comprehensive energy policy-making was moderate.

The structure of black participation and representation in energy policy-making accords well with Wolman and Thomas's observation about black participation and representation in the policy process generally: "Black participation and representation occurs primarily in the legislative-consideration and the implementation stages of the policy process. Black organizations and leaders have made little attempt to influence policy development at the innovative and formulative stage where meaningful choices between long-range alternatives are for the most part made."[49] However, this author disagrees with Wolman and Thomas's implicit assumption that the absence of black participation

bill nevertheless because he did not want to appear insensitive to blacks' desire to have a national holiday honoring Dr. King.

The above discussion provides support for all five pluralist propositions. Support for the proposition that political resources are unequally but noncumulatively allocated among interest groups seeking to influence the policy process (P_1) can be inferred from the success that black organizations had in influencing the policy process in several areas after 1965. Black organizations were centrally involved in the successful efforts to influence the enactment of additional civil rights legislation after 1965, which extended and expanded the civil rights protection provided to blacks by the pioneering governmental action of the mid-1960s. Blacks also experienced varying degrees of success in housing and energy policy-making.

Since 1965 black organizations have also influenced the actions of Congress and presidents in the nonpolicy areas of nominations to the federal judiciary and support for the King national holiday legislation. The success that blacks have achieved in both the policy and the nonpolicy realms since 1965 would not have been possible if blacks did not possess a significant amount of political resources. The principal resources that blacks used to achieve the success indicated were voting power, access to public officials, and knowledge of the political process. The fact that blacks were able to marshal these political resources in significant quantities strongly suggests that while other groups opposed to blacks' interests on various issues may have possessed substantial resources, these groups did not enjoy a cumulative advantage over blacks in this regard. By the same reasoning, the discussion also supports the proposition that multiple centers of power exist in the policy process but that none are sovereign (P_2). During this period examined, blacks attained some of their objectives, but not all of them. The same is true of groups that were opposed to black interests. No group was uniformly victorious in civil rights policy during this period.

The above discussion also supports the applicability of the multiple access points feature (P_3) to black politics during this period. During the period examined, blacks received most of their support from Congress and presidents. The discussion section also upholds the proposition that the policy-making process is characterized by bargaining and negotiation (P_4) and by incrementalism (P_5). Support for the latter proposition is best illustrated by several acts of government that extended federal protection of blacks' right to vote in the 1970s and 1980s and that led up to the passage of the fair housing entitlement of the 1968 Civil Rights Act.

The Utility of Pluralist Theory for Explaining Black Politics

This chapter has shown that pluralist theory consists of logically interrelated propositions that provide considerable insight for explaining black politics. Southern blacks overcame their exclusion from electoral politics in ways consistent with the five pluralist propositions identified here.

The arguments and conclusions presented in this chapter might raise several concerns. Space limitation allows a brief consideration of only three such concerns. One might be that it took too long for southern blacks to win back the right to vote. If the fifty years that most southern blacks remained without the franchise is compared to the fifty years that white males who did not own property did not have the right to vote between 1790 and 1840 and the 130 years between 1790 and 1920 that women did not enjoy a national right to vote, southern blacks have not fared too badly. Nevertheless, because the right to vote is such an essential criterion for a democratic society, the United States must be adjudged to have been a nondemocratic nation during the period that these groups were denied the right to vote. In reality, the United States did not become a democratic political order until southern blacks—the last major, previously excluded group to be incorporated into the political process—were reenfranchised in 1965.

In light of this explanation, a second concern may suggest an apparent paradox in finding pluralist propositions compatible with the political experiences of blacks while the nation was not considered a democratic polity. Dahl argues that pluralism is group specific, that is, it applies to particular groups, not to a polity as a whole. Therefore, Dahl would argue that the pluralist perspective applied to those groups that were incorporated into the political system before 1965 but not to ones that were not incorporated into the political system before then. This argument robs pluralist theory of its most useful value: its ability to serve as an indicator of whether a political system is democratic in its entirety. If all major groups except one were not incorporated into the political system of that society, to say that such a system is pluralistic and democratic with respect to that one group would be meaningless.

Charles Hamilton has appropriately criticized those who have characterized the United States before the 1960s as pluralist. Hamilton offers the following critique of such a characterization, which he imputes to Samuel Huntington[59] and Sidney Verba:[60]

> In contrast to the way some observers have pictured it, the development of black political participation from Reconstruction on has not been either smooth, stable, or free of violence. In 1890 ... southern states began revising their constitutions with the purpose of excluding blacks from political participation. Black Americans had to risk life and job to exercise the franchise most racial and ethnic groups in the United States took for granted. It is a matter of historical record that they frequently lost both . . . in the process. This story is too clear to excuse Huntington's and Verba's sanguine characterizations of the American participatory experience. America felt it had accommodated most if not all "significant" social and economic groups *only* because she had forcefully and deliberately denied the opportunity to blacks. Contrary to Huntington and Verba, it was the flagrant *abuse* of the pluralist model, not the operations of that model, that permitted this country to assume that it was dealing efficaciously with the matter of participation.[61]

Hamilton is correct in his assertion that the pluralist model was not in operation before the 1960s. In fact, as the discussion and analysis in this chapter show, the pluralist model was not in operation before the mid-1960s. While Hamilton's assertion in this regard is correct, it does not vitiate the argument that the process by which southern blacks reacquired the right to vote is fully consistent with the pluralist model. The process was pluralistic even though the United States cannot be said to have been democratic until after southern blacks had been reenfranchised. In other words, democracy closely followed a fully functioning pluralist process—it is that process which constitutes democracy.

The third objection that might be raised is that the gains blacks made from their increased participation in the political process were too small in scope to improve their social and economic conditions substantially. This is essentially a criticism of the incremental character of benefit allocation under the pluralist model. Three points are relevant here. First, it is true that the benefits blacks received from the national government were incremental in both their magnitude and their allocation.

Second, incremental benefits can add up to a rather significant change. This occurred with respect to the several initiatives by the national government to accord full voting rights to southern blacks. Third, the American political system is not generally inclined to produce major redistributive public policies for any group. Therefore, it is unrealistic to expect blacks to receive tangible benefits from the governmental process that would dramatically improve their life conditions.

In sum, the discussion and analysis presented in this chapter suggest that the pluralist model, properly understood, provides a useful perspective for explaining national black politics in the United States after 1965. After that time, blacks were able to pressure the political system to live up to the manifest meaning of the Fourteenth and Fifteenth Amendments, and, given the history of blacks in the United States, that is an extraordinary accomplishment. By contrast, the model does not apply to black politics in the United States before the mid-1960s, because before then practically all governmental and political processes were closed to the majority of blacks.

A good theory is capable of explaining different phenomena that fall within its domain. The pluralist perspective has been successfully used to explain the gradual incorporation of West European ethnic immigrants into the American political system. Pluralist theory is also useful for explaining the gradual incorporation of the working class and organized labor into American politics. This chapter shows that pluralist theory is also useful for explaining blacks' relationship with the American political system in the twentieth century and that this applicability of the pluralist perspective to twentieth-century black politics can be logically and qualitatively demonstrated.

Notes

1. John F. Manley, "Neo-Pluralism: A Class Analysis of Pluralism I and Pluralism II," *American Political Science Review* 77 (1983): 368; Minion K. C. Morrison, *Black Political Mobilization: Leadership, Power and Mass Behavior* (Albany: State University of New York Press, 1987), 3.

2. Michael Parenti, "Power and Pluralism: A View from the Bottom," *Journal of Politics* 32 (1970): 501–30; Harold L. Wolman and Norman C. Thomas, "Black Interests, Black Groups, and Black Influence in the Federal Policy Process," *Journal of Politics* 32 (1970): 875–97; Edward S. Greenberg, "Models of the Political Process: Implications for the Black Community," in *Black Poli-*

tics: The Inevitability of Conflict, ed. Edward S. Greenberg, Neal Milner, and David J. Olson (New York: Oxford University Press, 1971), 3–15; Dianne M. Pinderhughes, Race and Ethnicity in Chicago Politics (Urbana: University of Illinois Press, 1986), 253–61; Marcus D. Pohlmann, Black Politics in Conservative America (New York: Longman, 1960).

3. Pohlmann, Black Politics in Conservative America, 15.

4. Pinderhughes, Race and Ethnicity, 253–61.

5. Morrison, Black Political Mobilization, 3.

6. Parenti, "Power and Pluralism: A View from the Bottom," 501–30; Greenberg, "Models of the Political Process," 3–15; Pinderhughes, Race and Ethnicity in Chicago Politics, 253–61.

7. Huey L. Perry, "Pluralist Theory and National Black Politics in the United States," Polity 23 (summer 1991): 549–65; Huey L. Perry, "Black Participation and Representation in National Energy Policy," in Contemporary Public Policy Perspectives and Black Americans: Issues in an Era of Retrenchment Politics, ed. Mitchell F. Rice and Woodrow Jones, Jr. (Westport, Conn.: Greenwood Press, 1984).

8. Robert A. Dahl, Dilemmas of Pluralist Democracy (New Haven: Yale University Press, 1982), 107.

9. Dahl, Dilemmas of Pluralist Democracy, 116. Greenberg includes this proposition as his sixth and final element. See Greenberg, "Models of the Political Process," 11.

10. For an excellent quantitatively based analysis of the impact of these devices on restricting both black and white voting and eliminating party competition in the ex-Confederate South, see J. Morgan Kousser, The Shaping of Southern Politics: Suffrage Restrictions and the Establishment of the One Party South, 1880–1910 (New Haven: Yale University Press, 1974).

11. 238 U.S. 347 (1915).

12. 321 U.S. 649 (1944).

13. Steven F. Lawson, Black Ballots: Voting Rights in the South, 1944–1969 (New York: Columbia University Press, 1976), 52.

14. 347 U.S. 483 (1954).

15. For a thorough historical examination of Brown, including the role of the NAACP in the case, see Richard Kluger, Simple Justice (New York: Alfred A. Knopf, 1976).

16. Executive Order 8802, June 25, 1941, 3 Code of Federal Regulations, 1938–43 Compilation (Washington, D.C.: Government Printing Office, 1968), 824–30.

17. Dorothy K. Newman et al., Protest, Politics, and Prosperity (New York: Pantheon Books, 1978), 12.

18. Executive Order 9981, 3 Code of Federal Regulations 132 (Supplement 1948).

19. Newman et al., Protest, Politics and Prosperity, 14.

20. Samuel P. Huntington, *Political Order in Changing Societies* (New Haven: Yale University Press, 1968), 128–29.

21. Lawson, *Black Ballots,* 205–6, 212, and 231–32.

22. Ibid., 197.

23. Ibid., 183–86.

24. Ibid., 174–75, 187–88, 191–92, and 196.

25. Ibid., 271.

26. Ibid., 299.

27. Donald R. Matthews and James W. Prothro, *Negroes and the New Southern Politics* (New York: Harcourt, Brace and World, 1966), 19.

28. Ibid.

29. 446 U.S. 55 (1980).

30. Wolman and Thomas, "Black Interests, Black Groups, and Black Influence," 877.

31. Ibid., 881.

32. Ibid., 880. The citation for the article is: "Open-Housing Law Credited to Mitchell's Lobbying," *Congressional Quarterly Weekly Report,* April 26, 1968, 931–34.

33. Wolman and Thomas, "Black Interests, Black Groups, and Black Influence," 881–82.

34. Ibid., 877.

35. Ibid., 882.

36. Ibid., 884.

37. Ibid., 886.

38. Ibid.

39. Ibid., 894.

40. Ibid., 888.

41. Newman et al., *Protest, Politics, and Prosperity,* 139–40.

42. Ibid.

43. Ibid., 140–41.

44. Ibid. Title VIII was passed six days after King's assassination.

45. Perry, "Black Participation and Representation in National Energy Policy." See also Huey L. Perry, *Democracy and Public Policy: Minority Input into the National Energy Policy of the Carter Administration* (Bristol, Ind.: Wyndham Hall Press, 1985), and Wolman and Thomas, "Black Interests, Black Groups, and Black Influence," 875–97.

46. Perry, "Black Participation and Representation in National Energy Policy," 88.

47. Ibid.

48. Ibid., 88–89.

49. Wolman and Thomas, "Black Interests, Black Groups, and Black Influence," 894.

50. Equal Employment Opportunity Act of 1972, Public Law 92–261, 86 Statute 103, 42 *U.S. Code,* secs. 2000e et seq. (March 24, 1972).

51. Public Works Employment Act 1977, Public Law 1982, 42 *U.S. Code,* sec. 6701.

52. Newman et al., *Protest, Politics, and Prosperity.*

53. This quotation is excerpted from a quotation in J. Owens Smith, "Affirmative Action, Reverse Discrimination and the Court: Implications for Blacks," in *Contemporary Public Policy Perspectives and Black Americans,* ed. Mitchell F. Rice and Woodrow Jones (Westport, Conn.: Greenwood Press, 1984), 135.

54. Ibid.

55. Ibid., 136.

56. Omnibus Judgeship Act of 1978, Public Law 95–486; 28 *U.S. Code,* secs. 44, 81, 83, 86, 89, 93, 98, 102, 123, 133, 134.

57. Sheldon Goldman, "Reagan's Judicial Appointments at Mid-Term: Shaping the Bench in His Own Image," *Judicature* 66 (March 1983): 339, 345.

58. Bruce Adams and Kathryn Kavanagh-Baran, *Promise and Performance: Carter Builds a New Administration* (Lexington, Mass.: Lexington Books, 1979), 123.

59. Huntington, *Political Order in Changing Societies,* 128–29.

60. Sidney Verba, "Democratic Participation," *Annals* 373 (September 1967): 54.

61. Charles V. Hamilton, "Blacks and the Crises in Political Participation," *Public Interest* 34 (1974): 190–91.

■ *Part 2*

Black Political Attitudes, Behavior, and Participation

Chapter 3

Black Political Attitudes and Behavior in the 1990s

Wayne Parent and Paul Stekler

This chapter examines black political attitudes and the implication of those attitudes for understanding black partisan behavior in national politics. The national government's eventual guarantee of political rights to blacks, in response to the civil rights movement, has not resolved political conflict between blacks and whites; that conflict remains one of the most dynamic and visible elements of contemporary American politics.

Some recent studies suggest that, since the mid-1960s, issue clustering has grown among Americans largely because the two major political parties have clarified their differing racial stances.[1] No single cleavage in political attitudes in the United States today stands out as clearly as that between blacks and whites. In the aftermath of the civil rights movement and the urban unrest of the 1960s through the period of growing political conservatism in the 1980s and into the 1990s, public opinion polls have shown that blacks and whites live in different worlds, separated politically almost as much as geographically.

Blacks, the Democratic Party, and Presidential Elections

In 1992, Bill Clinton won the presidential election with 40 percent of the white vote, but was supported by 82 percent of blacks. In 1988, George Bush won the presidency with 59 percent of the white vote, but with only 12 percent of the black vote. Although Ronald Reagan won a forty-nine-state landslide reelection in 1984, blacks overwhelmingly disapproved of his job performance as president, giving him a 23 percent positive rating as compared with the 68 percent positive rating given to him by whites. Blacks gave the unsuccessful Democratic nominee, Walter Mondale, a strongly positive rating of nearly 90 percent. While the national Democratic party lost partisan identifiers and votes at the national level in recent decades, blacks have remained strong supporters of the national Democratic party (see Table 3-1). Norman H. Nie, Sidney Verba, and John R. Petrocik report that from the 1950s to the early 1970s, blacks were the only significant group of voters to move toward the Democratic party and not exhibit greater partisan independence.[2] As Table 3-1 clearly shows, blacks have continued to strongly support the Democratic party in presidential elections since 1964, although the overall level of support since 1964 has been lower than that given by blacks in the presidential election of 1964.

The effect of black Democratic partisanship on electoral politics is unmistakable. In 1976, Jimmy Carter would have lost the presidential election to Gerald Ford without strong black support. The 1992 presidential election followed a similar pattern. The difference in the white vote received by Clinton and Bush was only one percent. If black support for Clinton had been similar to his white support, Clinton's electoral college landslide victory would have been much narrower. Although Clinton would have still won the election, he would have done so by a much smaller margin. Black support was clearly an important component of Clinton's victory.

There were also some indications in 1992 that black support for the Democratic party was less than enthusiastic. Although Clinton was clearly the Democratic presidential candidate of choice for blacks in the 1992 presidential primaries, his support was not nearly so strong among blacks as was their 1984 and 1988 support for Jesse Jackson.[3] Black turnout in the 1992 Democratic presidential primaries, largely due to Jackson's absence, was as much as 75 percent lower compared with 1988 in some states.[4]

A similar trend was seen in the general election. Although black voters overwhelmingly chose Clinton over Bush and Ross Perot, black turnout was down. As Christopher Atherton noted, "In 1988, an estimated 8.3 million African Americans voted, constituting 10.5 percent of the national electorate; in 1992, these figures dropped to 8.1 million, or

Table 3-1. Black and White Support for the
Democratic Presidential Candidate, 1948–1992

1948	Black 81%	1972	Black 87%
	White 53%		White 32%
1952	Black 79%	1976	Black 83%
	White 43%		White 49%
1956	Black 61%	1980	Black 86%
	White 41%		White 36%
1960	Black 68%	1984	Black 87%
	White 49%		White 34%
1964	Black 94%	1988	Black 82%
	White 59%		White 41%
1968	Black 85%	1992	Black 82%
	White 38%		White 39%

Sources: National Election Studies, Center for Political
Studies, University of Michigan (1948–1988), and voter
research and surveys (1992).

eight percent of the [national] electorate."[5] One plausible explanation
for the decrease in black turnout between 1992 and 1988 is that black
voters were mobilized by Jackson's 1988 candidacy. In 1992, not only
was Jackson not a candidate, but the Clinton campaign did not focus on
blacks and other parts of the traditional Democratic base. The Clinton
campaign instead focused on, as Atherton notes, "the marginal votes
in the center."[6] The 1992 Democratic presidential strategy worked for
Clinton, but it did not strengthen black commitment to the Democratic
party.

Despite reduced black support for the Democratic party in the presidential elections in 1992 and 1988, black support for the Democratic
party in presidential elections since 1964, as previously indicated, has
been substantial. Blacks' association with the Democratic party is based
on a rational assessment of gains made by blacks during President
Franklin D. Roosevelt's New Deal and President Lyndon B. Johnson's
civil rights legislation and Great Society programs. Public welfare benefits directed at the black poor and black public sector employment,
disproportionately made up of middle-class blacks, are associated with
the beneficence of an active federal government generally preferred by
the Democratic party.[7] Blacks see the Democratic party as having sup-

ported policy positions favorable to them over the last thirty years. Conversely, blacks see the Republican party as having generally opposed their interests over the last thirty years.

Black Political Attitudes

The marked tendency of blacks to support the Democratic party is related to distinctive political attitudes held by blacks. That blacks had to overcome an oppressive political system in order to participate in electoral politics has some bearing on why black political attitudes are distinctive. Blacks' use of group protest during the civil rights movement to attain political rights as a group is quite similar to the process described by Seymour Martin Lipset and Stein Rokkan by which lower- and working-class groups forced their way into the political systems of European countries, forging bonds of group identity and then transforming those bonds into viable group-oriented political parties.[8]

The authors of *The American Voter* identified a three-step process in which the political attitudes and behavior of an individual become defined by his or her membership in a particular group. First, as an individual's identification with a group increases, the probability that he or she will think and act in ways that distinguish the group from nonmembers will also increase. Second, as the proximity between a group and the political world increases, the political distinctiveness of the group will also increase. Third, as the perception of proximity between the group and the political world becomes clearer, a group member's susceptibility to group influence in political affairs will increase.[9]

Much of the post–civil rights literature on black political participation has focused on the relationship between group consciousness and higher levels of participation by group members. Thus blacks who identify relevant political issues with race tend to have a greater awareness of their status as a deprived group and to be more active politically.[10] Racial consciousness among blacks at a lower socioeconomic level is associated with higher internal efficacy and a greater mistrust of government, factors that are also associated with greater political participation.[11] Higher levels of racial identification, specifically "us versus them" group feelings related to political issues, when combined with any combination of power deprivation feelings, dislike for "out" members, or other measures of racial polarization, is associated with higher presidential voting turnout among blacks.[12] So in this view, the fact of being black, among the racially conscious, produces behavior and attitudes that "define" the participation of black Americans in politics.

A closer examination of racial consciousness indicates that the impact of race on black behavior is more complex than the observation above indicates. A study of Jesse Jackson's only presidential primary victory in 1984, in Louisiana, reports that the standard reliance on self-reported claims of having voted in the primary indicates a strong relationship between measures of racial consciousness and higher-than-expected voting turnout among blacks, given their socioeconomic status. However, the use of validated voting data,[13] which were not used in Richard Shingles's work on black consciousness and political participation,[14] in the study of Jackson's Louisiana presidential primary victory in 1984 completely eliminated any connection between black voter turnout and black consciousness.[15] Race, however, was obviously important as Jackson's support among blacks approached monolithic status as the primary season progressed. Jackson's support surged in the last week of the primary among those blacks who actually voted, blacks with a personal history of higher turnout in previous elections. While Mondale had been an acceptable candidate to blacks, as evidenced by his very high positive ratings among them, Jackson's campaign had removed doubts about his lack of experience and convinced blacks that he was the best candidate.

Thus the link between racial consciousness and self-reported Jackson votes among blacks became stronger as time passed after the election. Jackson's race facilitated the development of racial consciousness among blacks. For black voters, Jackson's race helped make him one of the candidates to consider seriously, although it was his campaign ability that attracted black voters to him during the late stages of the primary campaign. For black nonvoters, race helped them to understand the election. For all blacks, race was used to clarify politics.

Black attitudes on racial issues diverge considerably from those of whites. This is especially true when principles associated with the civil rights movement of the 1960s are examined. Black attitudes normally differ substantially from white attitudes on race-relevant political principles—blacks display much stronger support for continued national civil rights progress.[16] However, differences between blacks and whites are not so stark when the attitudes of blacks and whites on specific race-relevant policy issues are examined. Specifically, black support for intervention by the federal government to promote school integration, to equalize job opportunities, and to provide economic aid to minorities has decreased during the last few decades and is approaching white attitudes.[17]

Among journalists and politicians, black attitudes are increasingly described as heterogeneous. Until recently, however, most scholarly studies concluded that race consciousness overshadowed socioeconomic differences among blacks. The notion that black political attitudes are relatively homogeneous was challenged in probably the most comprehensive recent work on the subject, Katherine Tate's *From Protest to Politics: The New Black Voters in American Elections*.[18] Tate found socioeconomic patterns that differentiated black political attitudes, explaining that "affluent Blacks were opposed to the principle of a minimum standard of living for every American as well as the expansion of most welfare programs, except Medicare."[19] Tate's findings in this regard provide additional support for the argument that economic class is becoming an important determinant of black attitudes toward government economic and welfare policy.[20] Tate concludes that "there appear to be two types of middle-class Blacks: those who remain racially identified and may even misidentify with the working-class and poor blacks, and those who identify with the upper classes and, as a result, are less race-conscious, viewing their lives as fairly independent of the group."[21]

One possible conclusion from this discussion is that so long as race is a relevant political issue, blacks will remain a distinctive group in American politics. However, the opening of economic opportunities for at least middle-class blacks allows an argument to be made that class, rather than race, is a more important determinant of life patterns among blacks.[22] The appearance of class division in politics among blacks nationally, however, is not evident on major issues or in partisan identification or behavior. While middle-class blacks have somewhat different orientations and attitudes from poor blacks, those differences are not pronounced. Middle-class blacks are disproportionately working in the public sector and are thus dependent on the same "big government" national spending priorities as poor blacks who are dependent on social welfare programs.[23]

Diversity in attitudes on political issues that are not specifically race-related have not received the close scrutiny of race-related issues, probably because the direct impact of these issues on voting behavior is much less significant than is the impact of race-related issues. While some have speculated that gender differences override racial differences, studies on topics ranging from the nomination of Clarence Thomas to be an Associate Justice on the U.S. Supreme Court, to abortion, to war have produced decidedly mixed findings.[24]

Summary and Conclusions

Race remains central to American electoral politics. Black and white differences in voting behavior, most obvious in differences in presidential choices and partisan identification, are likely to continue throughout the 1990s. These differences between blacks and whites reflect different attitudes on race-relevant political issues. However, these differences generally do not reflect significant racial disagreements on non–race-relevant issues.

Blacks' participation in presidential elections has provided them with important opportunities to influence governmental decision-making and has offered important points of access to that governmental decision-making, consistent with the major tenets of pluralist theory. As such, the uniformity in black voting for the Democratic party at the national level is strategically important for serving black interests. This is reinforced by the relative uniformity of political attitudes within the black community. The uniformity among blacks on most key political issues promotes blacks' interests by maximizing black power within the American political system. If black consciousness declines in the twenty-first century, blacks' attitudes may be no more germane to political discussion than those of people who are left-handed or tall. However, several decades of political struggle have created a strong, resilient uniformity of black electoral behavior and black political attitudes. That suggests that a long time will pass before black political attitudes and black voting behavior are no longer distinctive and important components of American pluralism.

Notes

1. See, for example, Edward G. Carmines and James A. Stimson, "Racial Issues and the Structure of Mass Belief Systems," *Journal of Politics* 44 (February

1982): 2–20, and *Issue Evolution: Race and the Transformation of American Politics* (Princeton: Princeton University Press, 1989).

2. Norman H. Nie, Sidney Verba, and John R. Petrocik, *The Changing American Voter* (Cambridge: Harvard University Press, 1976), 226–29, 233.

3. Ross Baker, "Sorting Out and Suiting Up: The Presidential Nominations," in *The Election of 1992,* ed. Gerald M. Pomper (Chatham, N.J.: Chatham House, 1993), 62.

4. Ibid.

5. F. Christopher Atherton, "Campaign '92: Strategies and Tactics of the Candidates," in *The Election of 1992,* ed. Pomper, 102.

6. Ibid.

7. Michael K. Brown and Steven P. Erie, "Blacks and the Legacy of the Great Society: The Economic and Political Impact of Federal Social Policy," *Public Policy* 29 (summer 1981): 321; and Pearl T. Robinson, "Whither the Future of Blacks in the Republican Party?" *Political Science Quarterly* 97 (summer 1982): 219.

8. Seymour Martin Lipset and Stein Rokkan, "Cleavage Structure, Party Systems, and Voter Alignments: An Introduction," in *Party Systems and Voter Alignments,* ed. Lipset and Rokkan (New York: Free Press, 1967).

9. Angus Campbell, Philip E. Converse, Warren E. Miller, and Donald E. Stokes, *The American Voter* (New York: John Wiley, 1960), 298–311.

10. Sidney Verba and Norman Nie, *Participation in America* (New York: Harper and Row, 1972): 149–51.

11. Richard D. Shingles, "Black Consciousness and Political Participation: The Missing Link," *American Political Science Review* 75 (March 1981): 84–86.

12. David B. Hill and Norman R. Luttbeg, *Trends in American Electoral Behavior,* 2nd ed. (Itasca, Ill.: F. E. Peacock, 1983), 90.

13. See Paul R. Abramson and William Claggett, "The Quality of Record Keeping and Racial Differences in Validated Turnout, *Journal of Politics* 54 (August 1992): 871–80.

14. Shingles, "Black Consciousness and Political Participation."

15. Doug Rose and Paul Stekler, "Validated Turnout and the Jesse Jackson Primary Victory in Louisiana," unpublished manuscript, 1989.

16. Howard Schuman, Charlotte Steeh, and Lawrence Bobo, *Racial Attitudes in America: Trends and Interpretations* (Cambridge: Harvard University Press, 1985), 141–43.

17. Schuman et al., *Racial Attitudes in America,* 148–49.

18. Katherine Tate, *From Protest to Politics: The New Black Voters in the American Electorate* (Cambridge: Harvard University Press, 1993).

19. Ibid., 43.

20. See, for example, Wayne Parent and Paul Steckler, "The Political Implications of Economic Stratification in the Black Community," *Western Political*

Quarterly 38 (winter 1985): 521–37; and Susan Welch and Michael Combs, "Intra-Racial Differences in Attitudes of Blacks: Class or Consensus," *Phylon* 2 (winter 1985): 91–97.

21. Tate, *From Protest to Politics,* 47.

22. William Julius Wilson, *The Declining Significance of Race: Blacks and Changing American Institutions,* 2nd ed. (Chicago: University of Chicago Press, 1980).

23. Brown and Erie, "Black and the Legacy"; and Robinson, "Whither the Future of Blacks in the Republican Party?" 207.

24. See Jane Mansbridge and Katherine Tate, "Race Trumps Gender: The Thomas Nomination in the Black Community," *PS* 25 (September 1992): 488–91; Susan Welch and Lee Sigelman, "A Black Gender Gap?" *Social Science Quarterly* 70 (May 1989): 120–33; and Pamela Johnston Conover and Virginia Sapiro, "Gender, Feminist Consciousness and War," *American Journal of Political Science* 37 (November 1993): 1079–99.

Chapter 4

Jesse Jackson's Campaigns for the Presidency: A Comparison of the 1984 and 1988 Democratic Primaries

Mfanya Donald Tryman

In 1988, Jesse Jackson entered the Democratic primaries as a serious candidate for the presidency of the United States, as he had done in 1984. The 1984 race was a unique occurrence, for never in previous U.S. history had there been a serious black candidate—that is, one who waged a competitive campaign—for the presidency. This chapter examines Jackson's 1984 Democratic primary campaign in terms of its strengths, weaknesses, and issues as well as its aftermath. The chapter also examines Jackson's 1988 candidacy and compares it to the 1984 campaign.

The 1984 Democratic Primaries

Jackson's 1984 primary race had four major objectives: 1) to increase black political participation; 2) to change party rules and state laws so that they would facilitate black political participation; 3) to take positions and raise issues of concern to minorities; and 4) to create a multiethnic coalition of progressive groups inside the Democratic party.[1] Jackson achieved varying degrees of success with the first three objectives but little success with the last.[2]

Before Jackson announced his candidacy for the Democratic presidential nomination in late 1983, several arguments were presented as to why he should not run. I have written elsewhere about the following four fallacies associated with criticizing Jackson's bid for the Democratic party presidential nomination. Jackson's critics argued that he would: 1) divide the black electorate; 2) alienate white allies; 3) divide the

Democratic party and allow the Republicans to win; and 4) create too many "risks and hazards."[3] Ironically, some criticisms of Jackson's decision to run for the presidency were very similar to those leveled at Martin Luther King during the civil rights movement of the 1960s— one of the most prominent being that the time was not right to pursue major civil rights advances.[4]

Jackson's 1984 presidential bid divided the black electorate and the Democratic party, but it was not the crucial factor that allowed the Republicans to win the presidential election. Ample evidence shows that Jackson's 1984 bid did not cause as much backlash among the white general population as it did among the white elite of the Democratic party.[5] His candidacy mobilized and consolidated the black electorate behind the Democratic party. However, two of the arguments against Jackson running for the presidency turned out, in part, to be true. His campaign did alienate some white voters (but not necessarily allies), according to one public opinion poll, and was "risky and hazardous" because of controversy surrounding his candidacy.[6] In particular, his "Hymie" and "Hymietown" remarks and his association with Louis Farrakhan of the Nation of Islam stigmatized his presidential bid and led some to ostracize him.[7]

Internally, many organizational problems plagued Jackson's candidacy, giving the impression that it was a "movement" rather than a political campaign for the country's highest public office.[8] These problems included inexperienced grass-roots activists, an organizational structure with the black church as its base, poor coordination and communications between national headquarters and local organizational structures, and the late start of the campaign.[9] The late announcement of the Jackson candidacy was a particularly difficult obstacle to overcome. Jackson did not announce his candidacy until November 1983, whereas serious contenders for the presidency traditionally initiate their campaign several months earlier. Other problems of Jackson's candidacy included fund raising, scheduling operations, and difficulty in obtaining "free media" coverage of the campaign (such as photo opportunities, talk shows, interviews, and morning news programs).

The media referred to Jackson as "the black presidential candidate,"[10] yet did not mention skin pigmentation when speaking of any white candidate. Some prominent black elected officials stated that Jackson should not run and threw their support behind Walter Mondale. However, by November 1983, Jackson had garnered substantial support among blacks. Ronald Walters notes that Jackson's black support included "half of the Congressional Black Caucus, a large contingent of mayors of smaller cities, many other black urban and state elected officials, some national black professional organizations, many local grassroots organizations, rank-and-file black labor, a wide network of religious institutions involving thousands of churches, and, as we have seen, . . . most black individuals."[11]

The print and television media often referred to Jackson's positions on issues collectively as the "black agenda," although his positions cut across racial, ethnic, religious, age, and class lines. The media may have characterized Jackson's issue positions as a black agenda because he, a black candidate, was a serious contender for an office that no black American had ever won; Mondale's and Gary Hart's issue positions were not characterized as a "white agenda." Statements Jackson made before and during the 1984 campaign contributed to the perception that he had a black agenda. In November 1983, when he announced his candidacy, Jackson stated in Washington, D.C., a city with one of the largest black population proportions in the country, that "our time has come." Thomas and Mary Edsall indicate that Jackson repeated this statement throughout the campaign. Similarly, they state that "Jackson repeatedly declared to cheering and applauding, overwhelmingly black crowds: 'We're not asking for welfare, we're asking for our share.' "[12]

The media also treated Jackson's 1984 candidacy differently on another issue. Jackson was repeatedly asked by reporters before and during the Democratic National Convention whether his delegates would disrupt or walk out of the convention during national, prime time television coverage if he did not get his way at the convention.[13] Presumably, getting his way meant that Jackson's platform planks would be accepted by the convention and that Jackson would be allowed to address the convention during national, prime time television coverage. The media did not ask Hart, for example, whether his delegates would disrupt or walk out of the convention if he did not get his way.

Jackson proposed four major planks for the Democratic party platform. These included no first use of nuclear weapons, a real cut in defense spending, the use of quotas in affirmative action, and strict enforcement of the voting rights laws.[14] Jackson also wanted second primaries, which were used mostly in the South, discontinued because they allegedly discriminate against blacks. The Mondale forces at the convention were willing to accept only the affirmative action plank, substituting the phrase "verifiable measures" for "quotas" in the plank on affirmative action.[15] They defeated Jackson's other planks. Jackson's wish regarding the discontinuation of second primaries was also not realized. Because blacks vote overwhelmingly Democratic, and because of the highly visible support Mondale received from well-known black political leaders, Mondale and his delegates felt little need to compromise with Jackson and his delegates.[16] However, Jackson was allowed to address the convention during national, prime time television coverage.

Jackson made critical mistakes in the 1984 race that damaged his campaign. But his run for the Democratic nomination also succeeded in some ways. In terms of electoral victories, Jackson won primaries in five states and placed second in nine others, most of these victories and near victories occurring in the South, where voter registration among blacks has increased dramatically since the mid-1960s.

He won all large cities with majority black populations. More than two million people were registered to vote as Democrats in 1984 as a result of Jackson's voter mobilization and registration drives. In the South alone, an estimated 869,000 blacks were registered to vote from 1982 to 1984, increasing by 20 percent the number of registered black voters in the South over this period. These numbers reflect the largest proportional increase of any two-year interval since 1964–66, when 524,000 blacks were registered to vote, increasing by 24 percent the number of registered black voters in the South. Most of the increase during the period is attributed to passage of the 1965 Voting Rights Act, which eliminated the most serious remaining legal barriers to black voter registration in the South. Jackson's voter registration drives and presidential candidacy in 1984 also led to a rise in black officeholding. According to the Joint Center for Political Studies, there was a 10 percent increase in the number of black mayors that could be related to the "coattail" effect of Jackson's candidacy.[17] Given the problems of Jackson's candidacy, these are significant accomplishments.

Although some critics asserted that Jackson's campaign was merely symbolic and that Jackson could not win, they overlooked the significance of symbolism in politics. As Lucius Barker points out:

Symbols influence people's thinking, guide their behavior, and shape the political environment. Symbols draw attention and get people to vote their interests. They may help reach people who are typically not motivated. Through his charisma and appeal, Jackson provided the sort of symbolism that activated large numbers. . . . Important political actions, such as running for president, serve and promote symbolic needs while simultaneously serving and promoting more material interests. . . . It was the very symbolism of Jackson's candidacy that gave it an importance far beyond what any ordinary candidacy could command.[18]

In addition, Jackson's run for the presidency may have important long-term benefits, such as " . . . black and [other] minority voter registration and turnout, and his contributions to increasing the political education and consciousness of those not previously activated."[19] Jackson's relentless efforts to inform American public opinion on South Africa is an example of his leadership in political education. Initially, Jackson repeatedly addressed the issue of apartheid in South Africa, which Mondale and Hart evaded. Jackson's repeated discussion of apartheid forced Mondale and Hart to address the issue late in the primary campaign and helped to raise American consciousness of apartheid. His education of the public, combined with the efforts of the Congressional Black Caucus and TransAfrica, were the catalysts behind the 1986 Anti-Apartheid Act passed by Congress.

Jackson's efforts to obtain the 1984 Democratic presidential nomination created a foundation for strategies for an African American Democratic candidate in the 1988 election. These included a balance-of-power strategy if the convention were deadlocked on two candidates, a dealignment of blacks as a consequence of their alienation from the Democratic party, and the possibility of blacks forming a third party to run for the presidency.[20]

The 1988 Democratic Race for President

Jackson's entry in the 1988 Democratic primaries for president, like his 1984 race, was criticized, but this time the criticisms were more subtle. More euphemistic statements were made in 1988 suggesting that Jackson should not run for the presidency. These statements began with the indication that Jackson was unelectable, which "logically" led to the question of what he was really after. Paul Simon (D-Ill.) and Richard Gephardt (D-Mo.) were not thought of as unelectable and were not asked what they hoped to gain.

Many felt that Jackson was unelectable because he had no prior experience in public office. Neither did President Dwight Eisenhower, now reappraised by some as one of the great American presidents.[21] This notion that Jackson was unelectable because he had not previously held public office may have disguised a deeper feeling that Jackson should not become president because of his race. This explanation was rarely mentioned until Jackson started winning and finishing a respectable second in important primaries.

Ben Wattenburg, a political analyst and conservative Democrat, expressed his frustration with Jackson's successes on Super Tuesday in the spring of 1988 by charging that Jackson's campaign involved "reverse racism," because initially no candidate would attack Jackson for fear of alienating black voters.[22] This changed as the presidential hopes of Senator Albert Gore (D-Tenn.) faded and he began openly to attack Jackson's lack of political experience. Michael Dukakis (then governor of Massachusetts) and Gore, who had been considered the front-runners, had ignored Jackson as a "noncandidate," often speaking of beating each other in primaries rather than Jackson, although Jackson had the second most delegates in early March 1988. This was similar to the campaign in 1984, in which Mondale and Hart had ignored Jackson during much of the Democratic primary season. Thus Wattenburg's reverse racism thesis lends itself to another interpretation. His opponents may have failed to attack Jackson because they did not consider Jackson a candidate worthy of their attentions. Jackson's past, his political rhetoric, his unconventional approach, and his controversial statements and stands on political issues may have contributed to this perception. Before the Democratic National Convention met in Atlanta, one high-ranking Democratic official argued that if voters perceived the Democratic nominee as the candidate Jackson wanted, it would be the "kiss of death" for the party in the general election.[23]

This could mean that race is still such a dynamic variable in American politics that the electorate will not give a black politician a pivotal role in decision-making to determine who is elected president of the United States.[24] Studies show, for example, a great deal of crossover voting in elections where black and white candidates are competing for the same office.[25]

Jackson's 1988 race was more successful than his 1984 race because of 1) better campaign organization and planning; 2) greater electoral support; 3) more whites in the campaign organization, including a white campaign manager; 4) utilization of expertise from the 1984 campaign; 5) the ability to tap issues that cut across racial and ethnic lines (e.g., drug use and the drug trade, and the plight of midwestern farmers losing land and jobs) with a strong populist appeal; and, inter alia, 6) an innovative strategy of bold campaigning in conservative areas such as Cicero, Illinois, and outside blue-collar factories in Alabama, with Jackson emphasizing his concern for plant closings, economic violence, and the loss of American jobs to foreign firms and countries. In addition, Jackson's charisma, ability to articulate issues, support by the black church, and political acuity were pluses in his 1988 campaign. While Jackson's personal attributes and support by the black church were present in the 1984 campaign, they were sharpened and refined in the 1988 primaries.

Jackson's 1988 primary campaign was also able to avoid major political controversy, which plagued his candidacy in 1984. After the Hymietown remarks and Jackson's association with Farrakhan during the 1984 bid, the media as well as Hart and Mondale became more concerned about Jackson's apologizing to Jews and disavowing Farrakhan than with Jackson's stands on issues. Controversy surrounding Jackson was limited in 1988. Anti-Semitism surfaced as an issue in 1988 in New York City, as it had in 1984. This issue was introduced by then Mayor Ed Koch. As the New York primary drew near in April 1988, Koch equated support for Jackson to support for racism and P. W. Botha of South Africa and declared that New York Jews would have to be crazy to vote for Jackson, just as South African blacks would be foolish to support President P. W. Botha.[26] After Koch's comments, the media again focused on whether Jackson was anti-Semitic, although a survey after the New York primary found that by a margin of two to one New York voters disapproved of what Koch had said about Jackson.[27]

Unlike in his 1984 campaign, Jackson made a strong showing in states like New Hampshire and Iowa, which have virtually no black population. On Super Tuesday, Jackson won primaries in five southern states: Alabama, Georgia, Louisiana, Mississippi, and Virginia. He also won his home state of South Carolina in the Democratic party caucus with 53 percent of the vote.[28] Jackson placed second in eleven other states: Florida, Maryland, Massachusetts, Missouri, North Carolina, Rhode Island, Tennessee, Texas, Hawaii, Idaho, and Nevada.[29] He placed first in the total popular vote among the Democratic candidates on Super Tuesday and was the only candidate to win delegates in all twenty Super Tuesday states.[30] Table 4-1 indicates the percentage of the vote won by Dukakis, Gore, Jackson, and Gephardt on Super Tuesday in the twenty states and the District of Columbia. In the wake of Super Tuesday, it became clear that Jackson's opponents would have to reassess his candidacy as a viable one. Table 4-2 provides data showing Jackson a distant third before Super Tuesday, with only 6.2 percent of delegate support, and after Super Tuesday, when he climbed to a close

Table 4-1. Super-Tuesday Voting Percentages

State	Dukakis	Gore	Jackson	Gephardt
AL	7.7	37.6	43.8	7.5
AK	18.9	37.2	17.1	12.0
FL	40.8	12.7	20.1	14.4
GA	15.6	32.4	39.7	6.7
HI*	52.7	1.0	37.0	2.2
IA*	37.6	8.3	19.4	1.1
KY	18.7	45.7	15.6	9.1
LA	15.2	28.0	35.2	10.2
MD	45.7	8.7	28.9	7.9
MA	58.6	4.5	18.6	10.2
MS	8.8	33.6	44.4	5.5
MO	11.7	2.8	20.1	57.8
NV*	26.1	30.0	23.3	2.0
NC	20.3	34.7	32.9	5.5
OK	16.9	41.4	13.4	21.0
RI	70.0	4.0	15.7	4.1
SC*	6.3	16.8	54.8	1.8
TN	3.4	72.3	20.7	1.5
TX	32.3	20.4	24.5	13.6
VA	21.8	22.5	45.0	4.5
DC*	44.0	2.4	34.6	−1.0

*Caucus states.
Source: Michael B. Binford, "Analysis of Super Tuesday in the South: Patterns of Campaign Spending," paper presented at the annual meeting of the Southern Political Science Association (Atlanta, Ga., November 3–5, 1988), 15.

Table 4-2. Delegate Support: Before and
After Super Tuesday

Candidate	March 1	March 9
Dukakis	14.2%	27.8%
Gephardt	10.4	8.7
Gore	3.8	21.2
Jackson	6.2	24.2
Others/unc.	65.4	18.1
(Delegates selected)	(451)	(1,638)

Note: Candidate delegate support percentage is based on delegates
selected through the date indicated.
Source: Charles D. Hadley and Harold W. Stanley, "Super Tuesday
1988: Hopes, Fears, and Facts," paper presented at the annual
meeting of the Southern Political Science Association Meeting
(Atlanta, Ga., November 3–5, 1989), 23.

second with 24.2 percent of delegate support. In Illinois, Jackson ran
second to favorite son candidate Paul Simon. In Michigan, in the Democratic party caucus, Jackson defeated Dukakis by a two-to-one margin
in an impressive victory, in which Jackson received 55 percent of the
vote compared with 28 percent for Dukakis, who had been the predicted
winner.[31] Turnout for the Michigan caucus consisted of only 212,000
voters out of a total electorate of 6.8 million. A majority of these votes
were from black precincts.[32]

At the end of March, Dukakis had only a slight lead in delegates over
Jackson. Despite Jackson's impressive performance, talk continued in
Democratic circles of a Dukakis-Gore or Dukakis-Gephardt presidential
ticket. Gephardt's chances of winning the nomination faded before
the Michigan caucus. Gore, the favored candidate of the South, was
decisively defeated by Jackson on his home turf on Super Tuesday. One
observer fully captured the apparent irony of Democratic leaders not
wanting to recognize Jackson's accomplishments: "There is no easy
explanation for such a lack of enthusiasm on the part of Super Liberals
who have been so busy bashing Reagan for his alleged opposition to
all Jackson symbolizes. Surely the same people who for eight years have
filled the air with cries of racism would not now try to draw a color
line at the White House door."[33]

Right before the Democratic National Convention, Dukakis chose as
his vice presidential running mate Texas Senator Lloyd Bentsen, who

had served three terms in the U.S. Senate. Jackson was informed by the media that he was not Dukakis's choice for the vice presidential nomination, although Jackson had made it clear to Dukakis that he did not want to be notified in this fashion. Of the potential nominees for the vice presidential nomination, Jackson was the last one to find out about Bentsen's selection, even though he had won the second-highest number of delegates.

Dukakis's decision to distance himself from Jackson was a calculated strategy designed to persuade blue-collar workers and southern white Democrats—popularly known as Reagan Democrats—to vote for him. From 1968 until 1992, blue-collar workers and southern whites defected from the Democratic party and voted for the Republican presidential candidate. The term "Reagan Democrats" described increasing numbers of those voters who voted for the Republican party in presidential elections because of Ronald Reagan's appeal. Like Mondale in 1984, Dukakis could not appear to be too close to Jackson or acquiescing to Jackson on issues for this strategy to be successful.

The Legacy of Jackson's Presidential Campaigns

Jackson's bids for the Democratic nomination for president in 1984 and 1988 left certain legacies and implications, as well as raising certain questions. Should a future black candidate use race in a subliminal manner to mobilize and consolidate a black base from which to expand his or her efforts? Will racism always surface when a black candidate runs for president, or is racism too easily confused with conservatism? Is Jackson partly responsible for the elevation to national stature of black political luminaries like L. Douglas Wilder (elected governor of Virginia in 1988) and Ronald Brown (appointed chair of the National Democratic Party and secretary of commerce in the Clinton administration), or would they have been just as successful in his absence? While these questions cannot be answered definitively, the following discussion, in part, addresses them and explores others.

One legacy left by Jackson's presidential campaigns is that a black politician can mount a serious campaign for president in the Democratic primaries and raise issues with national appeal. With regard to the latter, Jackson's emphasis on economic issues in the 1988 election presaged the 1992 election. The issue in the 1992 election was the economy. Most of the evidence suggests that President George Bush was defeated in 1992 because he had failed to provide domestic leadership on the economy, particularly concerning the prolonged recession and high unemployment that plagued the last year of his presidency.

Related to Jackson's example showing that a black politician can successfully run in the Democratic primaries and garner a significant percentage of the vote is the notion that charisma and leadership, particularly among the grass roots, can be used effectively in the absence of more traditional resources such as party support, an experienced cadre of campaign organizers, and adequate campaign financing. For example, of the six Democrats who ran on Super Tuesday in 1988—Dukakis, Jackson, Gore, Gephardt, Hart, and Simon—only Hart spent less money than did Jackson. Hart spent one percent of the total amount of money spent on the election, as compared with three percent for Jackson. Hart's and Jackson's spending proportions contrast significantly with those of Dukakis and Gore, who spent 47 percent and 25 percent, respectively, of the total amount spent on the election.[34] Yet Jackson was able to win five southern primaries, place second in eleven others, and win the overall Super Tuesday popular vote and delegates in all Super Tuesday primary states. Compared to the outcome for Dukakis, the biggest spender on Super Tuesday, who won only seven states and the District of Columbia, it is quite an accomplishment.

Jackson's campaign was much better organized in 1988 than it had been in 1984 and reflected more conventional practices. That improved organizational structure—including better planning, development of issues, fund raising, and media events—was complemented by his charismatic leadership style. Jackson's 1984 campaign organization has been characterized as a phenomenon rather than a legitimate campaign party organization.[35] Despite the problems of both campaigns, Marcus Pohlmann believes that Jackson achieved significant accomplishments: "Jesse Jackson broke several major party barriers. In 1984, he garnered 16 percent of the Democratic primary vote (more than 3 million votes) and gained nearly 400 convention delegates. In 1988, he fared even better, winning more than 29 percent of the primary vote (nearly 7 million votes) and gaining more than a thousand convention delegates."[36]

Pohlmann argues that blacks have four options in terms of political strategy: 1) *major-party strategy*—blacks work within the two-party system knowing that one of the two parties will always hold power, or work with the party that best represents their interests; 2) *third-party strategy*—blacks leave the two-party system and develop or support a third party, which can take various forms; 3) *black candidate strategy*—blacks run for office at various levels as a means of mobilizing, organizing, and nationalizing the black vote; and 4) *nonelectoral strategy*—blacks do not participate in conventional politics because it wastes scarce resources; rather, they participate in organized resistance and direct action tactics that help build mass-based organizations.[37]

The major-party and the black candidate strategies are the most rational for African Americans to pursue. Pursuing the major-party strategy would mean that blacks would work with only one party, the Democratic party, or would switch between the two parties to maximize influence so that neither party would take the black vote for granted. However, at present, for black Americans to place their faith in the Republican party does not seem rational. As of 1988, the Republican National Committee had only one black American who was a voting member, and he was from the Virgin Islands. Thus no black members of the Republican National Committee represented any of the fifty states or the District of Columbia at the 1988 Republican National Convention, and only 3.2 percent of the delegates to the convention were black. Compare this with 16 percent of the Democratic National Committee membership that was black and 23 percent of the delegates to the Democratic National Convention in 1988 who were black.[38]

The Republican party has never undergone the reforms that the Democratic party started in 1968 after challenges by the Mississippi Freedom Democratic Party at the 1964 convention; the Democratic party continues to undergo reforms in response to challenges by the Rainbow Coalition and other groups. The Republican party has continually disapproved proposals for reform that would make the party more representative of the U.S. population, under the guise that it does not cater to special interest groups; this ensures that white males continue to have disproportionate representation in voting and policy-making positions in the party.[39]

Hanes Walton argues that the 1984 and 1988 Jackson candidacies for president have affected African Americans in several ways: 1) they showed black youths that the presidency is a realistic goal for African Americans; 2) they brought newcomers into the political process at the mass and elite levels; 3) they increased the level of black participation in presidential primaries; 4) they made issues affecting blacks more salient and countermeasures to other issues in the party; 5) they articulated civil and economic rights for blacks and achieved results in this regard; and 6) they left a cadre of trained professionals who have gained critical local and national campaign experience and who may be utilized in future political campaigns.[40] Furthermore, Walton believes that Jackson's presidential candidacies highlight the importance of the black vote as a bloc that cannot be ignored in power, size, or turnout potential. Finally, Jackson's legacy can be found in his emphasis on humanistic issues and efforts to make government and the American public more aware of these issues, which are often absent from the political arena.[41]

Recent discussion has focused on the "politics of deracialization," which minimizes race and racial appeals that may alienate potential white support for black candidates.[42] Jackson increasingly appealed to blacks in 1984 to consolidate his electoral base once it became clear that he could not achieve more than 10 percent of the white vote in the primaries. Some have even argued that Jackson ran a racist campaign, suggesting that it was not just that he emphasized black issues, but that he did so *the way* he did—that is, he was unwilling to broaden his base of support among whites for fear that he would lose black support.[43] However, data collected and analyzed by Patricia Gurin, Shirley Hatchett, and James Jackson do not substantiate the racist charge that blacks would not have continued to support Jackson if he had reached out for more white votes. Their national survey of intergroup attitudes of a thousand blacks found that only a few Jackson supporters wanted no association with whites, most of them believing in group solidarity but not necessarily racial hostility to outgroups.[44] Therefore, in 1984, Jackson increased his appeal to blacks as the campaign progressed, not because of racial bias but because of his inability to persuade more whites to support his candidacy.

Jackson's Role in the 1992 Presidential Campaign

With Jesse Jackson on the sidelines as a candidate in the 1992 presidential campaign and election, the obvious question arose as to what role he would play vis-à-vis the black electorate. Would Jackson favor one candidate early in the Democratic primaries and campaign for him until the Democratic National Convention? Would he remain neutral until the convention and then endorse the eventual nominee? Would he openly support and campaign for the party after the convention as the presidential election approached? Two major components defined Jackson's role in the 1992 campaign: 1) political strategy and the black electorate; and 2) the Sister Souljah incident and the resultant conflict with Bill Clinton.

Early in the 1992 campaign, Jackson was noncommittal as to whom he would support. The Rainbow Coalition invited the Democratic candidates to a meeting in January to discuss their proposed policies, although the organization made it clear that it would not endorse any of the candidates. Jackson considered supporting the candidacies of Senator Tom Harkin (D-Iowa) and Edmund G. (Jerry) Brown, Jr., and in March, he campaigned for Harkin in the Democratic primaries. In early April, when Brown appeared before the Jewish Community Relations Council in New York City, his appearance turned into a disaster when he announced that he would like to have Jesse Jackson as his running mate. As he argued that this would help to heal the divisions between the Jewish and black communities, Brown was assailed with boos, heckles, and hisses from the audience. Jewish representatives replied that they had problems not with the black community, but with Jackson, whom they considered anti-Semitic based on his remarks during the 1984 presidential campaign and his association with Farrakhan and Palestine Liberation Organization chairman Yasir Arafat.[45] While Jackson did not openly campaign for Brown, his appearance with Brown at rallies fueled speculation that Brown might choose him as his running mate. Nevertheless, Jackson's tacit support for Brown in the New York primary in early April denied a clear-cut victory to Bill Clinton, who received only a plurality of the statewide vote and who was counting heavily on the black vote. Clinton had made numerous campaign appearances in black churches during the New York primary campaign in an attempt to woo black voters.

Friction between Jackson and Clinton had developed earlier in the campaign season when it was rumored that Jackson would endorse Harkin, which Clinton publicly referred to as a "stab in the back." Although Clinton apologized for the remark, animosity developed between Clinton and Jackson during the spring and continued throughout the Democratic primaries. In addition, Clinton did not allow Jackson to campaign directly on his behalf and refused to be closely associated with him. The Clinton camp feared that association with Jackson, an unabashed liberal, might alienate conservative Democrats and Reagan Democrats, whom Clinton was trying to attract back to the Democratic fold. This apparently was part of a larger debate in the Clinton camp as to whether Clinton should mobilize and organize the black vote or go after the vote of white conservatives. Lucius Barker and Mack Jones aptly sum this up in the context of Clinton's leadership position in the Democratic Leadership Council, which was committed to making the Democratic party more centrist:

> Governor Clinton too was careful to distance himself from special interests or groups, including blacks. Indeed, Clinton had obviously crafted a very deliberate "centrist-mainstream" strategy, carefully honed and promoted through the Democratic Leadership Council (DLC)—of which Clinton was a key leader. The apparent and open objective of DLC and this strategy was to recapture Reagan Democrats and appeal to the middle class and avoid too much focus on issues of relevance to the poor and underclass, who are disproportionately black, and minorities who live in urban areas.[46]

By late April Clinton and Jackson met and declared several common goals, including the defeat of George Bush. However, Jackson still refused to endorse Clinton for president and would not make an endorsement until just before the Democratic National Convention in New York in late July. Of course, by that time it had become clear that Clinton would win the nomination and, based on polls, had the best chance of defeating the incumbent president.

Just as it appeared that the Jackson-Clinton dispute was ending, Jackson invited Clinton to address a Rainbow Coalition meeting in mid-June. In his speech at the meeting, Clinton criticized remarks made by rapper Sister Souljah, a meeting participant, in an interview with the *Washington Post* after the Los Angeles riots.[47] She had stated that, rather than continuing to kill one another every day, blacks should take a week to kill whites. Clinton remarked that her comments had been filled with racial hatred.

Jackson responded that this criticism of Sister Souljah revealed a "character flaw" in Clinton and constituted a "sneak attack" in his attempt to attract the white suburban voter. Such behavior, Jackson argued, was part of a larger pattern, including posing with an all-black prison work crew in Georgia, playing golf at an all-white country club on several occasions earlier in the year, distancing himself from Jackson early in the campaign, and accusing Jackson of supporting Harkin. Jackson posited that this pattern of behavior was intended to send coded messages to whites.[48] His suggestion that Clinton had a character flaw came at a time when media reports were dying down that, among other things, Clinton had had an extramarital affair, had smoked marijuana, and was a draft evader during the Vietnam War—charges that had made him vulnerable early in his campaign for the presidency.[49] Nevertheless, he refused to withdraw his remarks about Sister Souljah. Then, in late June, after Clinton moved to reconcile differences with Jackson, Jackson openly supported Clinton's economic plan in a speech before the U.S. Conference of Mayors meeting.

After the Democratic National Convention, the question arose as to whether Jackson would actively campaign for the Clinton-Gore ticket. Jackson responded that he would have to meet with Clinton before determining what his role would be. Near the end of July, Jackson left on a two-day campaign tour, which included registering black voters in Mississippi, in preparation for a Democratic primary scheduled for the first week of August. The party provided Jackson with a plane, which by mid-October he had effectively used to campaign in twenty-seven states.

Did Jackson make a difference in the 1992 presidential election by not running? Was he a divisive factor in the campaign? Jackson's decision not to run made it easy for candidates Bush and Clinton to ignore racial issues in their campaigns. Although Clinton campaigned in black communities, he never addressed African Americans as a special constituency or issues primarily affecting the black community. As for Bush, addressing the concerns of black voters was out of the question for him and the Republican party in 1992. While the GOP often speaks of reaching out to minority constituencies, the Bush organization's invidious assault on Michael Dukakis in 1988 probably won few converts in the black community.[50] Did Jackson actually affect who won the presidential election? Perhaps. Barker and Jones note that the percentage of blacks among those who voted for the Democratic party played an important role in key states that may have determined the outcome of the presidential election, including Illinois (26 percent), Michigan (17 percent), Ohio (20 percent), Georgia (40 percent), and Louisiana (50.6

percent). Further, Clinton received a higher percentage of black Democratic voters in states where strong black candidates were running (Illinois, Georgia, Louisiana). Barker and Jones state that "this clearly suggests that a live and vigorous campaign of a Jesse Jackson could potentially have made for real differences (perhaps even outcome) in the 1992 presidential election."[51]

McCormick and Jones contend that several successful black candidates have recently won office because of the "politics of deracialization."[52] Clinton's strategy included deracialization in the context of nonadvocacy for black Americans as an interest group or special constituency. Yet it could be argued that he used race in a more symbolic way as a means to attract conservative white voters. Standing up to and criticizing Sister Souljah, playing golf at all-white country clubs, not allowing Jackson to campaign directly on his behalf, and distancing himself from Jackson could all be interpreted in a manner to attract white votes. It was George Wallace, in his races for the presidency, who talked about "sending a message to Washington." This may have been Clinton's means of "sending a message to the suburbs." However, the question of race arose more overtly because of the lingering controversy over Sister Souljah and the ongoing feud between Jackson and Clinton. In the end, it may be difficult to determine whether this public controversy ultimately did Clinton more harm than good, that is, whether he lost more black support than he attracted in white votes.

While it is not completely clear, Jackson's strategy may have been purposely elusive with the Democratic candidates early in the campaign, giving the impression that he was about to support Harkin at one point and Brown at another in order to persuade candidates to commit to a more specific agenda regarding the black community. At the same time, he remained noncommittal right up to the eve of the Democratic National Convention and on several occasions during the primary indicated that the Rainbow Coalition would not endorse any Democrat before the convention. If Jackson's strategy was to commit Clinton to publicly supporting a social and economic agenda that promoted the concerns of the black community, it failed. Nevertheless, it could be argued that Jackson's involvement in the campaign after the convention was a key factor in Clinton's victory. The political mobilization and registration of black voters in 1984 and 1988 may well have been a decisive factor that paid political dividends in 1992.

Summary and Conclusions

Jackson's victories in the 1984 and 1988 primaries were due, in part, to his own ability to understand and tap those substantive issues that have cut across a broad cross-section of America's dispossessed and disadvantaged. The attitudes and behavior manifested by mostly Democratic party officials and candidates to Jackson's candidacies in 1984 and 1988 were unfavorable. Paradoxically, what is most interesting is that while these Democrats acted adversely toward Jackson's candidacy, his positions on the major issues were closer to the traditional Democratic mainstream liberal positions than those of the other candidates, who were preoccupied with courting southern whites and blue-collar workers, the so-called Reagan Democrats.

Party leaders and candidates for national office stigmatized Jackson's candidacy and dissociated themselves from him philosophically during the 1988 campaign. Jackson's appeal regarding jobs, the downtrodden, the dispossessed, the role of government, and other traditionally liberal ideas put him in the classic New Deal Democratic party mode. Unlike in 1984, when Jackson made major blunders, in 1988 he exerted a much stronger influence on the course of the Democratic National Convention and the general election.

Although not a candidate in 1992, Jackson had an impact on the Democratic and Republican candidates in the presidential election that year. As a prominent black political figure, Jackson was almost able to manipulate racial concerns in the best interest of the Democratic party. Jackson's role in the 1992 election was one of consequence and uncertainty. Jackson, along with the Rainbow Coalition, refused to endorse any Democrat before the convention. His incentive for his noncommittal support was obscure. Rumors of Jackson's early support of the campaigns of Harkin and Brown were an apparent basis for the friction between Jackson and Clinton. Despite this friction, Jackson's involvement in the campaign was a key factor in Clinton's victory. After the Democratic National Convention, Jackson's campaign in several states registered a substantial number of black voters.

Since the presidency of Jimmy Carter, the Democratic party has been moving to the right in an attempt to recapture conservative blue-collar and southern white voters, who have been defecting from the party since 1968. Ironically, it was Jackson in 1988 who influenced Democratic candidates to move to the left to lessen Jackson's appeal among traditional Democratic supporters who had not abandoned the party. Jackson's base of electoral support was significant in 1988. Jackson raised important issues that both the Democratic party and, to a lesser extent, the Republican party addressed in the 1992 presidential election. Whatever the future holds for blacks and the Democratic party, Jesse Jackson significantly shaped the relationship between blacks and the party in his presidential campaigns of 1984 and 1988.

The African American voter has been a mainstay of the Democratic party since the election of FDR in 1932. Even as other Democratic constituents and interest groups began to defect to the GOP in the late 1960s and early 1970s, long before the Reagan Democrats, African Americans remained loyal to the party of the New Deal, the Fair Deal, and the Great Society. Beginning in the early 1970s, reforms in the Democratic party provided African Americans with additional influence and representation in party affairs and particularly at the Democratic National Convention. The Rainbow Coalition, headed by Jackson, was successful in getting the "party of the people" to make additional concessions in the 1980s. However, roughly coinciding with this same period from 1968 to 1988, the liberal party lost five of six presidential elections beginning with Richard Nixon's narrow defeat of Hubert Humphrey in 1968. In fact, as the Democratic party became more liberal and inclusive, the Republican party moved further to the right, becoming more conservative and exclusive. After Bush's defeat of Dukakis in 1988, when Bush painted Dukakis as an ultraliberal in the Willie Horton campaign ads and made *liberal* a dirty word by not using it, a strong movement began in the Democratic party to recapture the White House by restoring the conservative wing of the party. Clinton was successful not only in doing this but in formulating a policy agenda around economic, rather than social issues. Of course, this was also where Bush was most vulnerable, given the state of the American economy, which was suffering from recession and high unemployment.

Some have argued that although the American political system functions within a structure of democratic pluralism, it is a pluralism of an elitist nature. E. E. Schattschneider wrote that while the United States has a pluralist political process, it has an elitist ring. Surely, pluralist theory provides a better explanation for the gains made by African Americans in American politics than does elite theory. Nevertheless, it has not always been political pluralism for the masses, but elite pluralism. This argument applies not only to the political system as a whole but to the political parties as well. Although elite theory has greater applicability to the Republican party in terms of political philosophy, elements of elitism still pervade the apparatus of the Democratic party. In a two-party system without strong third parties, philosophical and ideological differences are found within as well as between political parties. This was demonstrated by the role of the Democratic Leadership Council in the Democratic party, a core group of party officials who influenced the party's shift to the right. This would explain the "recapturing" of the party by more conservative elements. It may remain this way if centrist Democrats feel it is necessary to maintain control of the White House.

Notes

1. Thomas Cavanaugh and Lorn Foster, *Jesse Jackson's Campaign: The Primaries and the Caucuses* (Washington, D.C.: Joint Center for Political Studies, 1984), 3.

2. Ibid.

3. Mfanya Donald Tryman, "Race and Presidential Campaigns and Elections: The 1984 Democratic Primaries," in *Institutional Racism and Black America*, ed. Tryman (Lexington, Mass.: Ginn Press, 1985), 151.

4. Lucius J. Barker, "Ronald Reagan, Jesse Jackson, and the 1984 Presidential Election: The Continuing American Dilemma of Race," in *The New Black Politics*, 2nd ed., ed. Michael B. Preston, Lenneal J. Henderson, Jr., and Paul L. Puryear (New York: Longman, 1987), 32.

5. John F. Zipp, "Did Jesse Jackson Cause a White Backlash Against the Democrats? A Look at the 1984 Presidential Election," in *Jesse Jackson's 1984 Presidential Campaign*, ed. Lucius J. Barker and Ronald W. Walters (Urbana and Chicago: University of Illinois Press, 1989), 223–24.

6. "Poll: Jackson's Run for Office Caused White Resentment," *Clarion-Ledger*, August 31, 1984, 3A.

7. Tryman, "Race and Presidential Campaigns and Election," 155–56. Jackson, in an off-the-cuff remark, referred to Jews as "Hymies" and to New York City as "Hymietown." Jackson's association with Farrakhan resulted in criticism because of Farrakhan's known anti-Semitic beliefs.

8. Adolph L. Reed, *The Jesse Jackson Phenomenon* (New Haven: Yale University Press, 1986).

9. Cavanaugh and Foster, *Jesse Jackson's Campaign*, 12.

10. Ibid., 12.

11. Ronald W. Walters, "The Emergent Mobilization of the Black Community in the Jackson Campaign for President," in *Jesse Jackson's 1984 Presidential Campaign,* ed. Barker and Walters, 49.

12. Thomas Byrne Edsall and Mary D. Edsall, *Chain Reaction* (New York: W. W. Norton, 1992), 206.

13. Tryman, "Race and Presidential Campaigns and Election," 159–60.

14. Ibid., 162.

15. Barker, "Ronald Reagan, Jesse Jackson, and the 1984 Presidential Election," 35.

16. Ibid.

17. Ibid., 52.

18. Ibid., 32.

19. Ibid., 33.

20. Hanes Walton, Jr., *Invisible Politics* (Albany: State University of New York Press, 1985), 164.

21. Fred I. Greenstein, *The Hidden-Hand Presidency: Eisenhower as Leader* (New York: Basic Books, 1982).

22. Cynthia Tucker, "Race Is the Silent Issue in Presidential Campaign," *Atlanta Journal and Constitution,* March 12,1988, 21A.

23. "The Power Broker," *Newsweek,* March 21, 1988, 21.

24. For a thorough analysis of the lingering significance of race in American presidential politics, see Edward G. Carmines and James C. Stimson, *Issue Evolution in American Politics* (Princeton: Princeton University Press, 1989).

25. For example, see Michael B. Preston, "The Election of Harold Washington: An Examination of the SES Model in the 1983 Chicago Mayoral Election," in *The New Black Politics,* ed. Preston et al., 139–71.

26. Micah L. Sifry, "Jesse and the Jews: Palestine and the Struggle for the Democratic Party," *Middle East Report* 18 (November–December 1988), 8.

27. Ibid., 8–9.

28. "Jackson's Victories in Caucuses Display His Appeal to Whites," *Savannah Morning News,* March 12, 1988, 1A.

29. "Super-Tuesday," *Atlanta Journal and Constitution,* March 10, 1988, 13A.

30. *Atlanta Journal and Constitution,* March 13, 1988, 2C.

31. "Michigan Just the Beginning, Jackson Vows," *Atlanta Journal and Constitution,* March 28, 1988, 1A.

32. Gerald M. Pomper, *The Election of 1988* (Chatham, N.J.: Chatham House, 1989), 44.

33. *Atlanta Journal and Constitution,* March 13, 1988, 2C.

34. Steven H. Haeberle, "Regional Primary or Multiple Campaigns in a Region: Lessons from Super Tuesday 1988," paper presented at the annual

meeting of the Southern Political Science Association Meeting, Atlanta, Georgia, November 3–5, 1988, 7.

35. Reed, *The Jesse Jackson Phenomenon*.

36. Marcus D. Pohlmann, *Black Politics in Conservative America* (White Plains, N.Y.: Longman, 1990), 141.

37. Ibid., 136–37.

38. Georgia A. Persons, "The Election of Gary Franks and the Ascendancy of the New Black Conservatives," in *Dilemmas of Black Politics,* ed. Persons (New York: HarperCollins College Publishers, 1993), 201.

39. Ibid., 201–2.

40. Walton, *Invisible Politics,* 106.

41. Ibid.

42. See Persons, *Dilemmas of Black Politics;* and Huey L. Perry, ed., "Exploring the Meaning and Implications of Deracialization in African American Urban Politics: A Minisymposium," *Urban Affairs Quarterly* 27 (December 1991): 181–215.

43. Patricia Gurin, Shirley Hatchett, and James S. Jackson, *Hope and Independence: Blacks' Response to Electoral and Party Politics* (New York: Russell Sage Foundation, 1989), 156.

44. Ibid., 161.

45. Maureen Dowd, "Candidate Is Tripped Up Over Alliance with Jackson," *New York Times,* April 3, 1992, A12.

46. Lucius J. Barker and Mack H. Jones, *African Americans and the American Political System,* 3rd ed. (Englewood Cliffs, N.J.: Prentice Hall, 1994), 346.

47. Beginning on April 29, 1992, south central Los Angeles was engulfed in a three-day insurrection reflecting the black residents' responses to the acquittal of four Los Angeles police officers who had used excessive force in subduing motorist Rodney King. The riots were marked by the beating of innocent citizens and the looting and destruction of local businesses.

48. Similar racial messages were conveyed to the electorate in presidential primaries in the 1970s and 1980s. While campaigning in Ohio in 1976, Jimmy Carter stated that he believed in "ethnic purity." In 1980, Reagan kicked off his campaign for the presidency in Meridian, Mississippi, by stating that he was for "states' rights." The Bush campaign in 1988 used the Willie Horton scenario to drive a message home to white voters (see note 50 below).

49. R. W. Apple, Jr., "Jackson Sees Character Flaw in Clinton's Remarks on Racism," *New York Times,* A1.

50. The Bush campaign's assault on Dukakis centered on an ad that featured Willie Horton, a black convicted felon who had been released from a Massachusetts prison and had subsequently raped a white woman. In the ad, the Bush campaign accused Dukakis (then governor of Massachusetts) of being lenient on criminals. Bush, who was criticized for the ad, indicated that it had not

been developed by his campaign committee, but by another organization that supported his candidacy.

51. Barker and Jones, *African Americans and the American Political System,* 348.

52. Joseph McCormick, II, and Charles E. Jones, "The Conceptualization of Deracialization: Thinking Through the Dilemma," in *Dilemmas of Black Politics,* ed. Persons, 66–84.

■ *Part III*

Blacks and National Institutions

Chapter 5

Blacks and Presidential Politics

Henry B. Sirgo

Parties and their presidential nominees prosper by putting together winning electoral coalitions. Winning presidential elections is the central objective of the Democratic and Republican parties as national organizations. Ironically, in terms of presidential elections, the Republican party, which was founded as an antislavery party, has become virtually disinterested in black support and the Democratic party, which long served as the leading instrument of black political subjugation in the South, has come to recognize support by blacks as indispensable to its electoral chances. The principal result of this ironic transformation is that blacks switched from overwhelmingly supporting the Republican party to overwhelmingly supporting the Democratic party. Since 1960, blacks have supported the Democratic party in presidential elections more than has any other population group.

This chapter examines how the struggle for racial advancement has influenced and been influenced by Democratic and Republican presidential electoral strategies since the election of 1932. The principal characteristic of black politics during this period is blacks' movement from being objects of the political process to being participants in it and the great sophistication that black leaders and voters have demonstrated in doing so. The transformation of the black vote from solidly Republican to solidly Democratic did not happen instantaneously, but rather over decades and in a manner that showed black awareness of efforts by presidents and party leaders to advance or retard their civil rights, or refrain from taking any action at all regarding their existing civil rights status. Consistent with the central propositions of pluralist theory out-lined in Chapter 2, U.S. government officials and black leaders have been measured in their responses to each other and pursued their interests fully conscious of the possible response of other groups in society.

Observers disagree as to whether current changes in the U.S. party system constitute "realignment," the development of new permanent voting blocs,[1] or "dealignment," the notion that party labels no longer exert much influence on the voting choice of individuals.[2] But analysts are unanimous in saying that the coalitional bases of the Republican and Democratic parties have altered over the past thirty years, at least in presidential elections. Domestic issues are usually the sources of shifts in partisan identification and voting choice.[3] The most commonly cited triggering factor for the current coalitional change is the emergence of civil rights and the place of blacks in U.S. society as a partisan issue.[4] Edward G. Carmines and James A. Stimson, in their analysis of the relationship between racial attitudes and long-term psychological at-tachment to party identification, classify race as a "long duration orthog-onal issue," or an issue that evolves over decades and can lead to fundamental change in the party system.[5] They maintain that race is the only such issue to arise since the New Deal realignment.[6]

Franklin D. Roosevelt and the New Deal Coalition

Blacks supported Franklin D. Roosevelt in 1932 less than they had supported Democratic presidential nominee Alfred M. Smith, whom the Ku Klux Klan had portrayed as a papist agent, in 1928. Little in Roosevelt's candidacy recommended him to black Americans. He had been part of the Woodrow Wilson administration (1913–21), which had aggressively implemented racially discriminatory policies. In 1933, Roosevelt did not mention blacks in his inaugural address. The white and largely fundamentalist South gave 82 percent of its vote to the Episcopalian Roosevelt in 1932, 1936, and 1940, with little variation by socioeconomic status. Roosevelt had closer connections to the South than any other northern candidate for the 1932 Democratic nomination. He had a home in Warm Springs, Georgia, and had served for seven years as assistant secretary of the Navy in the Wilson administration under Secretary of the Navy Josephus Daniels, an "ardent southern progressive." Through his service in the Wilson administration, Roosevelt became well acquainted with most southern Democrats.[7]

Roosevelt was unassailable in the South. The agencies he created, such as the Agricultural Adjustment Administration (AAA), the National Recovery Administration, the Tennessee Valley Authority, and the Rural Electrification Administration, were more important to the South than to any other region of the country.[8] Some of these agencies, like the AAA, ran programs administered by all-white local boards in a blatantly discriminatory manner. The activities of the AAA contributed to an increase in black farm tenancy and a decrease in black farm ownership.[9] Yet such notable New Dealers as Harold Ickes and Eleanor Roosevelt brought prominent blacks like Robert Weaver and Mary McLeod Bethune into the administration. Secretary of Interior Ickes and Mrs. Roosevelt were politically sophisticated and deeply experienced in the operations of civil rights organizations and were visibly concerned about the political and economic rights of black Americans.[10] Roosevelt was able to secure the nomination of the first black federal judge, William Hastie; the first female federal judge, Florence Allen; and two white males on the U.S. Supreme Court who compiled strong civil rights records, William O. Douglas and Hugo Black.[11] These actions notwithstanding, Roosevelt did not demonstrably promote the cause of black rights for fear that such advocacy would alienate powerful southern white congressmen and thus compromise his proposed economic and social reforms for the country. Two stark facts were that the South was the nation's most impoverished region and that blacks were almost totally disenfranchised in the region. Roosevelt never challenged the system of racial segregation in the South. To have done so would have substantially weakened his electoral support there, with a probably deleterious impact on his reelection effort.

Under pressure from the National Association for the Advancement of Colored People (NAACP) and the National Urban League, Roosevelt engaged in activities to reassure blacks that they were progressing socially and economically without diminishing his southern white political support. Shortly before the 1940 election, the post office issued a stamp commemorating the seventy-fifth anniversary of the ratification of the Thirteenth Amendment a few months earlier than scheduled, so that its issuance would precede the election. The post office also issued the first stamp with a black person on it: George Washington Carver.[12]

Roosevelt's subordination of civil rights issues to economic and social goals was a harbinger of later efforts by President John F. Kennedy.[13] Roosevelt believed that helping lower-income people generally was the only way he could help blacks without splitting the party. Roosevelt's legislative initiatives were assigned to House and Senate committees chaired overwhelmingly by white southerners. These white southerners acquired their powerful positions in Congress as a result of being re-elected several times in safe, majority white districts. Furthermore, before World War II, Roosevelt had to contend with white southerners who held the positions of vice president, Senate majority leader, and Speaker of the House. Roosevelt's only notable administrative action in the area of civil rights was the establishment by executive order of a temporary Fair Employment Practices Committee (FEPC), responsible for investigating complaints of discrimination in government employment and defense industries. Roosevelt issued this order only because of A. Philip Randolph's threatened march on Washington.

Randolph, a noted civil rights leader and president of the Brotherhood of Sleeping Car Porters, in 1940 "sought administration support for the inclusion of antidiscrimination clauses in all defense contracts negotiated by the Office of Production Management and for an end to segregation in the armed forces." A meeting between Randolph and Roosevelt failed to produce administration backing for the proposals. Subsequently Randolph turned his organizational skills to planning a mass demonstration in Washington, to be held on July 1, 1941. In mid-June 1941, negotiations resumed; the president issued an executive order on June 25, 1941. Executive Order No. 8802 forbade discrimination in the war industry on the basis of race, creed, or color and established the FEPC to oversee the enforcement of the antidiscrimination objective.[14]

Because the FEPC was not effective in preventing discrimination against blacks, it was later reorganized into a more effective committee. The Right Reverend Monsignor Francis J. Haas was appointed chairman of the new Committee on Fair Employment Practices in 1943.[15] The need for a vigorous Committee on Fair Employment Practices was underscored by the frequent attacks on black soldiers in uniform by whites. Such incidents provoked racial disorders in Los Angeles, Detroit, and other cities in 1943.[16] Paul V. McNutt, chairman of the Office for Emergency Management of the War Manpower Commission, maintained that such incidents endangered domestic support for the war effort and might squander minority manpower resources.[17] Robert Weaver was given responsibility for developing policies to address the issue of blacks and the military. Weaver developed a four-step program that consisted of the highly publicized announcement of policies of full protection for all military personnel everywhere, accepting the commissioning of black officers in the U.S. Navy and Marines, effectively handling labor union–originated discrimination against blacks, and utilizing black men and women in the nation's chronically discriminatory transportation and communication industries.[18]

Harry S Truman and the Emergent Civil Rights Movement

Harry Truman's candidacy depended on appealing to blacks and liberal northerners. Truman did far worse in the South than did Roosevelt in any of his campaigns. Truman's family background as a grandson of Confederate sympathizers did not inspire confidence among blacks; yet Truman moved forward far more decisively in the area of civil rights than had his predecessor.[19] Truman spoke out strongly during the presidential campaign of 1948 on his proposed anti–poll tax and antilynching legislation. Big-city machine Democrats in the Northeast urged the 1948 party convention to adopt a strong civil rights plank in order to mobilize black political support for the party's candidates at all levels. Truman saw the adoption of a strong civil rights plank in 1948 as a natural development. He served on the platform committees of the 1936, 1940, and 1944 Democratic National Conventions. The major problem he perceived was how to develop meaningful civil rights measures without driving away southern white supporters.[20] In this regard, Truman was a full step ahead of Roosevelt in his approach to how best to reconcile the interests of blacks, white southerners, and the Democratic party. Roosevelt chose a class-based approach to reconciling the three interests. Truman chose the far more difficult approach of favoring the development of specific government remedies for some of the problems of blacks in a way that would not drive away southern whites from the Democratic party.

The Truman campaign explicitly emphasized different issues in different sections of the country. The campaign stressed civil rights in the Northeast and California, the economic gains of the New Deal in the South, federal water projects in the West and Oklahoma, and labor policy and farm aid programs in the Midwest.[21] Truman and his chief campaign adviser, Clark Clifford, were primarily concerned about black support in order to carry the home state of his Republican opponent, Governor Thomas E. Dewey of New York. Truman's strategists perceived the black press as overwhelmingly Republican and black voters as amenable to a return to their traditional political home, the party of Lincoln. Even in the absence of such a development, the strategists feared that if Truman did not vigorously promote the moral cause of civil rights, the black vote in Harlem would go strongly for third-party candidate Henry Wallace; in this event, they believed that the electoral votes of New York, which they perceived incorrectly as a must-win state, would be won by the state's Republican governor.[22]

The Democrats also had to take a strong stand on civil rights because the Republican party was unassailable on civil rights and in some respects, even when excluding southern Democrats from consideration, had a better civil rights record than the Democratic party. Republicans in Congress had a slightly better voting record on civil rights and liberties issues than northern Democrats. Furthermore, in 1944 Governor Dewey signed legislation creating the first statewide fair employment practices commission. The chairman of the Republican National Committee in 1948 was Hugh Scott, who was sensitive to civil rights issues.

Truman's campaign advisers considered black-white coalitional voting essential for carrying New York, Massachusetts, Ohio, Illinois, New Jersey, Pennsylvania, and California.[23] The focus of the campaign was "the working people, the veterans, and the Negroes."[24] Truman's advisers anticipated that the only serious challenge to his reelection from within the ranks of the Democratic party would be from Wallace on the left and concluded that the central appeal of the campaign had to be to the liberal, progressive independent voter in the North who had supported Roosevelt.[25] It was assumed that the virtually all-white southern electorate would vote in its traditional fashion for the Democratic party, particularly since New Deal policies had benefited the region economically.[26]

Deductive evidence shows that, from the standpoint of traditional rank-and-file support for the Democratic party at the time, Truman and Clifford were quite rational in assuming that the South would support the Democratic ticket. The authors of *The Changing American Voter* indicate that in the 1950s, lower-class native white southerners were twenty-one points more liberal on social-welfare issues than the average American of voting age.[27] In addition, Bruce Campbell, in a study of the period from 1952 to 1972, found no change in partisanship attributable to civil rights issues among adult native white southerners.[28]

Given the dynamics of ideological and partisan shifts, these two observations were probably also applicable to the native white southern electorate in 1948. However, Truman and Clifford failed to take into account the roles of the Democratic members of Congress in the government and the party organization at the state level. Barbara Sinclair suggests that southern political elites and their financial supporters during this period were far more conservative than the southern masses.[29] Truman's campaign advisers overestimated the extent to which southern Democratic members of Congress perceived their own reelection prospects as dependent on Truman's reelection.[30]

The detachment of certain state party organizations to Truman's candidacy was even more pronounced than was the southern congressional relationship with the candidacy. Governor William M. Tuck of Virginia campaigned vigorously for the national Dixiecrat ticket and supported state legislation that would have given a party committee comprising leaders from the state's powerful Harry Byrd machine, which was decidedly anti-Truman, "the power to determine for whom Virginia's Democratic electors would be instructed to vote after the Democratic National Convention."[31] The Virginia State Central Committee publicly announced its refusal to campaign for the national Democratic ticket and instructed "the city and county committees to campaign only for the senatorial and congressional candidates."[32] Truman despised disloyalty, particularly as it pertained to party matters.[33] Given the nonsupport from the state party organization, organized black and labor support was vital to the successful outcome of Truman's campaign in Virginia in 1948.

Truman carried the South except for the four states that listed Governor Strom Thurmond of South Carolina on the ballot as the official Democratic presidential nominee: South Carolina, Alabama, Mississippi, and Louisiana.[34] In Alabama, Truman electors were not even listed on the ballot. Truman became the first Democrat elected to the presidency without winning New York. However, Truman won California, where the Republican party's vice presidential nominee, Earl Warren, was a popular governor. The only western state where the Democratic presidential ticket did not win was Oregon.[35]

Truman was concerned after his election that individuals who prospered electorally by association with the Democratic party were not supporting it in national campaigns. The 1948 campaign effort reinforced Truman's and his White House staff's notion that it was important to circumvent defiant state Democratic organizations by nurturing grass-roots support for the national party leadership. Because he could not accept having to bargain with uncooperative state party elites, Truman and his White House staff, supported by the Democratic National Committee, nurtured organizational bases that were independent of recalcitrant state Democratic party organizations, such as those of Virginia and Mississippi.[36]

Truman's strategy to target the black vote was successful. Before the Democratic convention, black voters were undecided; yet Truman won 70 percent of the black vote, which enabled him to secure the margin of victory in a state-by-state biracial coalitional pattern. Truman was not unmindful of the critical role that blacks played in his election, and he demonstrated his appreciation to them with favorable governmental initiatives, among them the issuance of two highly visible executive orders concerning civil rights on July 27, 1948. One created a Fair Employment Board in the Civil Service Commission to eliminate discrimination in the federal civil service and the other desegregated the armed forces. He also established through executive order a Committee on Government Contract Compliance. Its establishment meant that efforts were made for the first time to implement the nondiscrimination clauses in government contracts.

Eisenhower and Black Civil Rights

President Dwight D. Eisenhower, although not an enthusiastic supporter of civil rights, was the first president to appoint a black to an executive position in the White House. E. Frederic Morrow was on leave from a public affairs position with the Columbia Broadcasting System (CBS) in August 1952 when he joined Eisenhower's campaign staff. He campaigned vigorously with Eisenhower throughout the nation. Based on the promise of a White House job in the event of Eisenhower's election,

he resigned his position at CBS and experienced months of unemployment because of racial prejudice by some of President Eisenhower's
closest advisers, who temporarily prevented Morrow's appointment to
a position with the new administration.[37] Eventually, he was offered
the position of adviser for business affairs in the Department of Commerce and he accepted it.[38] In 1955, he accepted the position of administrative officer for special projects with the White House and served in
that position for the remainder of the administration. Morrow was an
outstanding campaigner for the Republican party, even during such
gloomy times for the party as the midterm elections of 1958, when it
endured a net loss of forty-five seats in the House of Representatives
and thirteen seats in the Senate.[39]

Morrow maintains that Eisenhower failed to fulfill his potential in
improving race relations because he was not politically savvy, owing to
his military background, and because of undue influence of southerners
who were Eisenhower's close friends during his administration and
his subordinates during his military career. Morrow was reluctant to
campaign for Eisenhower in 1952 until he explained why he had testified
before a congressional committee opposing the integration of the armed
forces in 1945. Eisenhower asked Morrow's forgiveness and said that
his views were based on the overwhelmingly negative viewpoints of his
field commanders, most of whom were southerners.[40]

The Eisenhower administration completed the desegregation of the
armed forces begun under Harry Truman and in 1957 brought about
the passage of the first civil rights legislation in nearly a hundred years.
That same year, President Eisenhower sent federal troops to Little Rock,
Arkansas, to enforce a federal court order to desegregate Central High
School, after Arkansas Governor Orval Faubus used the National Guard
to prevent nine black students from enrolling in the school. The federal
troops were stationed there until the school year was over.[41] Perhaps
Eisenhower's greatest contribution to the advancement of black civil
rights in the South was unintended: that is, his nomination of Republican
California Governor Earl Warren as chief justice of the U.S. Supreme
Court. The Warren Court from 1954 to 1969 was a vigorous advocate
of expanding civil rights for southern blacks.

President Eisenhower was able to increase his share of the nonwhite
vote from 21 percent in 1952 to 39 percent in 1956 as a result of Adlai
Stevenson's vacillation on civil rights issues in an effort to appease both

the northern and southern wings of the Democratic party.[42] Representative Adam Clayton Powell (D-N.Y.) switched his support to Eisenhower and influenced tens of thousands of black voters to support him as well. The lead person in the Eisenhower administration seeking black votes was Attorney General Herbert Brownell, whose service as chairman of the Republican National Committee led him to understand the strategic benefit to the Republican party of splitting the northern and southern wings of the Democratic party. Just as Truman and Clark Clifford had realized in 1948 when they were in the process of defeating Dewey, Brownell was aware that the black vote was crucial in large northern industrial states.

Morrow asserts that the Republican party never seriously courted black support, either during the Eisenhower administration or in subsequent Republican presidential administrations, and as a result, endured presidential defeats in 1960 and 1976. In 1960, Morrow tried to persuade the Republican presidential nominee, Vice President Richard Nixon, to send a letter offering his support to Mrs. Martin Luther King, Jr., when her husband was arrested in Georgia. His suggestion was ridiculed by Nixon's campaign staff. The Democratic presidential nominee, Senator John F. Kennedy of Massachusetts, offered support to Mrs. King, which was highly publicized nationally. Kennedy was elected president with strong black support in the closest presidential election in American history. Since Nixon was not viewed unfavorably by blacks at that point in his political career and many blacks were undecided on whom to vote for, Kennedy's telephone call to Mrs. King tipped the balance in his favor among many undecided blacks. This was an important factor in Kennedy's victory.

Ironically, in 1959, Martin Luther King, Jr., expressed admiration for Vice President Nixon and considered him the only likely presidential contender concerned about civil rights.[43] Vice President Nixon organized an effort to have the President's Committee on Government Contracts hold a conference on racial discrimination in employment with companies that contracted with the federal government in the spring of that year and invited King to speak.[44] King was impressed by the ringing declaration Nixon gave to the efforts to end such discrimination and by subsequent conversations they had on issues of civil rights. King believed Nixon, unlike President Eisenhower, would use the office of the presidency to strongly defend the Supreme Court's decision in *Brown v. Board of Education of Topeka* and the cause of civil rights.[45]

Democratic Presidents and the Black Vote in the 1960s and 1970s

John F. Kennedy's rapport with southern political leaders contributed to his margin of victory in the region in the 1960 presidential election. Paralleling Roosevelt's situation in 1932, Senator Kennedy had closer connections to the South than any other previous northern candidate for the Democratic presidential nomination except Roosevelt. Governor J. P. Coleman of Mississippi persuaded many southern delegates to the 1956 National Democratic Convention to support Kennedy for the vice presidential nomination over their fellow southerner, Senator Estes Kefauver of Tennessee. Kennedy spoke throughout the South during the late 1950s.[46] He voted with segregationist Mississippi Senator James Eastland, chairman of the Judiciary Committee, to refer the House-passed version of the bill that was to become the Civil Rights Act of 1957 to Eastland's committee and supported an amendment to the bill requiring jury trials in voting discrimination cases, which became part of the 1957 act. This amendment made implementation of the act virtually impossible.[47] The incorporation of jury trials into the legislation vitiated the act because during this period all-white juries in the South did not convict whites accused of violating blacks' rights.[48]

Kennedy chose the Senate majority leader and competitor for the 1960 nomination, Lyndon B. Johnson, as his running mate. Civil rights leaders at the 1960 Democratic National Convention found Kennedy's lukewarm support of civil rights and choice of Johnson (a southerner elected by a virtually all-white electorate) for vice president disappointing, although they were somewhat placated by a strong civil rights plank in the party's platform.

Kennedy's improved electoral performance among blacks over that of Adlai Stevenson, the Democratic presidential nominee in 1952 and 1956, as mentioned, can be attributed at least in part to his spontaneous decision to telephone Mrs. King during the campaign when her husband was arrested in Georgia.[49] Kennedy's share of the nonwhite vote was 68 percent compared with 61 percent for Stevenson in the 1956 election.[50] Kennedy's brother Robert then managed to secure King's release. Kennedy's margin of victory in Texas, South Carolina, and North Carolina was smaller than the black vote plurality received in each of those states. Given the historic closeness of the 1960 presidential election, Kennedy's increased percentage of the nonwhite vote was an important factor in his victory.

Lyndon Johnson, the first native and resident southerner to head a major party ticket in more than a hundred years, was the first Democratic nominee to perform better in the North than in the South. This was because he had championed and achieved the passage of the Civil Rights Act of 1964 and his Republican opponent, Senator Barry Goldwater, had voted against it. The law, among other provisions, provided access for all races to places of public accommodation engaged in interstate commerce and prohibited denial of the right to vote in any election for national public office because of minor errors on registration forms. Title VII of the Civil Rights Act of 1964 prohibited private sector employment discrimination on the basis of "race, color, religion, sex, or national origin."

The *Meridian Star* of Mississippi condemned Johnson to a notch lower than that of General William Tecumseh Sherman for his betrayal of the South.[51] Senator Ralph Yarborough of Texas, a Democrat, was the only senator from the South to vote for the legislation. While he was criticized for his action by his Republican opponent, George Bush, in the Texas Senate race in 1964, Yarborough won reelection handily. Johnson won the 1964 presidential election by a landslide. Johnson, acting on a mandate given to him by the voters in the 1964 election, which also greatly increased the ranks of northern Democratic liberals in Congress and reduced the contingent of southern Democratic committee chairmen in Congress, vigorously and successfully promoted passage of legislation that became the Voting Rights Act of 1965.

In part because of the Democrats' role in enacting the pathbreaking 1964 Civil Rights Act and the 1965 Voting Rights Act, and in part because of the subsequent marked increase in black voter registration in the South and continued black voter loyalty to Democratic presidential candidates—both of which alienated conservative blue-collar workers and southern whites from the party—Vice President Hubert H. Humphrey in 1968 and Senator George S. McGovern in 1972 both lost their presidential races. Humphrey carried only one state of the old Confederacy, Texas, and McGovern carried only one state in the nation,

Massachusetts. Only 38 percent of white voters supported Humphrey in 1968 and only 32 percent supported McGovern. Their respective levels of support from nonwhites were 85 percent and 87 percent.[52]

The Voting Rights Act of 1965 made possible a biracial coalition that enabled Democrat Jimmy Carter, a southerner, nearly to sweep the South in 1976. Carter could not have won the election without strong support from blacks in the presidential primaries and overwhelming black support in the general election.[53]

Carter was highly accessible to black groups, meeting with them thirty times during the first two-and-a-half years of his presidency.[54] President Carter regularly met with the Congressional Black Caucus and worked with the caucus to bring about the adoption and implementation of a $400 million Urban Development Action Grant (UDAG) program, which provided "HUD with discretionary funds to meet urgent needs of distressed agencies."[55] Patricia Roberts Harris, initially the Carter administration's secretary of housing and urban development and later its secretary of health and human services, headed an interagency task force that developed the UDAG program.

A veteran of the Kennedy and Johnson administrations, Harris became the first black female member of a presidential cabinet in U.S. history. Her two cabinet appointments demonstrated the Carter administration's efforts to place blacks and women in policy-making positions in the government. Other noteworthy black appointees included Eleanor Holmes Norton, chairwoman of the Equal Employment Opportunity Commission; Andrew Young, U.S. ambassador to the United Nations; Drew Days, assistant attorney general for civil rights; and Wade McCree, solicitor general of the United States. Had a vacancy occurred on the Supreme Court during Carter's presidency, McCree would have become the second black to serve on the Court in addition to being the second black in the nation's history to hold the office of solicitor general. President Johnson had appointed Thurgood Marshall to both positions. President Carter appointed thirty-seven black federal judges, more than all other presidents in American history.[56]

Blacks, Republican Presidential Strategy, and Richard Nixon

Republican actions encouraged the realignment of blacks into the Democratic party. Such an approach is questionable in light of the first two propositions of pluralist theory presented in Chapter 2. Proposition One states that political resources are noncumulative, and Proposition Two states that "the decision-making process is characterized by multiple centers of power." The notion that a "lily-white" Republican party can dominate U.S. politics makes implausible assumptions about blacks and whites.

Blacks clearly have political resources; most notably, they constitute a significant and growing part of the U.S. electorate and have a rich organizational life. Black organizations run the gamut from the NAACP to the Urban League to the church. A constant of U.S. political life has been that organizational vitality has a major influence on political power. White interests are not monolithic, and, in an increasingly varied society, white voting behavior cannot be expected to be nearly unanimous for long. Poor whites in Appalachia cannot be expected to have the same values as corporate chief executives and middle management officials; nor for that matter, are the interests of white small business people and multinational corporation officials, an overwhelmingly white group, the same. Given the coalitional nature of parties, one seeking long-term electoral success can neither alienate nor take for granted a sizable segment of the voting age population.

Republicans and northern Democrats had comparable civil rights voting records until the Seventy-Ninth Congress (1945–46).[57] The 1944 Republican party platform, four years ahead of the Democrats, called for fair employment practices legislation.[58] The Republican party's nominee that year and in 1948, Governor Dewey of New York, had earlier become the first governor in the nation to sign comparable state legislation.

In 1964 and 1965, Senate Republican leader Everett Dirksen of Illinois worked closely with Hubert Humphrey (D-Minn.) and northern Democratic senators to fashion civil rights legislation. More Republicans than Democrats voted for the passage of the Civil Rights Act of 1964 and the Voting Rights Act of 1965. Southern blacks voted Republican slightly more than the nation as a whole in the 1956 presidential election, and black voters in 1960 generally voted Democratic no more than did whites of comparable socioeconomic status.[59] In 1964, the Republican party chose Senator Barry M. Goldwater (R-Ariz.) as its presidential nominee, who had several years earlier embraced a "southern strategy" and declared, "We are not going to get the Negro vote as a bloc in

1964 and 1968, so we ought to go hunting where the ducks are."[60] The reaction of blacks was significant. The Republican share of the nonwhite vote dropped from 32 percent in 1960 to 6 percent in 1964.[61] Goldwater lost to Johnson by a landslide margin.

Despite Goldwater's huge loss, 1968 Republican presidential candidate and former vice-president Richard Nixon was impressed by the senator's victory in five southern states and made winning the South a fundamental component of his campaign strategy. The Nixon administration's pursuit of a southern strategy, which incorporated efforts to slow down the pace of public school desegregation, further alienated blacks from the Republican party.

The "New" Nixon and His Southern Strategy

Nixon campaigned vigorously against busing and the imputed excesses of the Earl Warren Court, which had been a champion of civil rights, from its unanimous verdict in the 1954 *Brown v. Board of Education of Topeka,*[62] which declared segregation in public schools to be in violation of the equal protection clause of the Fourteenth Amendment, to its 1966 ruling in *Harper v. Virginia,*[63] which outlawed the poll tax. Ironically, the pace of public school desegregation accelerated during Nixon's administration. This occurred despite Nixon's 1971 nomination of Warren Burger to succeed Earl Warren as chief justice. In *Swann v. Charlotte-Mecklenburg County Board of Education* a unanimous Court upheld the use of "busing" to achieve desegregation.[64]

Once in office, Nixon moved swiftly to have the Justice Department for the first time in its history enter school desegregation cases to slow down the pace of integration.[65] Moreover, the Voting Rights Act of 1965 was due to expire in 1970, and Nixon, in actions later mirrored by Gerald Ford and Ronald Reagan in 1975 and 1982 respectively, initially opposed its extension and sought without success to substitute a weaker measure for the protection of black voting rights. Congress, especially the Senate, resumed the dominant position vis-à-vis the presidency as guarantor of voting rights that it had occupied during the proposal and ratification of the Fifteenth Amendment to the Constitution. In his landslide victory in 1972, President Nixon's share of the black vote was 13 percent.[66]

Blacks and Post-Nixon Republican Administrations

President Gerald R. Ford, while displaying more sensitivity to black aspirations than had Nixon, had had a poor civil rights voting record as a member of the House of Representatives from Michigan. Ford, as minority leader of the House, voted against fair housing legislation in 1966, although by 1968 he had reversed his position.[67] Furthermore, he unsuccessfully led opposition to a Johnson administration reorganization plan for the District of Columbia, which was structured to ensure governance of the area by a " 'broadly representative' nine-member City Council" rather than by the then-used Board of Commissioners consisting of whites from the U.S. Army Corps of Engineers. Democratic Whip Hale Boggs of Louisiana was instrumental in upholding President Johnson's reorganization plan.[68] President Ford, however, had a supportive record with respect to the U.S. Civil Rights Commission.[69] On March 12, 1975, a meeting between President Ford and the Civil Rights Commission went well and reached a consensus that both sides should have more intimate collaboration.[70] In June 1975, President Ford issued Executive Order No. 11869, which exempted the commission's chairman, Arthur Flemming, a Republican with an outstanding record as a champion of civil rights, from mandatory retirement.[71]

President Reagan was not sympathetic to civil rights issues during his eight-year administration. He was not as kind to Flemming and the other liberal members of the commission as President Ford had been. He forced the resignation of Flemming and his liberal colleagues on the commission because they had criticized his administration's civil rights policies. Ironically, Flemming's successor on this commission was one of Reagan's few high-level black appointees, Clarence Pendleton. Pendleton, until his death in 1988, functioned as an aggressive critic of affirmative action programs and traditional black leadership groups such as the NAACP. Moreover, President Reagan nominated Robert Bork, a staunch conservative, to the Supreme Court in 1987. Bork wrote in a 1964 article that the then-pending Civil Rights Act of 1964, which would force white-owned businesses to serve blacks, constituted an unsurpassed kind of ugliness. Bork's nomination to the Supreme Court was blocked as a result of opposition from black and other liberal groups who viewed the nominee as too conservative and a threat to their interests. Reagan also appointed William Bradford Reynolds, also very conservative, to the position of assistant attorney general for civil rights. Reynolds saw his chief mission as trying "to narrow the remedies that can be used to correct discriminatory practices."[72]

Black electoral support for Reagan was low in 1980 (14 percent) and lower in 1984 (9 percent).[73] Reagan had been an outspoken critic of civil rights measures and Martin Luther King, Jr., during the 1960s. His administration's support of measures such as tax-exempt status for segregated educational institutions and his self-imposed isolation from civil rights groups further deteriorated his poor relationship with blacks.[74] As Robert Axelrod maintains, coalitions are fluid and Reagan's departure from the presidency presented opportunities for the Republican party to expand its support among blacks and to increase its competitiveness in elections at the state and local levels.[75]

Blacks were one of the few groups to increase their support, albeit slightly, for the Republican presidential candidate from 1984 to 1988. The level of support went from 9 to 12 percent.[76] This increase occurred despite the use of the notorious and effective Willie Horton political advertisement on behalf of George Bush's candidacy, which attacked Democratic opponent Michael Dukakis for his furlough program when he was governor of Massachusetts. The Republican advertisement carried the subliminal message that Dukakis and the Democrats were soft on black crime.

The Horton advertisement was incongruous with Bush's history of racial moderation. Bush had never been a race-baiter and had been accessible to blacks throughout his political career. He had won election to the House of Representatives in 1966 from Texas against a rabidly segregationist Democratic candidate.[77] For well over a year into his administration, he was the first modern Republican president to have had virtually the same job performance approval rating among blacks as whites.[78]

President Bush met far more frequently with black leaders than did President Reagan and appointed many blacks to high political office: Louis Sullivan, secretary of health and human services; Frederick D. McClure, assistant to the president for legislative affairs; and Colin Powell, chairman of the Joint Chiefs of Staff. The assistant attorney general for civil rights in the Justice Department, John Donne, and the solicitor general, Kenneth Starr, were far more sympathetic to black concerns than their respective predecessors in the Reagan administration, William Bradford Reynolds and Charles Fried, had been.[79] Donne, for example, argued that Section 2 of the Voting Rights Act as amended in 1982, which prohibits the dilution of minority group voting strength, covers all elections, including those for judicial positions. This view is now official policy.

President Bush failed blacks' litmus test when he vetoed the Civil Rights Act of 1990. The proposed legislation was a response to three decisions delivered in June 1989 by the Supreme Court. These cases, all decided by 5-to-4 majorities, shifted the burden of proof in Title VII employment discrimination cases from employers to employees. Bush's stated reason for vetoing the legislation was that the proposed legislation would have necessitated the use of quotas by employers.

President Bush repeated the quota charge when the House of Representatives passed similar legislation in June 1991.[80] Yet on November 21, Bush signed the Civil Rights Act of 1991, which did not differ significantly from the Civil Rights Act of 1990. Bush stated that he decided to sign the 1991 legislation because the objectionable part of the 1990 legislation with regard to quotas had been removed. Blacks were disappointed when Bush vetoed the 1990 legislation, and his approval of the 1991 legislation did not change their attitude toward him.

Blacks and the Clinton Presidency

Black support for President George Bush was minimal on November 3, 1992. White support for Bush was at its lowest level for a Republican presidential candidate since 1964. Governor Bill Clinton of Arkansas won the election with 43 percent of the vote, while Bush followed with 37 percent, and independent candidate Ross Perot received 19 percent.[81] Among white voters, 39 percent voted for Clinton, 41 percent for Bush, and 19 percent for Perot. Among black voters, 82 percent voted for Clinton, 11 percent for Bush, and 7 percent for Perot.[82] Clinton won 370 Electoral College votes, while Bush won 168, and Perot did not win any.[83] Clinton ran well in all regions of the nation while Perot was noticeably weakest in the South.[84] Perot's vote-getting ability was inversely related to the percentage of blacks in the voting age population at both state and county levels. For example, in Calcasieu Parish, Louisiana, which has a disproportionately small black population compared with the rest of the state, Perot garnered 15.6 percent of the vote compared with the 12 percent he received statewide. Respective figures for Clinton and Bush in Calcasieu Parish (CP) and Louisiana (LA) were 48.5 percent (CP)/46 percent (LA) and 35.9 percent (CP)/42 percent (LA).[85] The nonracial character of Ross Perot's campaign generated relatively little interest among either blacks or whites living in areas with substantial black populations. Consequently, his minor party campaign fared quite differently than did the efforts of segregationists Strom Thurmond in 1948 and George Wallace in 1968, both of whom carried four of the five Deep South states. Thurmond carried South Carolina, Alabama, Mississippi, and Louisiana. Wallace won Georgia, Alabama, Mississippi, and Louisiana. Perot stressed the economy, in particular the deficit, rather than segregation or racial code words (in contrast to Thurmond and Wallace).

Ross Perot's criticism of Reagan and Bush's economic policies worked to Bill Clinton's advantage.[86] Since the New Deal realignment, Democratic presidential candidates have been more successful in those elections where the electorate has considered the economy the most important issue.

Jesse Jackson, who had sought the nomination of the Democratic party for president in 1984 and 1988, played a major role in the 1992 election. In January 1992 his Rainbow Coalition conducted a forum where all announced Democratic presidential candidates were scrutinized.[87] Allen D. Hertzke has noted the following:

> Through tireless travel and exhortation, Jackson kept the Rainbow Coalition alive in 1992. Every one of the Democratic presidential candidates appealed for support from the Rainbow. They praised Jackson and echoed many of the populist economic [strategies] he had stressed in 1988—especially the "invest in America" theme, which was included in the 1992 Democratic platform.[88]

Other Jackson positions endorsed by then-Governor Clinton (D-Ark.) included statehood for the District of Columbia and the establishment of a national health care system.[89] Jesse Jackson endorsed Clinton for the presidency on the eve of the 1992 Democratic National Convention.[90]

Jackson worked diligently to increase voter registration and spoke in commercials sponsored by the Democratic National Committee on predominantly black listener radio stations to urge support for Clinton, vice presidential nominee Al Gore, senator from Tennessee, and the entire Democratic ticket. Shortly after the election, in a guest sermon at a Roman Catholic church in Little Rock, Arkansas, Jackson praised Clinton "as a leader who could 'make the nation whole.' "[91] Blacks played an important role in electing a president more sympathetic to their needs and the cause of civil rights.

President-elect Clinton chose Vernon E. Jordan, a prominent black with a distinguished record in civil rights, to serve as co-chairman of his transition team along with Warren Christopher. Christopher was a Los Angeles attorney who had served as deputy secretary of state in the Carter administration and would later become Clinton's secretary of state. Jordan had served in 1962 as field secretary for the NAACP in Georgia and from 1971 through 1981 as head of the Urban League.[92] He was also instrumental in the selection of Gore as Clinton's running mate, a choice that enhanced the competitiveness of the ticket in the South and apparently assisted it in carrying Tennessee, Louisiana, and Georgia.[93] President Clinton's cabinet, initially composed of four blacks, two Latinos, four women, and six white males, was the most diverse presidential cabinet in U.S. history. Given Jordan's lifelong dedication to increasing opportunity for blacks, he probably played a substantial role in helping to fashion the historic diversity of that cabinet. Black members of the original cabinet were Mike Espy, secretary of agriculture; Ronald H. Brown, secretary of commerce; Hazel R. O'Leary, secretary of energy; Jesse Brown, secretary of veterans affairs; and Lee Brown, drug policy coordinator. Blacks serving in important subcabinet positions included Drew Days, solicitor general; Ron Noble, assistant secretary of the treasury for enforcement; Joycelyn Elders, surgeon general; and Clifford R. Wharton, Jr., deputy secretary of state.[94]

On February 1, 1994, President Clinton nominated a black Boston attorney who had previously worked for the NAACP Legal Defense Fund, Deval Patrick, to be assistant attorney general for civil rights. Clinton's filling of this position was a slow and arduous task. In June 1993 he had withdrawn his nomination of black law professor Lani Guinier, whose scholarly writings had come under fire for allegedly calling for "novel forms of proportional representation and minority veto powers that would increase the political influence of the black community only at the expense of democratic principles."[95] U.S. Representative Kweisi Mfume, a Baltimore Democrat and head of the Congressional Black Caucus, criticized the president's action.[96] Nevertheless in remarks at the annual Congressional Black Caucus Dinner on September 18, 1993, Clinton advocated the drawing of district lines to "increase the empowerment of minorities,"[97] a view shared by Deval Patrick.[98] Representative Mfume spoke highly of the nomination shortly after its announcement, although he still found the administration's pace of filling this important position disappointingly slow.[99]

President Clinton's efforts on behalf of another issue important to blacks drew mixed reviews from black leaders. On November 21, 1993, the House of Representatives defeated "a bill to grant statehood to the District of Columbia."[100] Delegate Eleanor Holmes Norton (D-D.C.) spoke highly of the president's calling of members, at her request, to solicit their votes for the legislation. But Jesse Jackson saw his efforts yield only lukewarm response as the bill was defeated by a margin of 153–277.[101] Only one Republican, Wayne T. Gilchrist of Maryland, voted for the measure.

Blacks have been among those most favorably predisposed toward President Clinton's top legislative priority, his health care plan. The proposal to provide universal coverage was favored by a majority of the respondents to an Associated Press poll. But majorities in only three groups—blacks, Democrats, and those in families earning under $25,000 per year—reported that implementation of the plan would improve their health care coverage.[102]

Summary and Conclusions

Presidential support of black issues and black support of presidential candidates have been uneven from Roosevelt to Clinton. Not surprisingly, these two levels of support are linked. Presidential support of black issues has been most significant when black support provided the critical margin of victory, as in the presidential elections of 1948, 1960, 1976, and 1992. The presidential election of 1964 is an exception to this general rule in that blacks received benefits from the Johnson administration even though the strong electoral support he received from blacks was not critical to his election.

Presidents who have been most responsive to blacks have all been Democrats. In general, this has resulted in greater black support for the Democratic party than the Republican party in presidential elections and Democratic presidents more supportive of black issues than Republican presidents. This general trend, however, has not boded well for blacks because the Republican party, before the 1992 election, had controlled the presidency for twenty-eight of the forty years since Eisenhower's election in 1952.

If the Democratic party wishes to extend its success of 1992 to 1996 and into the twenty-first century, it must continue to stress economic issues in its campaigns and to have its candidates collaborate with black political influentials early in the election process. Governor Clinton did this when he secured the endorsement of Representative William Jefferson (D-La.) in January 1991.[103] This strategy is one reason why the Democrats have continued to be dominant in the South in most elections other than those for the presidency.

Blacks have serious economic problems, not all of which are exclusively theirs. Black family income was 62 percent of median white family income in 1975; by 1990, black family income was only 58 percent of white family income. Furthermore, in constant dollars black families in 1990 earned $39 less per year than they did in 1972.[104] Ideas for dealing with economic opportunities, and implicitly with race relations, include welfare reform as enunciated by President Clinton and empowerment as promoted by former Secretary of Housing and Urban Development Jack Kemp.

About as many whites as blacks are on welfare, but reality is often less important than perception in the conduct of campaigns.[105] David Duke garnered a majority of white votes in his Louisiana U.S. Senate and gubernatorial bids by condemning welfare "parasites." Gerald Wright, Jr., has observed that "the identification of welfare with blacks appears to be increasing" and that criticism of welfare provides a socially acceptable means for whites with antiblack feelings to express such attitudes.[106] If this "excuse" for white racism is taken away, perhaps the degree of white racism and racially polarized voting in the United States will decrease marginally.

The president's program, with its time limit of two years for the receipt of welfare and its work requirement, will probably have little effect on the size of the gross domestic product, but it may well ameliorate a noxious symbol and thus affect race relations in the United States. Kemp, who is expected to be a presidential candidate in 1996, has communicated with blacks and advocated the improvement of conditions for minorities through his advocacy of programs such as selling public housing units to tenants.[107]

The Republican party also must focus on the economy, but in addition it must address the causes of its poor image among blacks. The party is not only unpopular among working-class blacks but also among middle-class blacks.[108] The party must deal with civil rights issues with greater sensitivity. Ironically, the Republican party is in a prime position to make overtures to blacks without jeopardizing its current support base. The results of the 1992 election demonstrate that the party cannot rely on its current support base to win close presidential elections. If President Bush had received 30 percent of the black vote, as opposed to the 11 percent he received, he would have won reelection as president.

The Republican party is in an excellent position to appeal to blacks because the more conservative component of its current support base, which is the component most likely to oppose appealing to blacks, would not likely leave the party. It certainly would not leave for the Democratic party, because it was the Democrats' racially liberal orientation since 1964 that drove them away from it. The Republican party is well positioned to appeal to blacks for an additional reason. Blacks are becoming increasingly disenchanted with the Democratic party's seemingly growing reluctance to promote policies and programs that would improve their disadvantaged social and economic status. The percentage of black support of the Democratic presidential nominee has been decreasing for each nominee since Jimmy Carter in 1980. Although the decline has not been substantial, it is enough to suggest that overtures from the Republican party to attract blacks to the party may be received favorably. A second independent presidential candidacy of Ross Perot would not detract from a Republican party strategy to appeal to blacks. In fact, it would strengthen the wisdom of such an appeal. The Republican party would have an increased need for black support in order to recoup its loss of white voters to Perot.

If the Republican party appeals to blacks in a straightforward and nonpatronizing manner, it could succeed in attracting a substantial number of blacks to the party with only a minimal loss of white support. This state of affairs would benefit blacks because both the Democratic and Republican parties would have to compete for black voters in presidential elections. This would increase blacks' bargaining power regardless of who the winner is and would result in blacks receiving more consistent policy benefits from their participation in presidential politics.

No one is more aware of the need for a change in Republican strategy than black Republican party activists. That they have had some influence is indicated in the following passage:

> Prompted by moderate black Republicans from Massachusetts, the R.N.C. [Republican National Committee] is planning grassroots African American policy conferences in Chicago, Atlanta, and that bastion of the black middle class, Washington. The strategy emerged from the Massachusetts Black Republican Council, which held its first annual convention last fall. The council's most important recommendation: Repeal the delegate selection rules that short-change the most populous states, where blacks are more numerous. In 1993 only 3 of the R.N.C.'s 165 voting members were black— all three from the Virgin Islands.[109]

The process by which the black community shifted from being a part of the Republican party's coalition to constituting the most dependable component of that of the Democratic party exemplifies many tenets of pluralist theory. Coalitions are fluid and require bargaining between government officials and groups for their maintenance. President Franklin D. Roosevelt issued Executive Order No. 8802 forbidding discrimination in the war industry on the basis of race, creed, or color only because of A. Philip Randolph's threatened march on Washington.

Pluralist theory also indicates that change will usually be incremental. Democratic presidents and presidential candidates following Franklin Roosevelt reinforced and increased incrementally the black electoral shift to the Democratic party begun during his administration, usually by making discrete changes in civil rights policy and taking other actions supportive of the civil rights movement. This generally has been true with respect to civil rights policy and related electoral behavior. President Harry S Truman was able to win 70 percent of the black vote in the 1948 presidential election after he issued two highly visible executive orders, one dealing with racial discrimination in the U.S. Civil Service and the other desegregating the armed forces. A dozen years later John F. Kennedy obtained 68 percent of the nonwhite vote in part because he telephoned Mrs. Martin Luther King, Jr., with offers of assistance after her husband had been unjustly imprisoned. Both Truman and Kennedy thus obtained black support, which was indispensable to their victories. Truman required black votes for his margin of victory in several northern states; Kennedy needed them for his margin of victory in the southern states of Texas, South Carolina, and North Carolina. It became clear that racially diversified Democratic coalitions in all regions of the United States were necessary for Democratic victory.

It has also become clear in the mid-1990s that for the Republicans to build a sustainable governing majority, they must increase their party level of support from the black community. If the Republican party is to attract significant black support for its presidential candidates, the party will have to enhance its black support through the construction of substantive policy programs dealing with the economic well-being of the black community.

Notes

This work was made possible by grants from the Harry S. Truman Presidential Library Institute and the National Endowment for the Humanities. The author thanks Thomas Fox, Kenneth Goings, Otis Graham, Judith Haydel and Jo Richardson for their generous and excellent advice. I am responsible for any shortcomings or errors in this chapter.

1. John R. Petrocik, "Realignment and the Nationalization of the South," *Journal of Politics* 49 (May 1987): 373.

2. Stephen E. Frantzich, *Political Parties in the Technological Age* (New York: Longman, 1989), 30.

3. Nelson W. Polsby and Aaron Wildavsky, *Presidential Elections* (New York: Free Press, 1988), 42.

4. Edward G. Carmines and James A. Stimson, "The Racial Reorientation of American Politics," in *The Electorate Reconsidered,* ed. John C. Pierce and John L. Sullivan (Beverly Hills, Calif.: Sage Publications, 1980), 199.

5. Ibid., 201–2.

6. Edward G. Carmines and James A. Stimson, *Issue Evolution* (Princeton: Princeton University Press, 1989), 27–58.

7. Frank Friedel, "The New Deal, Southern Agriculture, and Economic Change," in *New Deal and the South,* ed. James C. Cobb and Michael C. Namorato (Jackson: University Press of Mississippi, 1984), 23.

8. Herbert S. Parmet, "Democratic Party," in *Franklin D. Roosevelt,* ed. Otis L. Graham, Jr., and Meghan Robinson Wander (Boston: G. K. Hall, 1985), 99.

9. Donald H. Grubbs, *Cry from the Cotton* (Chapel Hill: University of North Carolina Press, 1971), 97.

10. Nancy J. Weiss, *Farewell to the Party of Lincoln* (Princeton: Princeton University Press, 1983), 73.

11. Gilbert Ware, *William Hastie* (New York: Oxford University Press, 1984), 85–94.

12. Weiss, *Farewell to the Party of Lincoln,* 259.

13. Russell D. Renka, "Comparing Presidents Kennedy and Johnson as Legislative Leaders," *Presidential Studies Quarterly* 15 (fall 1985): 812–13.

14. Christopher L. Tomlins, "Asa Philip Randolph," in *Franklin D. Roosevelt: His Life and Times,* ed. Graham and Wandor (Boston: G. K. Hall, 1985), 342–43; United States President, "Reaffirming Policy of Full Participation in the Defense Program by All Persons, Regardless of Race, Creed, Color or National Origin and Directing Certain Action in Furtherance of Said Policy," Executive Order 8802, June 25, 1941, 3 *Code of Federal Regulations* 956, 1938–43 compilation (Washington, D.C.: Government Printing Office, 1968).

15. William E. Juhnke, "President Truman's Commission on Civil Rights," *Presidential Studies Quarterly* 19 (summer 1989): 597.

16. Robert C. Weaver to Jonathan Daniels, September 4, 1943, Box 10, Official File 4245g, War Manpower Commission, Franklin D. Roosevelt Library (FDRL), Hyde Park, New York, 1–3.

17. Paul V. McNutt to Jonathan Daniels, August 12, 1943, box 10, Official File 4245g, War Manpower Commission, FDRL, Hyde Park, New York.

18. Weaver to Daniels, 3.

19. Jonathan Daniels, *The Man of Independence* (Philadelphia: J. B. Lippincott, 1950), 40.

20. "Democratic Platform," 1953, Papers of Harry S. Truman, Harry S. Truman Presidential Library (HSTPL), 1–4.

21. Clark M. Clifford to the President (Harry S. Truman), November 17, 1948, Box 21, Papers of Clark M. Clifford, HSTPL, Independence, Missouri, 6–7.

22. William L. Batt, Jr., to Gael Sullivan, "Negro Vote," April 20, 1948, Box 20, Papers of Clark M. Clifford, HSTPL, Independence, Missouri, 1.

23. Batt to Sullivan, "Negro Vote," 2.

24. William L. Batt, Jr., to Clark M. Clifford, August 11, 1948, Box 20, Papers of Harry S. Truman, Files of Clark M. Clifford, HSTPL, Independence, Missouri, 1.

25. Batt to Sullivan, August 11, 1948, 5.

26. "1948 Campaign," August 17, 1948, Box 21, Papers of Clark M. Clifford, HSTPL, Independence, Missouri, 7.

27. Norman H. Nie, Sidney Verba, and John R. Petrocik, *The Changing American Voter* (Cambridge: Harvard University Press, 1977), 248.

28. Bruce A. Campbell, "Patterns of Change in the Partisan Loyalties of Native Southerners," *Journal of Politics* 39 (August 1977): 759.

29. Barbara Sinclair, "Agenda and Alignment Change," in *Congress Reconsidered*, ed. Lawrence C. Dodd and Bruce Oppenheimer (Washington, D.C.: CQ Press, 1981), 231.

30. Buchanan to Mathews, June 24, 1948, Box 1, Papers of William Boyle, Jr., Harry S Truman Presidential Library, Independence, Missouri.

31. Larry J. Sabato, *The Democratic Party Primary* (Charlottesville: University Press of Virginia, 1977), 46.

32. President (Harry S. Truman) to Bill [William] Boyle, "Democratic Presidential Campaign in Virginia," April 28, 1949, Box 1, Papers of William Boyle, Jr., HSTPL, Independence, Missouri, 2.

33. "Missouri Politics Post-Presidential," Box 4, Memoirs File, HSTPL, Independence, Missouri, 3.

34. James L. Sundquist, *Dynamics of the Party System* (Washington, D.C.: Brookings Institution, 1973), 249.

35. "The Votes in the 1948 Election," in *History of American Presidential Elections: Volume IV (1940–1968)*, ed. Arthur M. Schlesinger, Jr. (New York: Chelsea House, 1971), 3211.

36. President Truman to Boyle, ii–iii.

37. E. Frederic Morrow, *Black Man in the White House* (New York: Coward-McCann, 1963), 11.

38. Ibid., 13.

39. Harold W. Stanley and Richard G. Niemi, *Vital Statistics on American Politics* (Washington, D.C.: CQ Press, 1988), 89.

40. "Oral History Interview with E. Fredric Morrow by Dr. Thomas Soapes," February 23, 1977, Dwight D. Eisenhower Library (DDEL), Abilene, Kansas, 17.

41. Jack Bass and Walter DeVries, *The Transformation of Southern Politics* (New York: New American Library, 1977), 91–92.

42. Harvard Sitkoff, *The Struggle for Black Equality* (New York: Hill & Wang, 1981), 34.

43. David J. Garrow, *Bearing the Cross* (New York: Vintage Books, 1988), 118–19.

44. Ibid., 117–19.

45. 347 U.S. 483 (1954).

46. Mark Stern, "Black Interest Group Pressure on the Executive: John F. Kennedy as Politician" (paper presented at the annual meeting of the American Political Science Association, Chicago, Illinois, 1987), 11.

47. William R. Shaffer, "John F. Kennedy and the Liberal Establishment: Presidential Politics and Civil Rights Legislation in 1957" (paper presented at the Fourth Annual Presidential Conference, Hofstra University, Hempstead, New York, 1985), 3.

48. Huey L. Perry, "Pluralist Theory and National Black Politics in the United States," *Polity* (summer 1991): 549–65.

49. Stern, "Black Interest Group Pressure on the Executive," 30.

50. Stephen J. Wayne, *The Road to the White House* (New York: St. Martin's Press, 1980), 66.

51. Lois Lovelace Duke, "Racial Bias in Newsmaking" (paper presented at the annual meeting of the Southern Political Science Association, Memphis, Tennessee, 1989), 33.

52. Wayne, *The Road to the White House,* 67.

53. Lenneal J. Henderson, Jr., "Black Politics and American Presidential Elections," in *The New Black Politics,* 2nd ed., ed. Michael B. Preston, Lenneal J. Henderson, Jr., and Paul L. Puryear (New York: Longman, 1987), 4.

54. John Orman, "The President and Interest Group Access," *Presidential Studies Quarterly* 18 (fall 1988): 788.

55. Frank Moore and Stu Eizenstat to the President (Jimmy Carter), September 6, 1977, Box 151, Papers of Stuart Eizenstat, Jimmy Carter Library (JCL), Atlanta, Georgia, 3.

56. Sheldon Goldman and Thomas P. Jahnige, *The Federal Courts as a Political System* (New York: Harper & Row, 1985), 55.

57. Barbara Sinclair, *Congressional Realignment, 1925–1978* (Austin: University of Texas Press, 1982), 40.

58. Ruth P. Morgan, *The President and Civil Rights* (Lanham, Md.: University Press of America, 1987), 33.

59. Angus Campbell, Philip E. Converse, Warren E. Miller, and Donald E. Stokes, *American Voter* (New York: John Wiley, 1960), 302.

60. Pearl T. Robinson, "Whither the Future of Blacks in the Republican Party?" *Political Science Quarterly* 97 (summer 1982): 214.

61. Polsby and Wildavsky, *Presidential Elections,* 303–4.

62. 347 U.S. 483 (1954).

63. 383 U.S. 663 (1966).

64. Henry J. Abraham, *The Judiciary* (Boston: Allyn & Bacon, 1987), 183.

65. Bass and DeVries, *Transformation of Southern Politics,* 30.

66. Polsby and Wildavsky, *Presidential Elections,* 303–4.

67. "House Backs Quick Passage of Rights Bill" (*Washington Post,* March 15, 1968, A4), Gerald R. Ford Scrapbooks, 1929–1973, Reel 10, Scrapbook 24, Gerald R. Ford Library (GRFL), Ann Arbor, Michigan.

68. Ibid.

69. Bill Casselman to Bob Hartmann, August 21, 1974, Folder FG, Executive 90 (8/9/74–3/31/75), White House Central Files (WHCF), GRFL, Ann Arbor, Michigan.

70. WHCF, March 12, 1975, GRFL, Ann Arbor, Michigan.

71. Robert D. Linder to John Buggs, June 24, 1975, WHCF, GRFL, Ann Arbor, Michigan, 274.

72. Anthony Neely, "Government Role in Rooting Out, Remedying Discrimination Is Shifting," *National Journal,* September 22, 1984, 1772.

73. Gerald M. Pomper, "The Presidential Election," in *The Election of 1980,* ed. Pomper (Chatham, N.J: Chatham Publishers, 1981), 71.

74. Lincoln Caplan, *The Tenth Justice* (New York: Alfred A. Knopf, 1987), 53.

75. Robert Axelrod, "Where the Vote Comes from: An Analysis of Electoral Coalitions, 1952–1968," *American Political Science Review* 66 (March 1970): 17.

76. Gerald M. Pomper, "The Presidential Election," in *The Election of 1988,* ed. Pomper (Chatham, N.J.: Chatham Publishers, 1989), 134.

77. Chandler Davidson, *Biracial Politics* (Baton Rouge: Louisiana State University Press, 1972).

78. William Schneider, "Bush, the GOP, and the Black Voter," *National Journal,* May 26, 1990, 1318.

79. Neil A. Lewis, "Solicitor General's Career Advances at Intersection of Law and Politics," *New York Times,* June 1, 1990.

80. "Rights Bill Is Approved by House," *New Orleans Times-Picayune,* June 6, 1991.

81. "Here Are the Final Tallies for President," *St. Petersburg Times,* November 8, 1992.

82. "Portrait of the Electorate," *New York Times,* November 5, 1992.

83. David E. Rosenbaum, "What Can Clinton Change, and When?" *New York Times,* November 8, 1992.

84. "Portrait of the Electorate."

85. Memorandum from Drew Ranier to Southwest Louisiana Steering Committee and Workers of the Democratic State Central Committee of Louisiana, 1992.

86. F. Christopher Atherton, "Campaign '92: Strategies and Tactics of the Candidates," in *The Election of 1992,* ed. Gerald M. Pomper (Chatham, N.J.: Chatham House, 1993), 80.

87. Allen D. Hertzke, *Echoes of Discontent* (Washington, D.C.: CQ Press, 1993), 2.

88. Ibid., 186.

89. Lucius J. Barker and Mack H. Jones, *African Americans and the American Political System* (Englewood Cliffs, N.J.: Prentice Hall, 1994), 348.

90. Ibid., 347.

91. "Jackson Heaps Praise," *Lake Charles American Press,* November 23, 1992.

92. Neil A. Lewis, "Jordan: A Capital Insider with Civil Rights Roots," *New York Times,* November 7, 1992.

93. Gwen Ifill, "Clinton Appoints Two to Supervise Transition Group," *New York Times,* November 7, 1992.

94. *Weekly Compilation of Presidential Documents,* Administration of William J. Clinton, September 18, 1993, 1813.

95. Theodore J. Lowi and Benjamin Ginsberg, *Democrats Return to Power* (New York: W. W. Norton, 1994), 24.

96. Ibid., 25.

97. *Weekly Compilation of Presidential Documents,* Administration of William J. Clinton, September 18, 1993, 1813.

98. Michael J. Sniffen, "Boston Lawyer Nominated for Civil Rights Job," *Baton Rouge Morning Advocate,* February 2, 1994.

99. Kweisi Mfume, *C-Span* (broadcast), February 2, 1994.

100. "Despite Statehood Bill's Defeat, D.C. Avocates Claim Victory," *Congressional Quarterly Weekly Report,* November 27, 1993, 3261–62.

101. Ibid.

102. "Health Plan Still Popular," *Lake Charles American Press,* January 23, 1994, 1–2.

103. John McQuaid, "Clinton Is Winning Support of La. Democrats," *New Orleans Times-Picayune,* January 27, 1992.

104. Barker and Jones, *African Americans and the American Political System,* 35.

105. Thomas Byrne Edsall and Mary D. Edsall, *Chain Reaction* (New York: W. W. Norton, 1992), 162.

106. Gerald Wright, Jr., "Racism and Welfare Policy in America," *Social Science Quarterly* 57 (March 1977): 720–23.

107. Edsall and Edsall, *Chain Reaction,* 272–73.

108. Susan Welch and Lorn Foster, "Class and Conservatism in the Black Community," *American Politics Quarterly* 15 (October 1987): 334.

109. "The G.O.P.: Wising Up About Race?" *New York Times,* January 23, 1994, 4.

■ *Chapter 6*

Blacks and the National Executive Branch

Huey L. Perry
Tracey L. Ambeau
Frederick McBride

This chapter examines the participation of blacks in the executive branch of the national government from the presidency of Franklin D. Roosevelt to that of Bill Clinton. The general question that this chapter answers is: What influence, if any, have blacks had on the policy process in the national executive branch? While the chapter addresses the extent to which blacks participated in individual presidential administrations, the overarching contribution of the chapter is its delineation of general trends regarding blacks' influence in presidential administrations, until now absent from the scholarly literature.

An important component of presidential administrations is the president's cabinet. Among the oldest institutions in the American political system, the cabinet had its beginnings with George Washington and was firmly established as an institution for consultation and advice to the president by the end of 1793.[1] While the chapter is not limited to examination of blacks' influence in the executive branch to the cabinet, this examination forms its focus.

Before World War II, the Register of the Treasury, Auditor of the Navy, and Recorder of Deeds for the District of Columbia were the three jobs of any importance in the federal government that were thought of as "Negro jobs." That these jobs were set aside for blacks indicated a grudging recognition that a few blacks were able to handle significant government positions. Other than those positions, black employment with the federal government was limited almost exclusively to maintenance work and rarely included postings as junior-level clerks or other personnel.[2]

Given this situation before World War II, President Lyndon B. Johnson's announcement of the nomination of Robert Weaver as secretary of the newly formed Department of Housing and Urban Development on January 13, 1966, represented a major symbolic advancement in black federal employment. Johnson was the first president to nominate a black to a cabinet post, and upon Senate confirmation Weaver became the first black cabinet member. President Johnson's Great Society, however, was not the first presidential administration to understand the symbolic importance of black participation in the executive branch of government. That distinction belongs to the administration of Franklin D. Roosevelt, whose New Deal governance revolutionized the nature and function of the U.S. government.

FDR and Emerging Black Consciousness

Black influence in the New Deal can best be described as limited and largely informal. The formal influence of blacks was limited principally to one person, Ralph Bunche. Bunche was the senior social science analyst in the Africa Section of the Office of Strategic Services (OSS), which later became the Central Intelligence Agency. He was responsible for gathering information and keeping abreast of current events in the British Empire in Africa, which included Kenya, Uganda, Tanganyika, Nyasaland, Zanzibar, the Rhodesias, South Africa, the South African protectorates, and South-West Africa. Additionally, he wrote manuals on North Africa for the U.S. military. He later became a member of the State Department's Postwar Planning Unit, where he worked on the future of colonial territories. In 1945, he served as adviser to the U.S. delegation at the San Francisco conference that drafted the United Nations charter.[3] Bunche left the State Department for employment with the UN Secretariat, where he went on to achieve an illustrious career in foreign affairs.

The federal government generally did not support blacks' interests during the New Deal period, when racism and discrimination were prevalent. Roosevelt, for example, refused to support efforts to abolish lynching.[4] The Roosevelt administration's unwillingness to attack racial discrimination is also evident in the area of housing. The government got into the business of encouraging private lending institutions to provide loans for home purchase. The agency charged with providing guidance to underwriters issuing home insurance, the Federal Housing Administration, in its manuals warned insurance underwriters of the dangers to property values that would ensue from blacks entering white neighborhoods and gave detailed instructions on how to prevent this from happening. Similarly, the government's entry into public housing, as a result of the Housing Act of 1937,[5] was characterized by the provision of housing on a racially segregated basis consistent with local custom and practice.[6]

Although Bunche was the principal source of formal black influence in the Roosevelt administration, a few other blacks were involved in government during the New Deal era, but their role was extremely limited, consisting primarily of providing race relations advice to the administration. These blacks appointed by Roosevelt as informal advisers to his administration, comprising his so-called black cabinet, included Mary McLeod Bethune, Robert Weaver, William Hastie, Eugene Kinckle Jones, John P. Davis, and Walter White. There is no evidence that they were involved in any significant policy-making. Their role in the New Deal is best described by one historian: "They made white New Dealers marginally more sensitive to the needs of blacks; and they made the federal government seem more comprehensible and relevant to blacks." There are no formal records, but members of Roosevelt's black cabinet included several prominent and lesser-known blacks spread throughout the federal government.[7]

Mary McLeod Bethune is perhaps the best known of the black cabinet appointees in the Roosevelt administration. She was the most influential black in the New Deal in terms of domestic issues. A civil rights leader, Bethune was appointed to the Advisory Committee of the National Youth Administration. She pushed for nondiscrimination policies as well as for making the New Deal more sensitive to blacks. Ironically, black leaders like Bethune were successful in getting the government to begin to deal with problems of blacks because of the Great Depression.

The Depression forced the Roosevelt administration to deal with the long-term problems of blacks like unemployment, poverty, and inadequate housing using a race-neutral, class-based approach. Black leaders were successful in this regard mostly because these problems were shared by large numbers of people, both black and white. The

Depression created a much larger "lower class" than had existed in the United States before the 1930s. Roosevelt sought to aid the lower class by creating jobs and other forms of assistance to sustain citizens during those difficult years. The assistance that blacks received during the New Deal was never as a result of programs targeted specifically for blacks. The New Deal never challenged the racial status quo in the South.

President Roosevelt attempted to provide enhanced government employment prospects to blacks by using executive orders. Executive Order No. 8587 in 1940 had as its objective the ending of racial discrimination in the civil service.[8] In June 1941, Roosevelt issued Executive Order No. 8802, which sought to end racial, ethnic, and religious discrimination in the employment of workers in the defense industry and government.[9] The act established the first Fair Employment Practices Committee (FEPC) to accomplish this objective. Roosevelt issued Executive Order No. 8802 largely because of a threatened march on Washington by black labor leader A. Philip Randolph to protest employment discrimination against blacks in the defense industries.[10] These two executive orders were not effective because they lacked an enforcement mechanism. Although the FEPC was authorized to investigate discrimination complaints, during the first two years of its existence, it relied on the Civil Service Commission to conduct investigations, which rarely resulted in a finding of discrimination. The Civil Service Commission conducted investigations into allegations of discrimination for the FEPC between 1941 and 1943. It found discrimination in only fifty-eight cases of the nearly two thousand allegations of discrimination it investigated.[11] The FEPC was abolished in 1946.

Truman, Eisenhower, and Kennedy

Not much changed in the appointment of blacks to executive branch positions throughout the Truman, Eisenhower, and Kennedy administrations. Responding to growing fears of racial unrest, President Truman in 1946 created the President's Committee on Civil Rights to study civil rights issues in the United States and make recommendations for improving the civil rights climate. Robert Burk indicates that the real importance of the committee's recommendations was that their tenor marked a transition between earlier presidential actions to improve the well-being of blacks: the recommendations focused on aggregate economic issues and a new theme of presidential actions concentrating on political action in the civil rights arena as a means of improving the condition of blacks.[12] The committee's recommendations included the enactment of a civil rights bill, strengthening the Civil Rights Section of the Department of Justice, special training for police officers in handling civil rights–related disputes, ending Jim Crow laws, and withholding federal grants-in-aid from public and private agencies that practice discrimination and segregation. These recommendations did not become national government policy until many years later.[13]

The Truman administration was the first to demonstrate concern over the need for civil rights enforcement. Had the civil rights legislation that the Truman administration proposed to Congress been enacted into law, it would have significantly advanced the civil rights of blacks, particularly in the South. The legislation included a fair employment practice law, an anti–poll tax measure, and an antilynching law. Truman did not achieve much progress in this regard because of the absence of a national consensus favoring civil rights progress.

Truman, like Roosevelt, sought to increase the exercise of fair employment practices for blacks in the federal government. Because of his inability to get Congress to pass his legislative initiatives regarding civil rights, Truman, like Roosevelt, relied on the issuance of executive orders to provide favorable governmental action for blacks. Truman also issued Executive Order No. 10308, which created the Government Contract Compliance Committee to strengthen the enforcement of President Roosevelt's Executive Order No. 8802 barring discrimination by contractors with the government.[14] Truman's early executive orders, like Roosevelt's, were ineffective because they lacked an enforcement mechanism. Of the several Truman administration initiatives on behalf of blacks, the initiative for which the administration is best known is Truman's Executive Order No. 9981 in 1948, which provided the basis for the eventual abolition of segregation in the military.[15]

Although the Eisenhower administration was not as visible on civil rights issues as was the Truman administration, civil rights progress continued during its term in office. In general, Eisenhower was unenthusiastic about using the authority of the federal government to address civil rights issues. Eisenhower initially believed that racial change would occur as attitudes changed, not by passing laws. He modified his position on the capacity of government to effectuate positive change for blacks because of the influence of E. Frederic Morrow, a black assistant who advised Eisenhower on issues relating to blacks. Morrow began in the Eisenhower administration as an adviser on business affairs to the secretary of commerce. His job was to survey and investigate legislation proposed by the administration to see what effect it might have on the Department of Commerce. This was the first time a black had held an executive position in that department. Morrow also wrote speeches for Eisenhower. He continued at the Department of Commerce until July 1955, when Eisenhower asked him to become his executive assistant.

Early in Eisenhower's administration, Congress passed a bill to desegregate the army, which Eisenhower vetoed. Morrow was troubled by Eisenhower's veto, which the president justified by saying he had relied on the negative viewpoints of his field officers, who were mostly southerners. However, in 1954, Eisenhower desegregated the naval bases in the South to complete the efforts begun by Truman. He also desegregated veterans' hospitals.[16]

Morrow regarded President Eisenhower as a good, decent man who was concerned about civil rights. He indicates that Eisenhower had many "southern" friends with whom he often had to "fit in" on many issues and that sometimes there was a conflict between "old south" notions and civil rights issues.[17] Eisenhower was sympathetic to the efforts of blacks to attain economic and social opportunities. For example, Eisenhower appointed J. Ernest Wilkins, Sr., the first black assistant secretary of labor for international affairs. Moreover, in oral argument as *amicus curiae* before the Supreme Court for *Brown v. Board of Education*[18] in 1954, the Eisenhower administration's position was that public school segregation was unconstitutional, and that *Plessy v. Ferguson*[19] in 1896 had been wrongly decided. After the *Brown* ruling prohibiting racial segregation in public school, Eisenhower successfully pushed for desegregation of public schools in the District of Columbia.[20]

Eisenhower followed Truman's lead regarding efforts to advance black employment with the federal government. He also issued an executive order to prevent hiring discrimination. His Executive Order No. 10590 established the President's Committee on Government Employment Practices, which superseded Truman's order creating a Fair Employment Board and whose creation sought to strengthen the pursuit of equal opportunity in government employment.[21] Also by executive order, Eisenhower widened the scope of the Government Contract Compliance Committee.[22] Eisenhower abolished segregation in all federal employment and employment in the District of Columbia and took the lead in ending racial segregation in public accommodations in the District. Morrow, Max Rabb of the White House staff, and Samuel Spencer, Eisenhower's first appointee to the District of Columbia Board of Commissioners, implemented the desegregation of public accommodations in the District during the first year of the Eisenhower administration.[23]

In addition to completing the desegregation of the armed forces, President Eisenhower undertook two other major actions that advanced black interests. First, in response to the crisis in Little Rock, Arkansas, surrounding the attempt to desegregate the city's public schools, he issued a proclamation condemning the obstruction of school desegregation in the city, sent in federal troops to enforce the court order to desegregate the public schools, and nationalized the Arkansas National Guard to provide additional help.[24] As a result of Eisenhower's actions, public schools in Little Rock were desegregated. Second, the Eisenhower administration persuaded a reluctant Congress to enact the Civil Rights Act of 1957, the first national civil rights legislation since Reconstruction.[25] The 1957 legislation created a Civil Rights Division in the Department of Justice to enforce the new voting law contained in the legislation and a Civil Rights Commission to study discrimination in housing, voting, and education. The Eisenhower administration also enacted the Civil Rights Act of 1960 in response to the call of civil rights advocates for new legislation because of the weaknesses of the 1957 legislation.[26] The 1957 and 1960 acts were inconsequential in addressing the denial of the right to vote to southern blacks primarily because they both required a jury trial in voting discrimination cases. This was the case because at this time, juries in the South comprised only white jurors, which did not convict whites accused of interfering with the rights of blacks to vote.[27]

The Kennedy administration marked the beginning of a more significant number of blacks in policy-making positions in the executive branch. Robert Weaver worked in the Department of the Interior, as special assistant for Negro affairs to the administrator of the U.S. Housing Authority; Clifford L. Alexander, Jr., who was later to become secretary of the army under President Jimmy Carter, worked as a foreign affairs officer for the National Security Council. Although Weaver and

Alexander were the major black appointees in the executive branch during the Kennedy administration, they did not hold positions of policy influence on integration in education and public accommodations and equal employment for blacks. Alexander's position was in foreign affairs, and Weaver's position in the Negro Affairs Division of the Housing Authority did not afford him the ability to push for civil rights legislation.

Kennedy, like his predecessors since Franklin Roosevelt, issued an executive order to improve employment practices in the federal government for blacks. Executive Order No. 10925 combined the Committees on Government Contracts and Government Employment Practices into the President's Committee on Equal Employment Opportunity and gave the committee increased enforcement authority to combat discrimination in employment with the federal government.[28] The order directed the secretary of labor to implement equal employment practices in hiring federal employees and government contractors. The order for the first time emphasized affirmative action and incorporated mechanisms for hearings, appeal, review by independent authority, and the provision of counsel to employees who had grievances. But the order was ineffective because, like previous orders that sought to increase black government employment, its enforcement procedures were weak. Kennedy also undertook a major initiative to address racial discrimination in housing and in so doing became the first president to address this issue.[29] Like Eisenhower, Kennedy used federal marshals and the military, and nationalized state national guard units in connection with civil rights activities in Alabama and Mississippi.[30]

Kennedy's greatest contribution to blacks was his initiation of a strong civil rights agenda after efforts were made in the South to prevent black students from entering southern white universities. After the extensive protest of James Meredith's application to the University of Mississippi in 1962, Kennedy used his powers as president by ordering the National Guard to supervise Meredith's enrollment and attendance at the university. A similar incident occurred at the University of Alabama. On June 19, 1963, Kennedy sent to Congress one of the most extensive civil rights bills in the nation's history. The bill, later to become the Civil Rights Act of 1964, proposed to outlaw all forms of discrimination by race in public accommodations and employment, ban segregated education in schools and colleges, and protect the voting rights of blacks, among other provisions.

One pattern that stands out in the analysis of how blacks' interest in increased employment with the federal government was addressed in presidential administrations from Roosevelt through Kennedy is the use of executive orders to attempt to provide enhanced prospects of employment for blacks. The consistent use of executive orders during these administrations reflects the inability of getting desired actions through the legislative process and the unwillingness of presidents to lead the country on these issues as a means of facilitating congressional passage. The reason for this was largely that Congress was dominated by southerners who were vehemently opposed to progressive government initiatives in civil rights. Presidents did not want to challenge congressional intransigence in this regard for fear that their primary policy initiatives, which were not in the area of civil rights, would be scuttled by a vengeful southern-dominated Congress. Although Kennedy succumbed to this fear in the first two years of his administration, in 1963 he proposed to Congress the bold civil rights legislation that became the Civil Rights Acts of 1964.[31]

Kennedy's decision to push for a strong civil rights agenda during the third year of his administration was strongly influenced by the high tide of civil rights activity that year. Civil rights protest by blacks had been increasing every year in the United States, particularly in the South, ever since the successful black bus boycott in Montgomery, Alabama, in 1955.

LBJ and the Political Incorporation of Southern Blacks

The tragic circumstances in which Lyndon B. Johnson became president (the assassination of President Kennedy on November 22, 1963) prevented him from selecting a cabinet, inheriting that of his late predecessor. Johnson realized their symbolic value as a means of representing major social, economic, and political constituencies in the highest councils of administration when he was making cabinet appointments after his landslide election in 1964.[32] When Johnson appointed Robert Weaver as secretary of the newly created Department of Housing and Urban Development, he clearly understood that Weaver's selection as the first black to head a cabinet department symbolically embodied the political incorporation of blacks into the national U.S. government.[33]

Johnson was instrumental in securing the enactment of the most far-reaching civil rights legislation in the nation's history. This legislation included the Civil Rights Act of 1964,[34] which, as indicated, had been proposed by President Kennedy in 1963, the Economic Opportunity Act,[35] the Voting Rights Act of 1965,[36] and the Fair Housing Act of 1968.[37] These legislative enactments, particularly the Civil Rights Act of 1964, the Economic Opportunity Act, and the Voting Rights Act, have had a significant impact on improving the conditions of black life. The 1964 Civil Rights Act, among other provisions, accorded blacks equal access to places of public accommodation. The 1964 Economic Opportunity Act, created a Model Cities Program that served as an incubator for the development of black political leadership in the nation's cities.[38] The 1965 Voting Rights Act and its subsequent extensions and expansions have substantially contributed to the reincorporation of southern blacks into the political process.[39] The impact of the 1965 Voting Rights Act and its extensions and expansions on fully incorporating Southern blacks into the mainstream of political life are discussed in Chapter 9 of this book.

Johnson also made great strides in ensuring fair employment practices for blacks with the federal government. He issued Executive Order No. 11246 in September 1965, which directed the Civil Service Commission to guarantee equal employment opportunities with the federal government.[40] The order also directed the secretary of labor to implement the national government's nondiscrimination policies regarding contracts wholly or partly financed by the federal government.

Johnson's administration was the first to witness the movement of blacks in significant numbers into the middle levels of the federal civil service. As Norman Amaker recounts, Johnson's civil rights accomplishments were substantial: "There can be no question that the presidency of Lyndon Johnson exhibited the greatest amount of sustained executive leadership in this field in the nation's history. During the period from his succession [to the present] in November 1963 to his departure in January 1969, enforcement of civil rights by the executive branch of the government became a firmly established reality."[41]

The Nixon and Ford Administrations: Retreat from Civil Rights

Overall, the Nixon administration represented a retreat from the civil rights advances of the Johnson administration. However, Nixon did undertake some actions that benefited blacks. For example, the Nixon administration implemented the Philadelphia Plan, which expanded the concept of affirmative action to the point of implicitly supporting quotas. Moreover, according to one senior analyst of presidential appointments, in its early period the Nixon administration appointed a fairly significant percentage of blacks to subcabinet positions in the executive branch. In 1970, for example, about 13 percent of the Nixon administration's domestic discretionary appointments in the executive departments were black in contrast to about 3 percent of senior civil servants who were black. This analyst summarizes the Nixon administration's black appointment record in a favorable light: "Regardless of the Nixon administration's policy motives (and I think these were varied), [the administration's] actual appointments process was fairly open at the outset of the administration."[42]

Nixon also supported legislation to amend Title VII of the 1964 Civil Rights Act to increase the enforcement authority of the Equal Employment Opportunity Commission. The Equal Employment Opportunity Act of 1972[43] expanded the authority of the commission to allow it to seek court enforcement against prohibited discrimination and to ban discriminatory employment practices by federal, state, and local governments, and educational institutions.[44]

The Nixon administration's accomplishments indicated above were undercut by its policy initiatives in other areas, particularly school desegregation. As Amaker points out, the Nixon administration's initiatives to further strengthen the federal government to pursue equal employment opportunity for blacks were obscured by the administration's actions concerning school desegregation, including its publicly announced opposition to busing. Amaker describes the Nixon administration's action in this regard:

In 1979, the Nixon Justice Department, under the direction of Attorney General John Mitchell and Assistant Attorney General Jerris Leonard, went to court to oppose immediate implementation of the requirements of the *Brown* cases. It was the first time in the memory of civil rights lawyers since those decisions that lawyers for the United States and lawyers for the private plaintiffs . . . were on opposite sides in a school desegregation case. Although the Supreme Court rejected the position taken by the Justice Department in the cases, the action of the Justice Department, with the apparent approval of the president, signaled a rupture in what had been an alliance between the executive branch and the plaintiffs in school desegregation cases.[45]

The Nixon administration's policy position regarding school desegregation resulted in strained relations between the administration and blacks. These strained relations were exacerbated as a result of Nixon's failed attempts to secure the appointment of two southern conservative judges—Clement Haynesworth and G. Harrold Carswell—to the Supreme Court. Nixon sought these appointments because Haynesworth and Carswell were strict constructionists of the Constitution who, Nixon believed, would work to change the liberal tenor of the Court that had obtained during the fifteen-year tenure of Chief Justice Earl Warren. Blacks were appalled by the Haynesworth and Carswell nominations because they perceived them as a retreat from the government's commitment to civil rights in place since the passage of major civil rights legislation in 1964 and 1965. Black leaders and their allies mounted a successful campaign to block these two nominations.

President Gerald Ford assumed the presidency after Nixon was forced to resign from office as a result of the Watergate scandal. Ford inherited both the policies and executive staff that had been put in place by President Nixon. He did not have the opportunity to make a significant number of executive appointments. However, Ford did appoint William Coleman, Jr., as secretary of transportation, making him the second black cabinet member in U.S. history.

The Carter Administration and the Vestment of Blacks in the Executive Branch

The Carter administration made significant executive appointments in civil rights and was particularly interested in civil rights. As Amaker indicated, "For the first time in history of the civil rights enforcement effort, a substantial cadre of people drawn from the groups whom the civil rights laws were enacted to protect were appointed to positions in which they were able to exercise real enforcement authority."[46] The Carter administration represented the first real vestment of executive authority to blacks in the federal government in the country's history.[47]

The administration reinvigorated the commitment of the executive branch to both civil rights enforcement and increasing black representation in the executive branch. Carter's administration sustained its commitment to civil rights throughout its duration, unlike the Nixon and Ford administrations, which lapsed into dormancy in civil rights enforcement.

Patricia Roberts Harris, Carter's only black cabinet appointee, was appointed secretary of housing and urban development in 1977. Carter later appointed her to another cabinet post, secretary of health, education, and welfare, in which she worked from 1979 to 1981. Harris was the first black woman to head a cabinet department in the federal government. Carter also appointed Clifford L. Alexander, Jr., as secretary of the army, the first black to head a branch of the armed services, and named Wade McCree as solicitor general.

Carter's pathbreaking appointments to the federal government were actually at the subcabinet level, including Mary Frances Berry, assistant secretary for education in 1977; Azie Taylor Morton, national director, U.S. Savings Bonds Division of the Treasury; and Terence Todman, assistant secretary of state for Inter-American affairs (responsible for coordinating State Department matters in Caribbean, Central, and South American countries). Todman was the first black appointed to this position.

Carter's black subcabinet appointments significantly outdistanced those of other presidents. However, in addition to appointments, the Carter administration undertook policy actions that significantly advanced the interest of blacks. In equal employment opportunity enforcement, the Carter administration significantly strengthened the Equal Employment Opportunity Commission (EEOC), thus enabling it to fight discrimination in the workplace. The Carter administration "transferred to the EEOC from other governmental agencies all duties relating to equal pay enforcement; enforcement of the ban on age discrimination and discrimination against the handicapped; enforcement of nondiscrimination in federal government; and the overall responsibility for coordination of the equal employment opportunity effort accompanied by the appropriate transfer of budget, personnel, and files."[48] The EEOC thus possesses broad responsibility to enjoin employment discrimination and judicial action in all areas affecting employment in the private sector and with the federal government (the only exception to the latter is employment with federal contractors, which is the responsibility of the Office of Federal Contract Compliance Programs).

Regarding civil rights, the Carter administration created a civil rights unit in the Office of Management and Budget (OMB) to monitor enforcement and to advise the OMB director on funding and management resources needed for effective enforcement of civil rights laws.[49] Carter, by executive order,[50] gave the attorney general the "authority to enforce all federal laws mandating nondiscrimination in the provision of federal financial assistance and [made] the Justice Department responsible for coordinating the enforcement of these provisions by all agencies."[51] Carter considered the directive "an important step toward a comprehensive, coherent approach to the goal of distributing federal aid on a nondiscriminatory basis"[52] in order to "give the Department of Justice the leadership role in this area equivalent to that of the EEOC in employment."[53]

The Carter administration vigorously used the authority of the federal government to fight civil rights discrimination. Drew Days III was appointed as assistant attorney general in charge of the civil rights division of the Department of Justice. Days assertively filed lawsuits in order to implement the administration's goals in "housing (exclusionary zoning cases), voting (cases involving the dilution of minority voting strength), employment (hiring, promotion, and back-pay class relief), and education (busing and other mandatory pupil reassignment requirements)."[54] The Carter administration's civil rights commitment and accomplishments contributed significantly to restoring civil rights issues to the forefront of the nation's policy agenda, where they had been during most of the Kennedy-Johnson years. The combination of an unprecedented number of black subcabinet appointments and policy initiatives favorable to black interests distinguishes the Carter administration. Carter's performance in this regard surpasses all other presidents' administrations except Johnson's. While Johnson did not make nearly as many black appointments as Carter, his leadership role in the enactment of the Civil Rights Act of 1964 and the Voting Rights Act of 1965, among other legislation favorable to black interests, overall, places him above Carter. Johnson's legislative accomplishments, particularly the 1964 and 1965 laws, have had a greater impact than have Carter's black appointments on improving the political, social, and economic status of blacks. In fact, it could be argued that Johnson's pathbreaking legislative accomplishments in the interest of blacks created the political environment that allowed Carter's historic number of black appointments.

The Reagan Administration and the Assault on Civil Rights

Ronald Reagan's victorious bid for the presidency came about largely without black support. Accordingly, Reagan did not feel a sense of obligation to appoint blacks to influential positions in his administration. Moreover, the Reagan administration had only a minimal interest in civil rights. The American Civil Liberties Union conducted a two-year study on the Reagan administration's stand on civil rights issues. The study's report concluded that the administration had neglected civil rights issues. While the president portrayed himself as unbiased, sincerely dedicated to equal opportunity for minorities, his Justice Department betrayed his image by attempting to slow down, and even reverse, the civil rights gains of the twenty to thirty years before his administration.[55] Amaker indicates that Reagan's poor record on civil rights matters is not simply explained by the fact that Republican administrations are generally less supportive of civil rights than are Democratic ones. The Reagan administration's civil rights record was weaker than that of all his immediate predecessors, Republicans included.[56]

Part of the Reagan legacy in this regard is probably attributable to the absence in his administration of blacks in significant positions of civil rights enforcement. One senior analyst of presidential appointments describes the changing fortunes of blacks regarding presidential appointments to the executive branch during Reagan's tenure as president:

By 1986–87, the number of African Americans in senior civil service positions increased from 1970, but the percentage of those appointed by the presidential administration decreased even as those of other minorities—Hispanic Americans, Asian Americans, and women increased. The Reagan administration clearly felt none of the symbolic needs that the Nixon administration earlier had for significant African American representation in the Federal executive branch. That undoubtedly reflected the insignificant representation of African Americans in the Reagan constituency, the administration's own political goals, the ascendancy of other minority groups, and the temper of the times which I read as being less sympathetic to the specific concerns of African Americans in the 1980s than was the case in the 1970s.[57]

Reagan did cultivate a relationship with conservative blacks, particularly those opposed to affirmative action.[58] He did appoint to the executive branch conservative blacks who were at least publicly comfortable with the conservative positions of his administration. Reagan appointed Samuel R. Pierce, Jr., a black attorney, to head the Department of Housing and Urban Development (HUD). Unlike Patricia Roberts Harris, however, Pierce had experience in housing policy and administration. Evaluations of Pierce's performance are mixed, especially in view of the HUD scandal that surfaced after the Reagan administration had ended. Pierce was charged with allegedly committing fraud by giving construction projects to his associates and those of President Reagan. A different perception of Pierce is suggested by Lawrence Uzzell of the *National Review*. According to Uzzell, Pierce was the unsung hero and most effective cabinet member of the Reagan Revolution. Uzzell believes that Pierce reduced HUD's "spending, improved services, cleaned up the public housing 'boondoggle,' and persuaded Congress to accept housing vouchers." Pierce was also the only original Cabinet member to remain in the same post throughout Reagan's eight-year administration. Uzzell considers Pierce's low profile a principal factor in his being an effective administrator.[59]

Uzzell's favorable assessment of Pierce's performance suggests why he was held in such disregard by housing activists. Housing in the United States continues to be characterized by alarmingly high levels of racial segregation and discrimination. During the Reagan years, fair housing laws failed to change the deep-seated patterns in any significant way.[60] Many blacks considered Pierce's post one in which he could have made changes favorable to black interests in housing. Many blacks felt abandoned by the Reagan administration because Pierce was instrumental in cutting the budgets of certain housing programs and even eliminating others. According to Charles H. Moore and Patricia Hoban-Moore, "while the percentage of the [poor] population . . . [grew] from 11 to 15 percent . . . during the 1980s, overall budget authority at HUD fell from $36 billion in 1980 to $15 billion in 1988, the largest drop of any federal department" during that period. Moore and Hoban-Moore believe that not only were Pierce and other top-level political appointees at HUD during the Reagan administration inept managers but they were also ideologically hostile to the very programs that they were responsible for managing.[61]

Pierce's efforts were consistent with the Reagan agenda of reducing the size and influence of government to restore economic prosperity and improve national security.[62] The irony of the cuts in the housing programs under Pierce is that they occurred while a black official was at the helm of HUD.

Reagan appointed Clarence Thomas, a black Republican from Savannah, Georgia, chairman of the EEOC in May 1983. Before becoming EEOC chairman, Thomas was the assistant secretary for civil rights in the Department of Education. In comparing the EEOC's record of performance under the leadership of Thomas with that of his predecessors, one finds a "shift in emphasis rather than an actual decline in enforcement activity."[63] The number of cases the EEOC settled since 1980 increased, while the preceding year's backlog of cases decreased. Concomitantly, the number of settlements fell while the number of no-reasonable-cause determinations rose and the time committed to case processing increased.[64] (A "no reasonable cause" determination means that an investigation of a discrimination charge did not result in a substantiation of the charge.)

While Reagan's record is bleak with respect to the appointment of blacks to high-level positions in his administration, he did sign into law two pieces of legislation that were highly favored by African Americans. One was the legislation establishing a national holiday in honor of Martin Luther King, Jr. The other was the 1982 legislation extending the 1965 Voting Rights Act for an additional twenty-five years. The 1982 extension of the 1965 legislation was more than three times longer than the previous longest extension of seven years in 1975. Although President Reagan was philosophically opposed to both pieces of legislation, he nonetheless signed them into law because he did not wish to appear insensitive to the desires of blacks to be fully incorporated into the political system, both symbolically and substantively. The reason for President Reagan's actions regarding these two pieces of legislation is fully discussed in Chapter 9 of this book.[65]

The Bush Administration

President George Bush appointed only one black to his cabinet, Louis F. Sullivan, as secretary of health and human services. Bush's appointment of Sullivan caused controversy because Sullivan had expressed a pro-choice view on abortion policy whereas Bush's platform had been predominantly pro-life. Therefore, in order to secure the appointment, which would enable him to pursue an agenda of closing the gap in health care of minorities and the poor, Sullivan had to retract his position and renounce his pro-choice position. Sullivan is the first black medical doctor to hold the post and the second black to serve as secretary of health and human services (a position earlier called secretary of health, education, and welfare).

Sullivan worked most effectively to alert citizens to the danger of smoking, particularly, the danger of secondhand smoke. His efforts led to the prohibition of smoking on airplanes on all continental flights and the designation of smoking areas in restaurants, as well as in all federal government offices. Sullivan also initiated a new program called Healthy Start aimed at reducing infant mortality. The program targeted ten urban and rural sites over a five-year period with special initiatives designed to reduce the infant mortality rate by 50 percent.

In terms of black appointments to the executive branch of government, Bush is best known for his historic appointment of Colin L. Powell as the highest-ranking military officer—chairman of the Joint Chiefs of Staff of the Department of Defense. Powell is the first black ever to hold this post. As a result of his successful prosecution of the Persian Gulf War, Powell's stock militarily and politically increased enormously. Bush reappointed Powell as chairman of the Joint Chiefs for a second term.

Bush's other prominent black appointments to the executive branch included Constance Berry Newman as director of the Office of Personnel Management (OPM), whose responsibilities include formulating policies for all human resource–related issues for the federal government; and Gwendolyn King as commissioner of Social Security, responsible for all federal social security programs, including Old Age Insurance, Survivor's Insurance, Disability Insurance, and Supplementary Security Income for the needy, aged, blind, and disabled.

Bush's best known interaction with black political interests was his veto of the Civil Rights Act of 1990. His publicly stated objection to the bill, and his reason for vetoing it, was that the legislation mandated racial quotas in hiring in the private sector. African Americans, women, and their liberal allies were outraged at Bush's veto of the first major civil rights legislation other than extensions of the 1965 Voting Rights Act, since the civil rights legislation of the mid-1960s. These pro–civil rights groups claimed that the legislation did not mandate quotas and that Bush demagogically fueled racial and gender tensions by making the charge that it did. Pro–civil rights forces were able to get Congress to pass the 1990 legislation in 1991, with some modification of the alleged quota provision that was objectionable to Bush. Bush signed the revised legislation into law, making it the 1991 Civil Rights Act. Bush signed the legislation, according to Kerry Mullins and Aaron Wildavsky, "because he wanted racial inclusion" and he believed that the 1991 legislation, unlike the 1990 legislation, "did not mandate positive discrimination."[66]

Bill Clinton: Toward a Renewed Civil Rights Agenda

After twelve years of Republican presidents, Bill Clinton became the first Democratic president since Jimmy Carter. Black voters constituted a significant proportion of the coalition that elected Clinton in 1992. At a November 12, 1992, press conference, President-elect Clinton remarked that his cabinet would look more like America than had those of previous administrations. Clinton has seven major black appointees: Mike Espy, the first black elected to Congress from Mississippi since Reconstruction, was appointed secretary of agriculture. Ronald Brown, former chairman of the Democratic National committee and a principal architect of the Clinton victory, was appointed secretary of commerce. Hazel Rollins O'Leary, a former energy policy official and executive with a power company, was appointed secretary of energy. Jesse Brown, a Vietnam veteran, was appointed secretary of veterans' affairs. Joycelyn Elders, former director of the Health and Human Resources Department in the State of Arkansas, was appointed as surgeon general. Clifton Wharton, Jr.—the first African American president of a predominantly white university, Michigan State University, and the first African American to head a Fortune 100 company, Teachers Insurance and Annuity Association and the College Retirement Equities Fund, the largest private pension fund in the world with assets of $112 billion[67]—was appointed as deputy secretary of state. With these appointments, Clinton demonstrated a capacity to break new ground in the appointment of blacks to the executive branch. All of Clinton's black appointments are firsts for blacks in these positions.

Because a Democratic president had served during only four of the previous twenty years, Clinton did not have a rich pool of blacks with subcabinet level experience from which to select appointees. Therefore, Clinton had to choose them from the Democratic National Committee, Congress, and state and local government. By his appointments, President Clinton, like President Carter, reflected a keen awareness of the symbolic importance of presidential appointments representing diverse groups. Clinton's black cabinet appointments easily surpass that of all other presidents, not only in terms of number but also in terms of appointing blacks to cabinet positions in which blacks had not previously served. It remains to be seen whether the number of Clinton black subcabinet appointments will surpass the historical number of black subcabinet appointments by President Carter.

The reemergence of blacks as an influential group in presidential politics in the election of 1992 and the record number of black appointees to President Clinton's cabinet are fully consistent with pluralist theory. Blacks used the principal political resource available to them, the vote, to influence the outcome of the 1992 presidential election. Clinton rewarded this pivotal electoral support by appointing blacks not only to an unprecedented number of cabinet posts but also to head departments that no blacks had previously led. These appointees are thus in a position not only to direct the policies and actions of their agencies in ways that will benefit black interests, but also to influence the policies and actions of the overall Clinton administration in ways that will be beneficial to blacks. The capacity of the Clinton administration black cabinet appointees to do both these tasks provides additional support for the applicability of pluralist theory to national black politics in the post–civil rights period.

Blacks and Presidential Appointments: An Analytical Assessment

Black involvement in the executive branch of government since Roosevelt, overall, has been limited. The black appointments in the earlier presidential administrations reflected a philosophy to help blacks achieve administrative and policy experience at the national level of government. But they did not represent any real effort to accord blacks significant policy-making influence. Race relations advisers advised presidents on how they should handle certain issues concerning blacks. Moreover, until Clinton, black cabinet appointments showed a racially restrictive pattern. Of the five black cabinet appointees since Weaver in 1965, all but Coleman, who was appointed to head the Department of Transportation, have been appointed to two departments: the Department of Housing and Urban Development and the Department of Health and Human Services (or their predecessors). The pattern suggests that presidents believe blacks should be appointed to government departments that directly affect blacks. The Carter administration was the most prolific appointer of blacks to the executive branch, but primarily at the subcabinet level. The Clinton administration broke new ground in appointing blacks to executive positions where black representation had previously been absent.

Presidential administrations have differed substantially in terms of appointments of blacks to key policy-making positions in the executive branch of government. The data consulted suggest two general patterns: (1) Democratic presidents are more inclined than are Republican presidents to appoint blacks to significant executive positions; (2) Democratic presidents who receive critical electoral support from blacks are more inclined than are those who do not receive such support to appoint blacks in significant numbers to positions in the executive branch of government. These patterns also apply to blacks and favorable public policies. Democratic presidents are more inclined than are Republican presidents to support policy initiatives favorable to blacks. Democratic presidents who receive critical electoral support from blacks are more inclined than are those who do not receive such electoral support to support policies favorable to blacks.

Even within this general pattern, additional elaboration is needed. Although Democratic presidents who receive critical electoral support from blacks are generally more apt to appoint blacks in significant numbers to positions in the executive branch of government than are those who do not receive such support, blacks have been significantly represented in presidential appointments to the executive branch of government only in the administrations of first Jimmy Carter and now

Bill Clinton. President Carter appointed a record number of blacks to subcabinet positions in his administration. President Clinton appointed a record number of blacks to cabinet positions in his administration; his actions are further distinguished by his having appointed blacks to departments that they had not previously led. The gains that blacks have realized from their participation in presidential politics in the post–civil rights period supports the applicability of pluralist theory for explaining national black politics since the mid-1960s. This is especially the case with regard to the gains that blacks made in terms of presidential appointments to the executive branch of government during the Carter and Clinton administrations.

Notes

1. James E. Anderson, "A Revised View of the Johnson Cabinet," *Journal of Politics* 48 (August 1986): 529.

2. Dorothy K. Newman et al., *Protest, Politics, and Prosperity: Black Americans and White Institutions, 1940–75* (New York: Pantheon Books, 1978), 99.

3. Brian Urquhart, *Ralph Bunche, An American Life* (New York: W. W. Norton, 1993).

4. Benjamin Rivlin, ed., *Ralph Bunche: The Man and His Times* (New York: Holmes and Meier, 1990), 31.

5. 50 Statute 888 (1937).

6. United States Commission on Civil Rights, *Fair Housing and the Law* 6 (1972).

7. Otis L. Graham, Jr., and Meghan Robinson Wander, eds., *Franklin D. Roosevelt: His Life and Times* (Boston: G. K. Hall, 1985), 39.

8. United States President, "Amending Certain Provisions of the Civil Service Rules," Executive Order 8587, November 7, 1940, 3 *Code of Federal Regulations* 303, 1938–43 Compilation (Washington, D.C.: Government Printing Office, 1968), 824–30.

9. United States President, "Reaffirming Policy of Full Participation in the Defense Program by All Persons, Regardless of Race, Creed, Color or National Origin and Directing Certain Action in Furtherance of Said Policy," Executive Order 8802, June 25, 1941, 3 *Code of Federal Regulations* 956, 1938–43 Compilation (Washington, D.C.: Government Printing Office, 1968), 957.

10. Newman et al., *Protest, Politics, and Prosperity*, 11–12.

11. Samuel Krislov, *The Negro in Federal Employment: The Quest for Equal Opportunity* (Minneapolis: University of Minnesota Press, 1967), 33–34.

12. Robert F. Burk, *The Eisenhower Administration and Black Civil Rights* (Knoxville: University of Tennessee Press, 1984), 13.

13. Louis W. Koenig, *The Truman Administration* (Connecticut: Greenwood Press, 1979), 115.

14. Executive Order 10308, 3 *Code of Federal Regulations* 519 (Supplement 1951).

15. Executive Order 9981, 3 *Code of Federal Regulations* 132 (Supplement 1948), created the Committee on Equality of Treatment and Opportunity in the Armed Services. The committee's 1950 report *Freedom to Serve* was the basis for the later desegregation of the military. Norman C. Amaker, *Civil Rights and the Reagan Administration* (Washington, D.C: Urban Institute Press, 1988), 10.

16. Herbert Brownell, "Eisenhower's Civil Rights Program: A Personal Assessment," *Presidential Studies Quarterly* 21 (spring 1991): 235.

17. Frederic E. Morrow, interview by Thomas Soapes, February 23, 1977, Dwight D. Eisenhower Library, Abilene, Kansas.

18. 347 U.S. 483 (1954).

19. 163 U.S. 532 (1896).

20. Brownell, "Eisenhower's Civil Rights Program, 238.

21. Executive Order 10590, 3 *Code of Federal Regulations* (Supplement 1955).

22. Executive Order 10479, 3 *Code Federal Regulations* 97 (Supplement 1953); Brownell, "Eisenhower's Civil Rights Program," 241.

23. Ibid., 238.

24. Ibid., 241.

25. Public Law 85-315, 71 Statute 634, September 9, 1957 (codified as amended at 42 *U.S. Code*, secs. 197, 1975, 1975a–e, 1995).

26. Public Law 86-449, 74 Statute 86, May 6, 1960 (codified as amended at 42 *U.S. Code*, secs. 1971, 1974–1974e, 1975d).

27. Huey L. Perry, "Pluralist Theory and National Black Politics in the United States," *Polity* 23 (summer 1991).

28. Executive Order 10925, 3 *Code of Federal Regulations* 86 (Supplement 1961).

29. Newman et al., *Protest, Politics, and Prosperity,* 116.

30. For a brief discussion of these initiatives, see Amaker, *Civil Rights and the Reagan Administration,* 17.

31. Mark Stern, *Calculating Visions: Kennedy, Johnson, and Civil Rights* (New Brunswick, N.J.: Rutgers University Press, 1992), 233.

32. Amaker, *Civil Rights and the Reagan Administration,* 17.

33. Murray Edelman and Lucius Barker have discussed the importance of symbolism in American politics. Murray Edelman, *The Symbolic Uses of Politics* (Urbana: University of Illinois Press, 1967); and Lucius J. Barker, "Ronald Reagan, Jesse Jackson, and the 1984 Presidential Election: The Continuing American Dilemma of Race," in *The New Black Politics: The Search for Political Power,* 3rd ed., ed. Michael B. Preston, Lenneal J. Henderson, Jr., and Paul L. Puryear (White Plains, N.Y.: Longman, 1987), 32.

34. Public Law 88-352, 78 Statute 241, July 2, 1964 (codified as amended at 42 *U.S. Code,* secs. 2000a–2000e).

35. Public Law 88-452, 78 Statute 508, August 20, 1964 (codified as amended at 42 *U.S. Code,* secs. 2701, 2711–20, 2731–36, 2751–56, 2766, 2781–91, 2801–7, 2821, 2822, 2831, 2841, 2851–54, 2861, 2871, 2881, 2901–7, 2921–33, 2941–49, 2961–66, 2981).

36. Public Law 89-110, 79 Statute 437, August 6, 1965 (codified as amended at 42 *U.S. Code,* secs. 1971, 1973–1973b).

37. Public Law 90-284, Title VIII, 82 Statute 81, April 11, 1968 (codified as amended at 42 *U.S. Code,* secs. 3601–19).

38. Albert K. Karnig and Susan Welch, *Black Representation and Urban Policy* (Chicago: University of Chicago Press, 1980).

39. See also Perry, "Pluralist Theory and National Black Politics," for a full discussion of how voting rights actions by the national government have resulted in full reincorporation of southern blacks into the political process.

40. Executive Order 11246, 3 *Code of Federal Regulations* 339 (1965).

41. Amaker, *Civil Rights and the Reagan Administration,* 19.

42. Bert A. Rockman, May 21, 1991, private correspondence.

43. Equal Employment Opportunity Act of 1972, Public Law 92-261, 86 Statute 103, March 24, 1972 (codified as amended at 42 *U.S. Code,* 2000e et seq).

44. Ibid., sec. 2, 42 *U.S. Code,* sec. 2000e as amended.

45. Amaker, *Civil Rights and the Reagan Administration,* 23.

46. Amaker, *Civil Rights and the Reagan Administration,* 25.

47. J. David Greenstone and Paul E. Peterson were the first scholars to employ the vestment concept to refer to the incorporation of black interests within the governmental decision-making process. See J. David Greenstone and Paul E. Peterson, *Race and Authority in Urban Politics: Community Participation and the War on Poverty* (Chicago: University of Chicago Press, 1973), 170, 286–94, 307, and 314.

48. Ibid., 26.

49. Amaker, *Civil Rights and the Reagan Administration,* 26.

50. Executive Order 12250, 3 *Code of Federal Regulations.*

51. Amaker, *Civil Rights and the Reagan Administration,* 26.

52. Ibid.

53. Ibid.

54. Amaker, *Civil Rights and the Reagan Administration,* 26–27.

55. American Civil Liberties Union, *Civil Liberties in Reagan's America* (New York: American Civil Liberties Union, 1982), 34–35.

56. Amaker, *Civil Rights and the Reagan Administration,* 5.

57. Bert A. Rockman, private correspondence, May 21, 1991.

58. The lead author of this chapter is grateful to Professor James C. Garand of the Department of Political Science at Louisiana State University in Baton

Rouge, Louisiana, for reminding him of this point in private correspondence critiquing an earlier draft of this manuscript, May 1, 1991.

59. Lawrence A. Uzzell, "The Unsung Hero of the Reagan Revolution," *National Review,* December 9, 1988, 31.

60. Ibid.

61. Charles H. Moore and Patricia Hoban-Moore, "Some Lessons from Reagan's HUD: Housing Policy & Public Service," *PS: Political Science and Politics* 23 (March 1990): 14.

62. John L. Palmer and Isabel V. Sawhill, eds., *The Reagan Record* (Cambridge, Mass.: Ballinger Publishing Company, 1984), 2.

63. Amaker, *Civil Rights and the Reagan Administration,* 109.

64. Lynn Burbridge, *The Impact of Changes in Policy on the Federal Equal Employment Opportunity Effort* (Washington, D.C.: Urban Institute, Discussion Paper, 1984), 39 and 41, Chart 3. See also Burbridge, "Changes in Equal Employment Statistics Tell Us," *Review of Black Political Economy* (summer 1986): 76–77.

65. See also Perry, "Pluralist Theory and National Black Politics," 561, for a full discussion of President Reagan's action regarding these few pieces of legislation.

66. Kerry Mullins and Aaron Wildavsky, "The Procedural Presidency of George Bush," *Political Science Quarterly* 107 (spring 1992): 37.

67. Joint Center for Political and Economic Studies, "An Administration That Looks Like America," *Political Trendletter,* in *Focus* 21 (April 1993): 2–3.

Chapter 7

The Evolving Congressional Black Caucus: The Reagan-Bush Years

Richard Champagne
Leroy N. Rieselbach

Formed in 1971 during President Richard Nixon's administration, when many of the civil rights victories of the 1960s were under direct attack, the Congressional Black Caucus (CBC) has become a visible and viable force in congressional politics. Its members now serve on virtually every congressional committee and increasingly in important leadership positions. While the members of the CBC have climbed the seniority ladder and find themselves in positions of genuine power in the House of Representatives, they have struggled to resolve an "identity crisis" that has beset the CBC since its founding: Should CBC members act as a collective body, play a nonpartisan role, representing both inside and outside Congress the interests of the national black population, or should they engage in the fragmented world of pluralistic congressional politics, in which compromise and accommodation of black interests are necessary norms of conduct? This dilemma shapes the strategies, tactics, and roles of black legislators in an overwhelmingly white institution. This chapter focuses on the ways the CBC addressed its identity crisis during the administrations of Ronald Reagan and George Bush.

The Nature of CBC's Identity Crisis

The identity crisis that confronts the CBC is best captured in the words of two of its most prominent members.[1] In March 1971, the late Charles Diggs (D-Mich.-13) announced to Congress the formation of the CBC, asserting that "the issues and concerns of this caucus are not partisan ones." Instead, he proclaimed, the CBC's concerns include those of "citizens living hundreds of miles from our districts who look on us as Congressmen-at-large for black people and poor people in the United States."[2] Diggs's announcement was a clear declaration that the CBC was an organization that would not be limited by partisan politics, that would seek allies wherever it could find them, and that would serve as the symbolic voice for the interests of blacks and the poor. By 1985, the situation could not have been in sharper contrast. On assuming the chairmanship of the powerful House Budget Committee, William Gray III (D-Pa.-2) outlined his new legislative role: "I represent not the Black Caucus. I represent the House of Representatives. The House of Representatives is a multicolored, multisexed situation."[3] In contrast to Diggs's depiction of CBC members as "congressmen-at-large" for blacks and the poor, Gray saw himself, first and foremost, as a member of the House, representing the interests of the Democratic party.

Others who have studied the CBC have recognized this dilemma. Barnett distinguished three stages in CBC's development.[4] In the first phase, in 1971 and 1972, the CBC adopted a "collective" model of group action, in which the caucus envisioned itself as *the* leadership forum of the "national black community." Its sphere of action was not confined to the narrow corridors of Congress. While the CBC was to press for legislation of direct benefit to blacks, it was also, and perhaps more importantly, to mobilize and articulate the interests of blacks both inside and outside Congress. In short, the CBC was not a mere legislative caucus, but rather the organizational embodiment of what remained of the civil rights movement after the murders of Malcolm X and Martin Luther King, Jr. As such, it was above partisan politics.

In the second stage, from mid-1972 through 1974, the CBC acted on an "ethnic" model of group action, in which it saw itself as a legislative caucus, representing discrete and insular black interests. CBC members pursued their individual legislative careers, in ways similar to members of white ethnic groups, adopting, for example, the congressional norm of specialization in substantive policy areas. As Louis Stokes (D-Ohio-21) asserted, "If we are going to make a meaningful contribution to minority citizens and this country, then it must be as legislators."[5] Thus, CBC members adapted to the congressional process, engaging in legislative politics, in the hope of securing better positions from which to advance black interests.

The third stage, from 1975 through 1994, is a synthesis of the collective and ethnic models of group action. While working within the legislative process, the CBC also tries to retain its position as leader of the national black political community. A clear example of this new role involved the 1978 struggle over the Humphrey-Hawkins full employment bill. In its initial form, this legislation called for the federal government to become the employer of last resort. CBC members championed this bill as a symbolic and substantive measure of direct benefit to the black community, since black unemployment was (and remains) at depression levels. But in the partisan struggle to secure its passage, black legislators found themselves forced to compromise on the substantive provisions of the legislation. The result, as Barnett argued, was a public law that "was utterly meaningless as a vehicle to aid the black unemployed."[6] Although CBC members assumed the lead in passing this legislation, the final result of their actions had little effect on the economic condition of black Americans. For that reason, Barnett contends, the CBC faces a crisis. By engaging in partisan legislative politics, in which bargaining, logrolling, and compromise are necessary norms of strategic conduct, the CBC may be undermining its position as the leadership forum for the black community.

The framework we use to examine the CBC differs from Barnett's in two important ways. First, we reject the notion that discrete stages of development can be empirically demarcated in a period as brief as the twenty-four years that the CBC has been in existence. The CBC is not a monolithic organization, whose actions are subject to clear and precise categorization. Rather, the CBC consists of many individual black legislators, who pursue in very different ways the goals of racial equality and the amelioration of the dire economic condition of black Americans. As the former CBC chairman, the late Mickey Leland (D-Tex.-18), put it:[7] "We all have basically the same goals. The question is how to attain these goals."[8] In other words, in any given session of Congress, CBC members adopt various legislative roles. For that reason, we prefer to examine the dilemma confronting the CBC not in developmental terms but rather as an unresolved tension concerning the most apposite mode of legislative action. The dilemma is whether CBC members should remain above the fray of conventional partisan politics or engage in legislative politics as party members who actively participate in committee activities, building coalitions with other members of Congress to realize the substantive goals of racial equality and economic justice.

Our second point of departure from Barnett's framework is one of theoretical emphasis. She holds that a proper understanding of the CBC must presuppose "the caucus first as a part of Afro-American political life and only secondarily as a part of congressional politics."[9] While the CBC does exist as an authority structure within the larger black political community, it is also an organization within a legislative setting. Congress is not a neutral arena, whose essential features are subject to the whims of individual legislators in any given session. Rather, it is an institutional structure with a compelling system of rewards and incentives that shapes, and sometimes transforms, the behavior of individual legislators. For that reason, Congress cannot be treated in a secondary fashion in explaining the actions of the CBC and its members. Indeed, as we demonstrate, that system of rewards and incentives profoundly affects the ways in which the CBC is resolving its "identity crisis."

Our argument is that specific institutional arrangements in Congress are increasingly compelling the CBC to resolve its crisis in favor of ordinary legislative politics. Congress is a pluralistic institution; it divides power widely, but not equally, among its members. Individual representatives, regularly ensconced in safe seats that virtually guarantee them extended congressional careers, attain positions of authority from which they can influence some segment of legislative policy-making and oversight.[10] Though no longer inviolate, the seniority tradition—which rewards the majority party member with the longest continuous service on a committee or subcommittee with the best chance of assuming the committee's or subcommittee's chair—allows members of Congress who win re-election several times to advance to formal positions of leadership.[11] Such positions provide vantage points for senior members, also presumably specialists on the subject matters within their committee and subcommittee jurisdictions, to be key players in congressional deliberation and decision-making. As CBC members have risen in the seniority system to assume major positions of power, they have increasingly been drawn into the maelstrom of bargaining, compromising, and coalition-building politics that characterizes an individualistic House of Representatives.

When the CBC was organized in 1971, only one of its members held a leadership post. Consequently, caucus members had few incentives or opportunities to engage in conventional legislative politics; they did not have the leverage to impose their liberal policy preferences on a more conservative institution. They lacked the ability to bargain from positions of strength and instead were forced to make their views known outside the normal legislative process. They engaged in "symbolic" efforts, such as boycotting President Richard Nixon's 1971 State of the Union Address.[12] The CBC's current situation is strikingly different from what it was in 1971; black legislators now occupy some of the most powerful positions in Congress. As William Clay said, "We don't have to go hat in hand begging anymore. In fact, it's just the reverse. Now a lot of people have to come hat in hand [to us] asking for favors."[13] As they have acquired expertise, seniority, and institutional power, CBC members have attained congressional positions of strength; they have become increasingly successful participants as skilled "insiders" in ordinary, Washington-based legislative politics.

The CBC in the 101st Congress

The improved circumstances of CBC members are evident from their status in the 101st Congress (1989–90), as the Reagan administration gave way to that of George Bush. The caucus in the 101st Congress consisted of an all-time high of twenty-four members: twenty-three members of the House, all Democrats, from thirteen states, plus Walter Fauntroy, also a Democrat, the nonvoting delegate from the District of Columbia. The black legislators represented heavily black districts: seventeen had black majorities, and several others (notably in California and New York) had sizable Hispanic populations, which give the CBC members minority-dominated constituencies (Table 7-1, column 3). Only two members—Ronald Dellums (Cal.-8) and Alan Wheat (Mo.-5)—represented districts with white majorities.[14] These constituencies, moreover, are mostly urban (those of Dellums and Mike Espy [Miss.-2] were the exceptions) and mostly poor—all twenty-three had median family incomes below, and most well below, the national average (Table 7-1, column 4).[15] Such districts are heavily Democratic, and CBC members, once in office, experience little difficulty in retaining their seats. Indeed, only three—Dellums, Wheat, and Espy—received less than 70 percent of the vote in 1988, and each of them captured 60 percent or more (Table 7-1, column 5). The CBC members' congressional power rests firmly on electoral security.

In social terms, black representatives are similar to their white colleagues. They are well educated; all but two have college or graduate degrees (Table 7-1, column 6). Most pursued professional occupations (Table 7-1, column 7) before winning seats in the House, and many had previous experience in the public sector—at the state and local levels or with the federal government. By contrast, CBC members are ideologically distinctive. They are all strongly liberal, scoring at the low end of the American Conservative Union rating scale (Table 7-1, column 8).[16] Overall, CBC members are a homogeneous lot: liberal Democrats, of high educational and occupational accomplishment, representing poor, central city constituencies. These basic facts shape their behavior in Congress.

CBC members have pursued various courses in a decentralized Congress. Electoral longevity has enabled them, over the years, to attain substantial status, to develop considerable expertise, and to exert considerable influence in the legislative process. Table 7-2 notes the achievements of the caucus members at the start of the 101st Congress (in January 1989). Several have served for extended periods: The former dean of the CBC, Augustus Hawkins (Cal.-29) served fourteen terms, and stood twelfth (of 260) on the Democratic seniority ladder. John Conyers (Mich.-1) had won thirteen electoral victories and had risen to eighteenth in seniority among his party colleagues. Lengthy tenure allowed several CBC members to assume important committee chairmanships. Hawkins headed the Education and Labor Committee, which has jurisdiction over matters of special concern to the constituents of black legislators—education, employment, and welfare programs. Julian Dixon (Cal.-28) chaired the Committee on Standards of Official Conduct (Ethics), charged with investigating alleged ethical improprieties of, among others, such important House figures as Speaker Jim Wright (D-Tex.).

Overall, CBC members, during the 101st Congress, held the chairmanship of four standing committees, two select committees (Hunger and Narcotics), and sixteen subcommittees. In addition to the Budget (Gray) and Ethics Committees, CBC members chaired the District of Columbia (Dellums) and Government Operations (Conyers) Committees. CBC subcommittee chairmen were on such "power" committees as Appropri-

Table 7-1. Congressional Black Caucus, 101st Congress Outside the House

Member	Dist.	% Black Population	Median Family Income ($)	% 1988 Vote	Education	Prior Occupation	Ideology (1988 ACU)*
William Clay	1-Mo.	52	18,108	72	B.S.	Real estate, insurance	0
Cardiss Collins	7-Ill.	67	16,074	100	"attended" college	Auditor, accountant	0
John Conyers	1-Mich.	71	18,689	90	LL.B.	Lawyer	0
George Crockett	13-Mich.	71	12,825	87	J.D.	Lawyer	0
Ronald Dellums (Chrm.)	8-Cal.	27	23,127	67	M.S.W.	Social worker	0
Julian Dixon	28-Cal.	39	15,649	75	LL.B.	Lawyer	0
Mervyn Dymally	31-Cal.	34	19,212	76	Ph.D.	Teacher	0
Mike Espy	2-Miss.	58	12,270	65	J.D.	Lawyer	12
Walter Fauntroy	Del.-D.C.	70	19,099	71	B.D.	Clergy	—
Floyd Flake	6-N.Y.	50	19,656	86	B.A.	Clergy	0
Harold Ford	9-Tenn.	57	15,230	82	M.B.A.	Mortician	0
William Gray	2-Pa.	80	13,800	94	Th.M.	Clergy	0
Augustus Hawkins	29-Cal.	50	13,717	83	A.B.	Real estate	0
Charles Hayes	1-Ill.	92	14,017	96	high school grad.	Labor official	0
Mickey Leland	18-Tex.	41	15,449	93	B.S.	Pharmacist	0

Table 7-1. continued

Member	Dist.	% Black Population	Median Family Income ($)	% 1988 Vote	Education	Prior Occupation	Ideology (1988 ACU)*
John Lewis	5-Ga.	65	15,431	78	B.A.	Civil rights activist	0
Kweisi Mfume	7-Md.	73	15,072	100	M.A.	Radio personality	4
Major Owens	12-N.Y.	80	12,690	93	M.S.	Librarian	0
Donald Payne	10-N.J.	58	14,729	77	B.A.	Community development exec.	0
Charles Rangel	16-N.Y.	49	10,720	97	LL.B.	Lawyer	0
Gus Savage	2-Ill.	70	20,074	83	B.A.	Journalist	0
Louis Stokes	21-Ohio	62	18,005	86	J.D.	Lawyer	0
Edolphus Towns	11-N.Y.	47	9,542	89	M.S.W.	Social worker	0
Alan Wheat	5-Mo.	23	20,462	60	B.A.	Public service	0
Total	U.S.	10.9	24,525				

*ACU is the acronym for the American Conservative Union.

Sources: Congressional Directory, 101st Congress (Washington, D.C.: Government Printing Office, 1989); P. Duncan, ed., Politics in America 1990: The 101st Congress (Washington, D.C.: Congressional Quarterly, 1989); Congressional Quarterly, Congressional Districts in the 1980s (Washington, D.C.: Congressional Quarterly, 1983).

Table 7-2. Congressional Black Caucus, 101st Congress Inside the House

Member	Term	Democratic Seniority	Committees (Seniority)	Committee Leadership	Party Leadership	1988 Party Unity	1988 Presidential Support
Clay	11	28	Education and Labor (4) House Administration (8) Post Office (2)	Subcomm. chair Subcomm. chair	DCCC*	68	12
Collins	9	48	Energy & Commerce (11) Government Operations (2) Select Narcotics (5)	Subcomm. chair		87	16
Conyers	13	18	Government Operations (1) Judiciary (4) Small Business (17)	Full & subcomm. chairs		83	13
Crockett	5	123	Foreign Affairs (7) Judiciary (11) Select Aging (17)	Subcomm. chair		82	14
Dellums	10	35	District of Columbia (1) Armed Services (4)	Full Comm. chair Subcomm. chair		88	19
Dixon	6	101	Standards of Official Conduct (1) District of Columbia (5) Appropriations (19)	Full Comm. chair		85	17
Dymally	5	124	District of Columbia (5) Foreign Affairs (9) Post Office (11)	Subcomm. chair Subcomm. chair Subcomm. chair		83	16

Name			Committees	Chair	Leadership			
Espy	2	211	Agriculture (22) Budget (12)		At-large whip	78		20
Fauntroy	10	—	Select Hunger (10) Banking (3) District of Columbia (2) Select Narcotics (9)	Subcomm. chair Subcomm. chair Subcomm. chair	DCCC DCCC	—		—
Flake	2	211	Banking (25) Small Business (20) Select Hunger (11)			82		14
Ford	8	53	Ways and Means (7)	Subcomm. chair	Steering & Policy Comm.	61		12
Gray	6	101	Select Aging (4) Appropriations (25) District of Columbia (4)		Majority whip Steering & Policy Comm.	78		4
Hawkins	14	2	Education and Labor (11)	Full & subcomm. chairs		79		14
Hayes	4	194	Education and Labor (11) Small Business (16)			91		14
Leland	6	101	Energy and Commerce (10) Post Office (5) Select Hunger (1)	Subcomm. chair Full comm. chair	At-large whip DCCC	77	15	
Lewis	2	211	Interior (21) Public Works (18)		At-large whip	93		13
Mfume	1	211	Banking (26) Education and Labor (22)		At-large whip	93		23

Table 7-2. *Continued*

Member	Term	Democratic Seniority	Committees (Seniority)	Committee Leadership	Party Leadership	1988 Party Unity	1988 Presidential Support
Mfume			Select Narcotics (19) Small Business (16)				
Owens	4	146	Education and Labor (10) Government Operations (13)			79	13
Payne	1	240	Education and Labor (14) Foreign Affairs (28) Government Operations (22)				
Rangel	10	35	Ways and Means (4) Select Narcotics (1)	Subcomm. chair Full comm. chair	Deputy whip	80	14
Savage	5	124	Public Works (9) Small Business (10)	Subcomm. chair		82	18
Stokes	11	28	Appropriations (7)			81	16
Towns	4	146	Government Operations (14) Public Works (14) Select Narcotics (14)			76	13
Wheat	4	146	District of Columbia (6) Rules (7) Select Children (13)	Subcomm. chair		79	15
House Dem X̄						80	30

Sources: Same as Table 7-1 and *Congressional Quarterly Weekly Report* 47 (1989): 3540–50.
*DCCC is the acronym for Democratic Congressional Campaign Committee.

ations (Dixon) and Ways and Means (Charles Rangel, N.Y.-16) as well as on important policy committees like Foreign Affairs (George Crockett [Mich.-13] and Mervyn Dymally [Cal.-31]), Armed Services (Dellums), Banking (Fauntroy), and Public Works (Gus Savage, Ill.-2). In sum, by the time of the 101st Congress in 1989–90, CBC members had earned several positions of power and influence in the House committee system.

By 1989–90, CBC members had also assumed prominence in the Democratic party organizational hierarchy in Congress. During the 101st Congress, William Gray built on his selection as chairman of the Budget Committee and election as Democratic Caucus chairman to win the party's majority whip position, the third-ranking post in the party leadership in Congress. Charles Rangel was a deputy whip, and Mickey Leland, Mike Espy, John Lewis (Ga.-2), and Kweisi Mfume (Md.-7) were at-large whips.[17] In addition, Gray and Harold Ford (Tenn.-9) served on the Democratic Steering and Policy Committee, a major advisory body to the Speaker with important committee assignment powers in addition. Finally, Leland, Fauntroy, Clay, Dymally, and Espy were members of the House Democratic Congressional Campaign Committee (DCCC), the party's body responsible for promoting election of Democrats to the House.

CBC members have obtained positions of power and influence in the Democratic party organizational hierarchy in Congress because Democrats in Congress have sought to reflect the diversity of their party and because they have been loyal Democrats in recent years in their leadership positions. In terms of party loyalty, the twenty-two voting CBC legislators' average party unity score of 81 percent in 1988 was essentially the same as the 80 percent average party unity score for all Democrats.[18] Thirteen CBC members were above the party mean, nine below; their scores ranged from 93 percent party support (Lewis and Mfume) to 61 percent (Ford). Similarly, the CBC opposed Reagan administration policy initiatives. Its members' average presidential support of 15 percent in 1988 was well below the mean of 25 percent for all Democrats. Only two CBC members (Mfume, 23 percent, and Espy, 20 percent) supported President Reagan on one vote out of five. Overall, CBC members, as devoted Democratic partisans holding several important legislative and party positions, were well situated to work inside the legislative system to promote their policy and other aims during the 101st Congress.

The CBC as an "Informal Caucus"

The Congressional Black Caucus is one of the oldest of the informal, ad hoc groups that have sprung up in Congress over the past two decades—there are at present more than a hundred such organizations, which the House designates as either "legislative service" or "congressional membership" organizations. Like-minded members band together, often very loosely, to foster common interests: to promote consideration of causes they favor; to push for particular policies, using their numerical strength to bargain in support of favored legislative provisions; to encourage the exchange of information among their members; and to represent ethnic, regional, or broad national constituency interests outside Congress.[19] As such, informal organizations (caucuses) supplement the activities of political parties and external interest groups, often collaborating with the latter in efforts to build successful policy coalitions.

The caucuses survive financially by assessing members, who contribute from their regularly available office funds. They often draw on member staff and pool other facilities such as telephones. The CBC, in the Ninety-Ninth Congress, collected four thousand dollars from each member's office account; the caucus had a staff of three full-time employees of its own. Its activities centered on helping members prepare legislation, writing and distributing a newsletter to members' constituents and other interested groups, and serving as an "informal clearinghouse of information" for the national black political community.[20] The CBC chairman (Leland) sought to hold weekly meetings of the caucus to exchange information and plan strategy.

In 1976, the CBC established the Congressional Black Caucus Foundation to organize and administer a legislative internship program. The foundation raises money to sustain its operations from private, noncongressional contributors. It stages an annual legislative weekend—"three days of seminars, speeches and dinners devoted to the black political agenda."[21] In 1982, the House Administration Committee decreed that no legislative service organization could both use House facilities and solicit outside funds. As a result of this decree, the formal relationship between the CBC and the foundation was discontinued, an action that qualified the CBC as a legitimate informal House organization. The foundation operates beyond the formal control of CBC members, but some of them serve on its board of directors. The foundation has an annual budget of some $550,000 and a full-time staff of nine. It engages in policy research and aids CBC members in writing legislation.

Both the CBC and the foundation stress "inside" politics—that is, promoting their black political agenda in Congress. But both also address the concerns of the national black population. The CBC maintains a "brain trust," a "network of professional and academic advisers" that keeps it in touch with extra-legislative points of view as well as enabling it to draw on expertise beyond Capitol Hill.[22] It also has established an "action alert communications network" to enable it to reach 150 or so black grass-roots political organizations. The communication network enables the CBC to encourage citizens to lobby Congress for preferred policies.[23] Overall, the CBC and the foundation possess modestly significant resources that they commit mostly but not exclusively to pursuing preferred policies within the usual rules, formal and informal, of congressional politics.

The CBC and Legislative Politics

The identity crisis the CBC confronts is most apparent with respect to the federal budget. The evolution of CBC strategy and tactics appears clearly in its approach to budgetary politics, which emerged as a central concern in the Reagan era of high deficits. Caucus activity after 1981 amply demonstrates the perhaps insurmountable constraints on members' participation in conventional congressional processes.[24]

In 1974, Congress enacted the Budget and Impoundment Control Act, significantly restructuring the budget process and specifically establishing new Budget Committees in the House and Senate as the central congressional forums for budgetary and fiscal policy. From the formation of the House Budget Committee in 1975 to 1980, the CBC had been well represented on the committee, having secured the appointment of Louis Stokes and William Gray to the committee. But in 1980, Stokes's term expired, and Gray chose to leave the committee.[25] As the Ninety-Seventh Congress (1981–82) inaugurated the Reagan era, with its fiscal stringency, the CBC was excluded from the central locus of the budget process.[26]

Outside the normal channels of the budget process, the CBC adopted an innovative budget strategy under the leadership of Walter Fauntroy. The CBC surprised many people in 1981 when it introduced its own budget for fiscal year 1982. While this was clearly a symbolic gesture, reflecting CBC displeasure with both the Democratic and the Republican budget alternatives, it was also an effort by the CBC to make itself heard. The CBC budget restored money for many social programs, reduced defense spending by $2 billion, and provided for $56.4 billion in tax relief. While CBC members called their budget the "most equitable" budget alternative, not all House members appreciated the CBC alternative or the fact that the CBC had used valuable floor time in introducing its budget to Congress.[27] Ron Dellums responded to that criticism by saying, "We are going to take some time here even if we only get 18 or 19 votes." Moreover, in response to House antagonism, Parren Mitchell (Md.-7) charged that some House members "are so racist they cannot accept a constructive alternative budget which emanates from a Congressional Black Caucus."[28] In the end, the CBC budget alternative received only 69 votes, all from Democrats. A similar scenario followed in 1982 when the CBC again offered its own budget alternative. CBC's 1982 budget alternative called for no increase in defense spending, more funds for domestic programs, and increased federal taxes. The budget received only 86 votes, again all from Democrats.

The CBC budget strategy in 1981 and 1982 is best viewed as a reaction to the caucus's exclusion from the House Budget Committee, coupled with its unhappiness with the Reagan budget proposals. Forced outside normal policy-making channels, the CBC, to maintain its organizational visibility, had little recourse other than to adopt a nonpartisan strategy, opposing both the Democratic and Republican budget alternatives. At the very least, proposing an alternative budget permitted the caucus to demonstrate its concern for black economic progress to its national black constituency.

The situation was different in 1983. During the Ninety-Eighth Congress (1983–84), William Gray was reappointed to the Budget Committee, allowing an articulation of CBC's interests and diminishing the need for the CBC to continue introducing its budget alternative with the same fervor. Although CBC chairman Julian Dixon introduced a CBC budget for fiscal year 1984, it was never debated or subjected to a House vote. Instead, in light of the Gray's active and visible committee role, CBC members, for the first time, unanimously voted for the Democratic budget.[29] Moreover, during the House-Senate conference on the final budget bill, Gray assembled a coalition of CBC and liberal House members and successfully bargained for the restoration of funds cut from social programs. Acting in the legislative arena, Gray achieved a victory for the CBC and played a major role in shaping the fiscal year 1984 budget. This assessment is supported by a House Budget Committee aide, who commented on the process that produced the fiscal year 1984 budget, "Gray was a key in pulling things together."[30]

However, some CBC members, such as John Conyers and Gus Savage, were uneasy about CBC's foray into the partisan world of budget politics. Instead, they wanted the CBC to introduce its own, nonpartisan budget. This division partly reflected generational differences among CBC members. Conyers and Savage began their political careers during the tumultuous years of the civil rights movement, when blacks were marching and fighting for the minimal right to participate in the political process. Their struggles were against the institutions and practices of *both* political parties; this confrontational and collective political style carried over into their legislative actions. In contrast, other members, such as Gray and Dixon, began their political careers after the civil rights movement, having benefited from the universal extension of the franchise to black Americans. They perceived their legislative roles in very different terms. As Gray argued, "We see ourselves not as civil rights leaders, but as legislators."[31] For that reason, less senior CBC members were more predisposed to partisan politics.

With Gray on the Budget Committee, the CBC was represented in the partisan budget process. But several CBC members did not find this sufficient for the CBC to abandon its independent budget strategy. After all, Gray was only one of several dozen Budget Committee members, and his influence was at best limited. For that reason, in 1984 and subsequently, the CBC championed its own budget, calling for defense spending cuts, tax increases, and substantially greater funds for domestic programs. During House floor debates, CBC members and several other liberal Democrats praised the substantive provisions of the CBC budget, but the results were always the same: the budgets were not taken seriously, received scant attention outside Congress, and were overwhelmingly defeated, never receiving more than a hundred votes.[32] House Democrats who backed the CBC budget alternatives would, subsequently, vote for their party's budgets.

During the first term of the Reagan administration, the CBC had not resolved its identity crisis; it wanted both to represent broad black interests and to shape actual budgetary allocations. In terms of the CBC's congressional power, the alternative budget strategy raised two serious problems. First, the introduction of the CBC budget was increasingly regarded as a sideshow in a larger congressional performance, whose denouement was virtually assured to result in House passage of the Democratic budget. Second, the CBC budget strategy was a clear affront to the committee system. By offering its own budget, the CBC directly challenged the authority of the Budget Committee.[33] This had serious implications for CBC's congressional power. Several senior CBC members had assumed powerful committee positions, and their success as leaders depended on the viability of the committee system, in which majority party members would not oppose legislation written in committee. The CBC budget strategy, however, was an unabashed attempt to circumvent the committee process, to challenge the jurisdictional autonomy of the Budget Committee. Thus the CBC was pursuing a strategy that, if applied universally to all committees in all policy areas, could have undermined the power of its own members who held committee leadership positions.

CBC's identity crisis became more acute in 1985, when William Gray became the chairman of the Budget Committee.[34] His election reflected his legislative skills. Observers described him as "a superb politician, adept at building coalitions"[35] and as possessing "keen understanding and significant mastery of the political process in the House."[36] Gray himself defined his role not as "one who legislates his own personal ideological perspective," but rather as "one who is able to build consensus."[37] In seeking consensus on the budget, he held regional hearings throughout the country. He circulated to Democratic House members a budget-options survey, appropriately called an "Exercise in Hard Choices," asking them to rank their budgetary preferences. His strategy was a clear departure from precedent: He tried to forge not only a Democratic response to the Reagan administration budget but also a *bipartisan* response. He held the Budget Committee markup in executive (closed) session, out of the public eye, in an attempt to find a bipartisan agreement. It was a return to the yesteryear of congressional politics, when committees met behind closed doors to bargain over legislation in private, far removed from the klieg lights of the media. In the end, Gray's bipartisan strategy failed, as the Budget Committee voted out a Democratic fiscal year 1986 budget, largely along party lines. When the

CBC introduced its budget alternative—it declined to follow Gray's lead and fall in line behind the party proposal—he broke ranks with the CBC by voting "present" (abstaining, in effect) on the roll call vote for the CBC budget alternative.

While the House enacted the Budget Committee alternative, the House and Senate versions were fundamentally different. Gray prepared himself for the House-Senate conference by again adopting an unprecedented budget strategy; he transformed the budget battle into an institutional struggle between the House and Senate, rather than a contest between Democrats and Republicans. He enlisted the aid of conservative Republicans, as well as the Democratic leadership, and he met with administration officials. The result was that the Reagan administration backed away from its previous support of the Senate budget. So bipartisan were Gray's efforts that one House member, Butler Derrick (D-S.C.), remarked: "It's the most bipartisan group I've seen since I've been on the Budget Committee."[38] In the end, the House prevailed. The domestic programs cut by the Senate were restored, and cost of living increases were retained for Social Security recipients.

An overwhelming majority of House Democrats and Republicans voted for the budget compromise. Support for the budget compromise was so great in the House that the CBC's votes were not needed to ensure its adoption. Since the CBC had relegated itself to the sidelines during the budget process, its members faced a dilemma as to how to vote on the final budget. Twelve members voted against the budget; voting for it were seven members who were among the most powerful, or fastest-rising, in the CBC: Gray, Dixon, Hawkins, Wheat, Rangel, Stokes, and Ford. Three chaired their own committees, while the others served on the powerful Rules, Appropriations, and Ways and Means Committees.[39] The mere fact that these members split with the CBC, especially when their votes were not needed by the Democratic leadership, underscored the emerging legislative orientation of many CBC members.

The increasing inclination of CBC members to choose "inside" legislative strategies over ideological politics is visible in other ways as well. In the late 1980s, black lawmakers began "branching out," looking to move beyond race to other matters. "For blacks coming to Congress, civil rights issues are still very important, but we also want to pursue other activities, and we've done a good job of that."[40] Charles Rangel made a credible but unsuccessful bid for the Democratic whip job. Dixon achieved prominence as chairman of the Committee on Official Standards (Ethics), presiding over difficult investigations of House Speaker Jim Wright and Barney Frank (D-Mass.). Columnist David Broder described Rangel as a man who "makes his way not by the militance of his advocacy of civil rights or other racially linked issues, but on the basis of personal and intellectual qualities which cross racial and ideological divisions and make him an effective bridge builder." He has demonstrated "his ability to forge a consensus."[41]

The newer, less senior CBC members seem especially inclined to "bring a different style to Washington."[42] They—Kweisi Mfume, Floyd Flake (N.Y.-6), John Lewis, and Mike Espy, in particular—constitute a "new breed" of pragmatists who "have become issue activists and coalition builders eager for influence."[43] Mfume, for instance, is described as "a collegial operator who tries to help the needy by making legislative allies."[44] The search for allies has led caucus members to play conventional electoral politics. William Gray formed a personal political action committee and disbursed campaign funds to Democratic incumbents and aspiring challengers alike.[45] Espy, in his second term, took to the stump on behalf of party colleagues, including white, relatively conservative southerners like Charlie Rose (N.C.) and Richard Ray (Ga.).[46] Such activities may translate into influence for these CBC members and support for their legislative initiatives. Even the more senior CBC members seem to have "mellowed" with "age and government experience" and to have become "powerful players in an institution they once distrusted."[47]

The chief symbol of the integration of CBC members into the mainstream of House politics is William Gray. Moving on from the Budget Committee chairmanship, he first won election as secretary of the Democratic Caucus and then, in 1989, as majority whip, ranking him third in the party leadership hierarchy. His rapid rise reflected his talent as a player of inside politics. Observers continually described him as "pragmatic," "skilled at avoiding and managing conflict," able "to forge consensus," always eager "to work something out," and "a leadership team member."[48] Gray himself described his success as majority whip as being "based on my competence and abilities to bring people together."[49] He noted that "if I am successful as whip in establishing coalitions and building priorities of . . . fundamental principles . . . , that is important. When I give a speech in a Member's district, that strengthens my colleagues locally, and I am communicating to other Democrats about our policies and positions."[50] In short, Gray, while not eschewing symbolic politics entirely, operated comfortably within the confines of a decentralized Congress where pragmatism commonly triumphs over ideology.

This is not to say, however, that the Congressional Black Caucus is unconcerned about issues; it is only to suggest that the CBC members often seek policy influence more as individuals than as a collectivity. For instance, in 1986, the CBC engaged in discussions with Jack Kemp (R-N.Y.) about his pending proposals for housing legislation.[51] The same year, Dellums and Gray were instrumental in the adoption of economic sanctions against South Africa's apartheid policies. Dellums played a major part in the House passage of a strong bill, while Gray charted a strategy, requiring acceptance of more moderate Senate provisions, that helped sustain a coalition able to override President Reagan's veto of the legislation.[52] The same two lawmakers, and other CBC members, were active in a revolt among Democrats against Les Aspin (Wisc.), chairman of the Armed Services Committee; they sought, unsuccessfully, to have Aspin removed from the chairmanship and have Marvin Leath (Tex.) appointed in his place. These lawmakers sought to replace Aspin in the hopes of reducing the overall defense budget and improving the prospects for arms control agreements.[53] In addition, several members of the caucus, including Dellums, fought the Reagan administration's efforts to aid the Nicaraguan contra rebels on the grounds that it was not in the national interest to bring down the Sandinista government in that country.[54] In the 101st Congress (1989–90), the CBC proposed, and the Foreign Affairs Committee accepted, an amendment to a fiscal year 1990 supplemental appropriations bill allocating $1 billion to development aid in Africa.[55]

If the Congressional Black Caucus, and its individual members, focused increasingly, and pragmatically, on specific policies, operating within the confines of traditional methods of conducting legislative business (bargaining and brokering), they were unwilling to relinquish entirely the articulation of broader black interests. For example, the CBC continued to offer an annual alternative budget calling for increased spending on social welfare needs for the poor (and William Gray, after his term as Budget Committee chairman had ended, returned to voting with his CBC colleagues in support of the budget alternative). In 1986, caucus members pointedly declined to meet with Angolan rebel leader Jonas Savimbi, citing his close connection with the government of South Africa and its apartheid policies.[56] CBC members expressed concern, in 1988, that articles of impeachment initiated against Alcee L. Hastings, a black federal judge, were racially motivated. While most eventually supported impeachment—John Conyers, a Judiciary Committee member, found the evidence against Hastings compelling—George Crockett (Mich.-13) cast the lone dissenting vote on the committee, and on the floor Gus Savage and Mervyn Dymally provided two of the three votes against impeachment (and Harold Ford voted "present").[57] Moreover, when George Bush, eager to improve Republican party relations with black Americans, invited the caucus to the White House for the first time in eight years, CBC members chastised the president for his neglect of the inner cities and for his "intransigent" foreign policy approach toward the Soviet Union.[58] In 1990, when the Senate was considering a motion to shut off debate on a major civil rights bill, several members of the CBC—including Gray, Mfume, and Rangel—took the floor to encourage wavering senators to invoke cloture (that is, force an end to debate).[59]

The Past and Future Congressional Black Caucus

Thirteen black members of the House of Representatives, liberal Democrats representing urban constituencies, came together in 1971 to establish the Congressional Black Caucus. Largely outside the power structure of the House, the CBC organizers sought to articulate the sentiments of the national black constituency that lacked a clear voice within the halls of the national legislature. By 1989, as the Reagan era ended, their number had grown to twenty-four and their skill and seniority had elevated many of them to important leadership positions in a decentralized Congress. Given ordinary attrition rates in Congress and their relative electoral safety, a majority of caucus members may soon hold leadership posts. This rise to prominence, symbolized by William Gray's rapid advance to the top of the Democratic party hierarchy, created a dilemma, an "identity crisis," for the CBC: whether to continue to represent a broad extra-legislative national black population or to pursue programs that benefit black America within the framework of conventional House policy-making. We argue that increasingly, but not exclusively, caucus members have opted to play "inside" politics, to exploit the positions of influence they have attained to bargain and compromise to obtain favorable policy results.

By the end of the Reagan-Bush years, the CBC had come to resemble other informal legislative caucuses. It worked to raise important issues and to place them on the congressional agenda. It conducted research on these matters and disseminated the information produced to members and nonmembers. It sought to pool its collective resources and to build coalitions in support of the programs it favored. In these efforts, the CBC has not always been entirely successful in surmounting the individualism that characterizes contemporary congressional decision-making. As John Lewis put it, "We have to do more than come together on a particular issue—we have to use our votes as leverage."[60] Augustus Hawkins expressed the sentiment in another way: "It's pretty difficult to get individual politicians . . . to subordinate their own egos to group activity."[61] CBC members increasingly have engaged in the give-and-take of conventional legislative conflict resolution.

How the CBC will adapt to its members' growing congressional power is uncertain. If it is true that acquisition of authority inclines members to the inside, institutional game of coalition-building—and the budget experience, at least since 1985, suggests it is—then it is reasonable to expect the CBC's cohesion and ideological fervor to decline. Some, perhaps most, black legislators may find it difficult to oppose legislation written in committees that blacks chair or on which blacks have exerted substantial influence. On at least some issues, CBC members may have to choose between conventional legislative politics and ideological purity. To the extent that they opt for the former, CBC organizational solidarity will suffer.

On the other hand, budgetary politics illustrates the CBC's difficulty in fully resolving its identity crisis. Although members, given their rise to positions of congressional prominence, act more as individual legislators than as members of a collectivity, they still feel an obligation to represent the national black population. They win election in economically disadvantaged, urban, heavily minority constituencies; the voters "back home" are inevitably among the least likely to prosper economically.[62] To the extent that conventional legislative politics, with its frequent incremental outcomes, enables CBC members to serve their districts, they should exploit their congressional power and influence to benefit their actual constituents. However, if economic gains for black Americans are not forthcoming, if civil rights progress ebbs, CBC members may well feel obliged to eschew the machinations of ordinary politics and engage in efforts to articulate the interests of blacks nationally.[63] In the words of Kweisi Mfume, the Congressional Black Caucus "raises crucial issues affecting black Americans that may not be raised as forcefully or as often."[64]

In sum, the CBC in the 1990s faces the same dilemma it did at its founding in 1971: Should it work within the legislative system, where compromise and accommodation prevail, or should it be an organization articulating the interests of black citizens? The passage of time, the increase in the number of CBC members, and changed congressional circumstances have increased the incentives for the former course, and these incentives can be expected to increase further in the years ahead. Most CBC members seem to stress participation in conventional legislative politics; the "synthesis," if there is one, of partisan and nonpartisan strategies seems clearly tipped toward ordinary congressional routines and away from symbolic politics.

Congress is the epitome of American pluralistic politics. It distributes influence widely, but unequally, among its members. Its decentralized decision-making process offers numerous opportunities for lawmakers to exert their authority. It reaches decisions through bargaining and negotiation, leading most commonly to incremental rather than sweeping and innovative public policies. The CBC has increasingly adapted to this pluralist setting. Its members have attained positions of power in Congress; they have used their authority to negotiate with other influentials; and they have settled regularly for compromise, piecemeal solutions to issues of concern. Yet, as the budget battle demonstrates, not all CBC members have found the pluralist institutional game compelling or rewarding enough to abandon entirely the role of "congressman-at-large" for black Americans. The CBC identity crisis may well have receded, but it is unlikely to disappear.

Epilogue: The CBC in the Clinton Era

The 101st Congress was, in one sense, the CBC's high-water mark; its members had attained positions of genuine influence in the House and positioned themselves to play the "inside" political game effectively. While the 1990 elections increased the caucus' membership by two—including the first black Republican, Gary Franks (Conn.-5)—to twenty-six, in other ways, the CBC lost some stature in the 102nd Congress. Augustus Hawkins, chairman of the important Education and Labor Committee, retired after twenty-eight years in the House. William Gray, majority whip, suddenly resigned from Congress (amid unsubstantiated rumors that his office was under investigation for ethical improprieties) to become president of the United Negro College Fund. In addition, several CBC members were caught in the coils of the House banking scandal as "abusers" of the banking privilege. In 1993, President Bill Clinton appointed Mike Espy as secretary of agriculture, resulting in the loss of another influential member of the caucus. These developments, particularly the departure of its two most visible and powerful members in Hawkins and Gray, and the loss of Espy reduced, at least temporarily, the stature of the caucus.

The 103rd Congress (1993–95), however, will surely mark a great change for the caucus. Amendments to the Voting Rights Act mandated both protection of existing House districts represented by African Americans and creation of new "minority-majority" constituencies wherever possible. As a result, thirteen newly created districts sent blacks to Congress; an additional three blacks retained the seats of departing CBC members. Moreover, Carol Moseley Braun (D-Ill.) became the first black woman elected to the Senate. Thus, the CBC has forty members: thirty-nine representatives and one senator. Organizing for the new Congress for the first time included competition for the CBC chairmanship. After a "spirited" contest, Kweisi Mfume defeated Craig Washington (Tex.-18) on a 27-9 vote, moving up, as custom has dictated, from the CBC vice-chairmanship.

Although speculation is always risky, the initial signs suggest that the caucus is poised to continue to emphasize a conventional rather than an ideological strategy. Most of the thirteen new districts, in contrast to the older constituencies, are rural and so add diversity of outlook to the CBC. Members, however, insist that they will have little difficulty in forging consensus on the issues they will confront.[65] On the other hand, of the CBC sixteen newcomers, fifteen had prior experience in elective office.[66] They have been aggressive in seeking positions of authority and influence inside Congress. In the Mfume-Washington race for the CBC chairmanship, both men promised to "join other minorities" in coalitions and to work to put CBC members on all important committees.[67] With respect to the former goal, the caucus sought allies from "other progressive caucuses" and from "associate members" (affiliated, but not formal members) that the CBC has enrolled since 1988.[68] In pursuit of widespread influence, the CBC has been singularly successful. Representative-elect Carrie Meeks (Fla.-17), waging a conventional lobbying campaign aimed at the Democratic leadership, secured a place on the prestigious Appropriations Committee, bringing the number of blacks on the panel to three.[69] Freshman Mel Reynolds (Ill.-2) joined two incumbent CBC members (John Lewis and William Jefferson [La.-2]) in winning seats on the Ways and Means Committee; five African Americans are now on the tax writing committee. The House Energy and Commerce Committee, where much action on trade, health, and environmental issues will occur, has four black members, including two freshmen. In addition, Louis Stokes, Eleanor Holmes Norton (Del.-Washington, D.C.), and Floyd Flake seem in line for significant subcommittee chairs on the Appropriations, Post Office and Civil Service, and Banking Committees, respectively. Finally, and perhaps most important, Ron Dellums was appointed chairman of the influential Armed Services Committee, replacing Les Aspin, whom President Clinton appointed as secretary of defense.

Caucus members gained noncommittee leadership positions as well. Speaker Thomas Foley (Wash.-5) appointed the newly elected Melvin Watt (N.C.-12) to the powerful Steering and Policy Committee and named freshman Bobby L. Rush (Ill.-1) a deputy whip. Representatives James A. Clyburn (S.C.-6) and Eva Clayton (N.C.-1) share the chairmanship of the Democratic freshman class of 1993. Black Caucus members were poised to use these several positions of strength to further their policy goals more as loyal Democrats than as ideologues. As Clayton put it, "We are reform-minded, change-oriented, but all of that within the system." Watt echoed the theme: "We are going to be responding, at least in the short term, to the agenda of the President of the United States."[70]

In 1993, the CBC did just that; it emerged as a major player as Congress took up the Clinton administration's agenda. Its tactics reflected its enlarged commitment to the inside, pluralist policy-making game. The caucus did not always achieve its objectives, but its thirty-nine voting members made their presence felt regularly.[71] Caucus members delayed for two weeks floor debate on an "enhanced rescission" bill giving the president new power to cut appropriated funds,[72] arguing that the measure would tip the executive-legislative balance significantly in favor of the former; the bill eventually passed. The CBC compelled the Democratic leadership to include $920 million for an urban youth job training program in a supplemental appropriations bill. Most importantly, after winning assurances that five favored social programs were "nonnegotiable," it provided 37 votes for the Clinton budget reconciliation package, which passed only by only two votes (218–216). "We can win now," observed Ron Dellums. "We've gone beyond just being 'the conscience of the House.' "[73]

In addition, the CBC has made common cause with other groups— the Hispanic Caucus on enhanced rescission, the Concord Coalition[74] on a successful effort to cut funds for the superconducting supercollider, and women's groups on abortion questions. It has supported controversial nominations of African Americans—Lani Guinier as head of the Justice Department's Civil Rights Division (unsuccessfully) and Joycelyn Elders as surgeon general (successfully). It forced the administration to abandon the nomination of its second choice for the civil rights post, John Payton, also a black, because many members were unimpressed with his views on the creation of majority black electoral districts.[75] Finally, the caucus has staked out clear positions on major issues and has fought for them. It opposes campaign finance reform that eliminates political action committee contributions, on which minority members representing poor districts depend heavily. John Lewis has introduced legislation to require the Environmental Protection Agency to be sensitive to the excessive exposure of minority communities to toxic pollutants.

Pursuing pluralistic politics purposefully calls for group cohesion, and the CBC closed ranks impressively in 1993. But not always. Because they believed that the administration was neglecting domestic needs, eighteen members, including CBC Chairman Mfume, voted to cut aid to Russia. Moreover, the increased size and diversity of the CBC contains the seeds of potential discord. The urban and rural contingents may not always see eye to eye; the older members, ensconced in the Democratic leadership, may be less inclined than their younger colleagues to bargain forcefully. Individualistic members may opt to go their own way rather than submit to group discipline. To date, however, CBC unity, and thus its negotiating leverage, has been high.

To say that the Black Caucus has stressed pluralistic politics is not to suggest that it has abandoned its wider audience. In September 1993, the CBC entered into a "sacred covenant" with the Nation of Islam, headed by the controversial Louis Farrakhan, to work for meaningful social change, such as revitalization of the black community.[76] The Black Caucus will, as it deems appropriate, continue to speak out on behalf of broader African American interests. Still, while it will surely not forgo its role as the outspoken voice of the nation's black population, the Congressional Black Caucus seems more likely to serve its constituency by seeking to move policies and programs successfully through a legislative system in which its members are increasingly well entrenched and wield substantial influence.

Notes

1. For a useful historical treatment of African American representation in Congress, see Carl M. Swain, "Changing Patterns of African American Representation in Congress," in *The Atomistic Congress: An Interpretation of Congressional Change,* ed. Allen D. Hertzke and Ronald M. Peters, Jr. (Armonk, N.Y.: M. E. Sharpe, 1992), 107–42.

2. *Congressional Record,* 92nd Congress, 1st sess., 1971, 8710.

3. D. D. Fears, "A Time of Testing for Black Caucus as Its Members Rise to Power in House," *National Journal* 17 (1985): 910.

4. Marguerite Ross Barnett, "The Congressional Black Caucus," in *Congress Against the President,* ed. Harvey C. Mansfield (New York: Praeger, 1975), 34–50; and Barnett, "The Congressional Black Caucus: Illusions and Realities of Power," in *The New Black Politics,* ed. Michael B. Preston, Lenneal J. Henderson, Jr., and Paul L. Puryear (New York: Longman, 1982), 28–54.

5. Quoted in Charles F. Henry, "Legitimizing Race in Congressional Politics," *American Politics Quarterly* 5 (February 1977): 167.

6. Barnett, "The Congressional Black Caucus," 45.

7. In mid-1989, during the 101st Congress, Mickey Leland died tragically in a plane crash in Africa while on a fact-finding mission in his capacity as chairman of the House Select Committee on Hunger. Craig Washington, a longtime political ally of Leland, won a special election in December 1989, and became the newest member of the CBC. He later won assignment to the Judiciary and Education and Labor Committees.

8. Quoted in Nadine Cohodas, "Black House Members Striving for Influence," *Congressional Quarterly Weekly Report* 43 (June 1985): 680.

9. Barnett, "The Congressional Black Caucus," 30.

10. Gary C. Jacobson, *The Politics of Congressional Elections*, 3rd ed. (New York: Harper Collins, 1992).

11. Steven S. Smith and Christopher J. Deering, *Committees in Congress* (Washington, D.C.: CQ Press, 1984).

12. Henry, "Legitimizing Race in Congressional Politics," 167.

13. Quoted in Cohodas, "Black House Members Striving for Influence," 675.

14. Dellums's district consists mainly of liberal, upper-class suburbanites in the San Francisco Bay area (e.g., Berkeley); Wheat's constituency includes the "heart of Kansas City," a relatively poor urban industrial center. See Michael Barone and Grant Ujifusa, *The Almanac of American Politics, 1994* (Washington, D.C.: National Journal, 1994).

15. Indeed, eight of the districts electing CBC members in the 101st Congress fell among the 16 "poorest" constituencies in terms of median family income. Alan Ehrenhalt, "New Black Leaders Emerging in Congress," *Congressional Quarterly Weekly Report,* 41 (1983): 1643.

16. Many rating scales exist, and they are usually strongly intercorrelated; we use the American Conservative Union scores to denote conservative ideology. Keith T. Poole, "Dimensions of Interest Group Evaluation of the U. S. Senate, 1969–1978," *American Journal of Political Science* 25 (1981): 49–67.

17. The whip arrangements—a whip plus deputy and at-large whips—serve to link party leaders and rank-and-file Democrats. They act as communications channels to keep both leaders and followers aware of each other's views, to promote attendance on the floor, and generally to facilitate party cohesion. See Barbara Sinclair, *Majority Leadership in the U.S. House* (Baltimore: Johns Hopkins University Press, 1983).

18. The twenty-third member, Donald Payne (N.J.-10), was a freshmen in the 101st Congress, and thus did not have a party unity score in 1988.

19. Susan Webb Hammond, Daniel F. Mulhollan, and Arthur G. Stevens, "Informal Congressional Caucuses and Agenda Setting," *Western Political Quarterly* 38 (1985): 583–605; and Burdett A. Loomis, "Congressional Caucuses and the Politics of Representation," in *Congress Reconsidered,* 2nd ed., ed. Lawrence C. Dodd and Bruce I. Oppenheimer (Washington, D.C.: CQ Press, 1981), 204–20.

20. Cohodas, "Black House Members Striving for Influence," 681.

21. Ibid.

22. Dianne M. Pinderhughes, "The President, the Congress, and the Black Community, or Logic and Collective Politics" (paper presented at the annual meeting of the Midwest Political Science Association, Chicago, April 1979).

23. Hammond et al., "Informal Congressional Caucuses and Agenda Setting."

24. For a thorough analysis of CBC budgetary strategy, see John C. Berg, "The Congressional Black Caucus Budget and the Representation of Black Americans" (paper presented at the annual meeting of the Midwest Political Science Association, Chicago, April 1987).

25. The *New York Times* (January 5, 1985) reported that Gray's decision to leave the Budget panel reflected his "frustration with the committee's reluctance to support social spending."

26. The CBC mounted a challenge to the Democratic Steering and Policy Committee's committee assignment recommendations, supporting Harold Washington (Ill.-7) for the Budget Committee. But the Democratic Caucus rejected the CBC initiative. Irvin B. Arieff, "House Continues Dispute on Committee," *Congressional Quarterly Weekly Report* 39 (1981): 197.

27. *Congressional Record,* 97th Congress, 1st sess., 1981, 8672.

28. *Congressional Record,* 97th Congress, 2nd sess., 1982, 8677, 8682.

29. Richard E. Cohen, "What a Difference a Year—and an Election—Make in Producing a Budget," *National Journal* 15 (May 1983): 696–99.

30. Quoted in Diane Granat, "Representative Gray: Junior Conferee at Center Stage," *Congressional Quarterly Weekly Report* 41 (April 1983): 1271.

31. Quoted in Alan Ehrenhalt, "New Black Leaders Emerging in Congress," *Congressional Quarterly Weekly Report* 41 (April 1983): 1643.

32. John C. Berg, "The Congressional Black Caucus Budget and the Representation of Black Americans."

33. Steven S. Smith, *Call To Order: Floor Politics in the House and Senate* (Washington, D. C.: Brookings Institution, 1989), finds that the Budget Committee was one of the least likely to confront floor amendments, suggesting the audacity of the CBC in mounting its regular challenges to the committee's resolutions.

34. Gray's rise to the chairmanship of the Budget Committee is one of the most amazing success stories of the postreform Congress. When the chairmanship became vacant (Jim Jones [D-Okla.] was required to give up the position because his limited tenure on the panel had expired), Gray mounted an immediate campaign. He secured the backing of the Democratic leadership and went after the support of party factions that might not have been amenable to his accession to so powerful a position. He campaigned actively for southern Democrats in the 1984 elections. When the Democratic Caucus convened in early 1985, it selected Gray as Budget Committee chairman, making him, after only six years' service in the House, one of its most influential figures. Stephen Gettinger, "Bill Gray Builds a Political Career on Paradox," *Congressional Quarterly Weekly Report* 44 (1986): 1739–43.

35. "New Budget Chairman An Unswerving Fighter," *New York Times,* January 5, 1985, 7.

36. Milton Coleman, "Gains in the House Hailed as a 'Coming of Age' for Black Lawmakers," *Louisville Courier-Journal,* January 11, 1985, A15.

37. Quoted in Pamela Fessler, "New House Budget Chief Gray Weighs Local, National Claims," *Congressional Quarterly Weekly Report* 43 (1985): 185–87.

38. Quoted in Jacqueline Calmes, "Social Security Issue Splits Each Party As House Opposes Senate on Budget," *Congressional Quarterly Weekly Report* 43 (1985): 1469.

39. Lawrence C. Dodd, "Coalition Building by Party Leaders: A Case Study of House Democrats," *Congress and the Presidency* 10 (1983): 147–68, suggests that members of the House who have achieved "career success"—"whose movement into positions of influence and authority has been more rapid than that of their peers with whom they entered the House"—are particularly responsive to party leaders and appeals to party loyalty. The CBC members voting for the 1985 budget resolution clearly qualify as successes and this may account for their adherence to institutional norms in preference to making symbolic gestures with respect to the budget.

40. Julian Dixon, quoted in S. V. Roberts, "Blacks in Congress Are Branching Out," *New York Times,* June 22, 1986, sect. 4, p. 4.

41. David S. Broder, " . . . and Healthy Signs of Change," *Louisville Courier Journal,* April 12, 1989, A11.

42. Beth Donovan, "The Wilder-Dinkins 'Formula' Familiar to Blacks in House," *Congressional Quarterly Weekly Report* 47 (1989): 3099.

43. Richard E. Cohen, "A New Breed for Black Caucus," *National Journal* 19 (1987): 2432–33.

44. Donovan, "The Wilder-Dinkins 'Formula,'" 3099.

45. Richard E. Cohen, "Moving Up the Ladder," *National Journal* 20 (1988): 3158.

46. Tim Curran, "Some Surprising Guests Turn Out on the Stump," *Roll Call* 36, no.18 (1990): 1, 10.

47. Donovan, "The Wilder-Dinkins 'Formula,'" 3099.

48. Gray's impressive movement into the Democratic leadership attracted substantial journalistic attention. See, inter alia, Cohen, "A New Breed for Black Caucus," 2432–33.

49. Quoted in Cohen, "A New Breed for Black Caucus."

50. Ronald E. Cohen, "Gray's Game: Playing Democratic Ball," *National Journal* 22 (1990): 30.

51. Ronald Brownstein, "Kemp and Poverty," *National Journal* 18 (1986): 2531.

52. John Felton, "House Accepts Senate's Anti-Apartheid Bill," *Congressional Quarterly Weekly Report* 44 (1986): 492–97.

53. Jacqueline Calmes, "Aspin Ousted as Armed Services Chairman," *Congressional Quarterly Weekly Report* 45 (1987): 83–85; and "Aspin Makes Comeback at Armed Services," *Congressional Quarterly Weekly Report* 45 (1987): 139–42.

54. John Felton, "All But a Favored Few Feel Pain of Aid Cutbacks," *Congressional Quarterly Weekly Report* 46 (1988): 492–97.

55. John Felton, "Funds for Panama, Nicaragua Move Down Hill Runway." *Congressional Quarterly Weekly Report* 48 (1990): 1007–10.

56. John Felton, "Savimbi: Selling Washington on Angola's War," *Congressional Quarterly Weekly Report* 44 (1986): 264–65.

57. Nadine Cohodas, "Judiciary Committee Votes to Impeach Hastings," *Congressional Quarterly Weekly Report* 46 (1988): 2100–2101, and "By Wide Margin, House Impeaches Hastings," *Congressional Quarterly Weekly Report* 46 (1988): 2205.

58. Maureen Dowd, "Black Caucus, Back in the White House, Uses Straight Talk, *New York Times,* May 24, 1989, A29.

59. Steven A. Holmes, "Senate Votes to Limit Debate on Provisions of Rights Bill," *New York Times,* July 18, 1990, A17.

60. Cohen, "A New Breed for Black Caucus," 2433.

61. Quoted in Steven A. Holmes, "Veteran of Rights and Poverty Wars Tastes Bitter Fruit of Many Battles," *New York Times,* September 28, 1990, A10.

62. Alphonso Pickney, *The Myth of Black Progress* (New York: Oxford University Press, 1984).

63. Barnett, "The Congressional Black Caucus," makes the case for the desirability of this approach.

64. Cohen, "A New Breed for Black Caucus."

65. Jeffrey L. Katz, "Growing Black Caucus May Have New Voice," *Congressional Quarterly Weekly Report* 21 (1993): 5–11.

66. Ronald Smothers, "A New Diversity for Congress's Black Caucus," *New York Times,* November 10, 1992, 9.

67. Graeme Browning, "Strength in Numbers for Hill Group?" *National Journal* 24 (1992): 2732–33.

68. Mary Jacoby, "Battle Is on for Black Caucus Chair," *Roll Call* 38, no. 39 (1992): 1, 12.

69. Jill Zuckman, "All the Right Moves," *Congressional Quarterly Weekly Report* 50 (1992): 3786.

70. Phil Duncan, "Quietly Assertive Freshmen Arrive for Orientation," *Congressional Quarterly Weekly Report* 50 (1992): 3746–47.

71. On the CBC in the Clinton administration, see David A. Bositis, *The Congressional Black Caucus in the 103rd Congress* (Washington, D.C.: Joint Center for Political Economic Studies, 1993); Kitty Cunningham, "Black Caucus Flexes Muscle on Budget—And More," *Congressional Quarterly Weekly Report* 51 (1993): 1711–15; Graeme Browning, "Flex Time," *National Journal* 25 (1993): 1921–25; and Kenneth J. Cooper, "For Enlarged Black Caucus, a New Kind of Impact," *Washington Post,* September 19, 1993, A4.

72. Enhanced rescission, a less stringent form of the line item veto, would

permit the president to rescind (cancel) single items in appropriations bills unless both houses of Congress voted to disapprove the rescission.

73. Quoted in *Washington Post,* September 19, 1993, A4.

74. The Concord Coalition is a public interest organization, formed to promote deficit reduction and headed by former senators Warren Rudman (R-N.H.) and Paul Tsongas (D-Mass.).

75. Neil A. Lewis, "Clinton's Choice for Rights Chief Is Withdrawing," *New York Times,* December 18, 1993, 1.

76. Lynn Duke, "Congressional Black Caucus and Nation of Islam Agree on Alliance," *Washington Post,* September 17, 1993, A3. Some CBC members, however, worried that the embrace of the Nation of Islam, widely criticized as anti-Semitic, would jeopardize collaboration with Jewish and other liberal groups on issues of more immediate concern, and the caucus backed away from any formal association. Kevin Merida, "Black Caucus Says It Has No Official Working Ties with Nation of Islam," *Washington Post,* February 3, 1994, A16.

★ Chapter 8

The Supreme Court, African Americans, and Public Policy: Changes and Transformations

Michael W. Combs

In a sense, the Supreme Court permitted the entrance of African Americans into the body politic at the national level by putting their interests and rights on the national agenda. Because African Americans had been excluded from participation in the political, social, and economic life of the United States, they have disproportionately lacked political resources. An examination of key resources (e.g., income, wealth, status, popularity of demands, education, and organizational connections) that determine outcomes in the political process reveals extreme inequalities when African Americans are compared with whites.[1] Since the American political process is greatly influenced by the extent to which groups or individuals can marshal resources at decisive points in the process, African Americans have been severely disadvantaged in this regard.

Moreover, the aggregation of political resources within a group affects its choice of arena for the protection of rights and advancement of its interests. The limited availability of resources within the African American community, including the level of systemic support for its agenda, has influenced its choice of the Supreme Court as the forum to obtain favorable policies, especially since the 1930s. The Supreme Court is a plausible choice to accomplish this for two major reasons. First, the resources necessary to prevail in the Supreme Court are different in kind and in amount from those necessary to prevail in Congress or in the executive branch of government. In order to win in the Supreme Court, it has been said, "all that is needed are a good cause, a client, and a good lawyer." This means that the Supreme Court is accessible to nearly everyone. Second, the justices of the Supreme Court must justify their decisions in language different from that of other policy-makers. Consider the language of the Supreme Court: fairness, equality, individualism, freedom, due process, discrimination, and "the Constitution says." This language holds tremendous symbolic importance because it reflects the foundation of the American political system.[2]

Because of the separation of powers and federalism, the Supreme Court is an avenue for pursuing advancement of African Americans' rights. The Court is an important participant in the formulation of national public policy. Scholars argue that the Supreme Court has the capacity to: (1) affect the course of national policies; (2) regulate the political process when elected officials behave in a hostile or prejudicial manner against the politically weak; and (3) represent the interests of the unrepresented, the underrepresented and the downtrodden.[3]

This chapter analyzes how the status and policy interests of African Americans have been influenced by the Supreme Court. The first section of the chapter outlines changes in the personnel of the Supreme Court since the early 1950s and how these changes have affected the status, rights and policy interests of African Americans. The second section of the chapter examines the last forty years of policy-making by the Supreme Court in the area of race, divided into the first twenty years and the second twenty years. The final section of the chapter is the conclusion.

Personnel and Policy Changes: An Overview of Four Decades

Changes in the composition of the Supreme Court have enormous ramifications for policy emanations from the Court. For example, in 1935 and 1936, the Supreme Court nearly nullified President Franklin D. Roosevelt's New Deal policy agenda. To overcome these devastating defeats in the Supreme Court, Roosevelt proposed what was eventually labeled the "court packing" plan. The president's proposal would have permitted him to nominate and the U.S. Senate to confirm a new justice for every justice who was at least seventy years of age, up to a total Supreme Court membership of fifteen. Roosevelt knew that at least six justices were more than seventy years old. This meant that Roosevelt could have appointed six new justices, gaining him a majority on the Court that could be expected to support his New Deal programs. The proposal, however, became unnecessary. Chief Justice Charles Evans Hughes and Associate Justice Owen Roberts switched to President Roosevelt's position, thus allowing Roosevelt's New Deal to win by a majority of 5 to 4 rather than losing by 6 to 3.[4]

Presidents and other participants in national policy-making have long realized how new incumbents on the Court can bring about sharp breaks from the status quo. Because of the Supreme Court's influence on the governmental process, presidents carefully consider their nominees to the Court. Presidents, however, have not developed a foolproof method of nominating justices who will promote their ideological or policy objectives. President Dwight D. Eisenhower, for example, nominated Governor Earl Warren of California to succeed Chief Justice Fred Vinson, who died suddenly in September 1953. Eisenhower used the nomination of Warren to promote the "New Republicanism," which Eisenhower advocated during the first years of his administration. Compared to the New Deal of President Roosevelt and the Fair Deal of President Harry S Truman, Eisenhower's New Republicanism called for limiting the role of the national government in domestic matters. Eisenhower's nomination of Warren was also influenced by Warren's earlier involvement in securing Eisenhower's nomination as the Republican candidate for president.[5] Moreover, because Warren had the political skills and know-how to become California's gubernatorial nominee of both the Democratic and Republican parties, Eisenhower correctly reasoned that Warren would also be acceptable to the Democrats in the Senate who would vote on his confirmation. To Eisenhower's considerable dismay, Warren transformed the Supreme Court into a great supporter of the rights of African Americans. Under Warren's leadership, the Supreme Court announced unprecedented rulings expanding the involvement of the federal government in ending the denial of blacks' fundamental rights.[6]

Although President Eisenhower also appointed Associate Justices John Harlan, Charles Whittaker, Potter Stewart, and William Brennan, of these, Brennan had the greatest influence on the development of racial policy. Unlike most new justices, Brennan did not position himself at the center of the Court for a few terms before gravitating toward the right or the left. Rather, Brennan became a part of the Warren voting bloc, which also included Hugo Black and William O. Douglas. Even after these justices left the Court, Brennan continued to be a chief advocate of the expansion of African Americans' rights. The controversy over affirmative action revealed perhaps Brennan's greatest contribution to the development of policy regarding the rights of African Americans. Brennan, in the late 1980s, wrote opinions that removed some of the ambiguity on actual victimization.[7]

To replace Associate Justices Felix Frankfurter, who died in office, and Charles Whittaker, President John F. Kennedy nominated Arthur Goldberg and Byron White. Goldberg served until appointed by President Lyndon Johnson as U.S. ambassador to the United Nations in 1965. For most of his tenure, White was right of center on racial issues, particularly in the 1970s and the 1980s.[8] In 1967, President Johnson appointed Thurgood Marshall to succeed Justice Tom Clark, who had resigned to allow his son to serve as attorney general. Marshall had an impressive career as chief counsel for the National Association for the Advancement of Colored People (NAACP) Legal Defense and Educational Fund, solicitor general of the United States, and a judge on the Court of the Appeals for the Second Circuit. Marshall was the first African American to serve on the Supreme Court. He brought to the Court a rich background in civil rights litigation as well as the perspective that law is a necessary and legitimate agent of social change. Marshall immediately became a part of the majority Warren bloc on the court. However, as the liberal and moderate justices (Hugo Black, John Harlan, Abe Fortas, and Chief Justice Warren) left the Court and were replaced by conservatives, Marshall increasingly became part of the minority bloc on the Court and subsequently seldom wrote majority opinions. This does not mean that Marshall did not make a significant contribution to the overall decision-making of the Supreme Court while he was part of the minority bloc—he remained a strong advocate of justice for disadvantaged citizens.

In the late 1960s and 1980s, appointments to the Supreme Court became key issues in several presidential campaigns. Upon winning the presidential election of 1968, President Richard Nixon tried to appoint only justices who were strict constructionists (that is, interpreted the Constitution narrowly) or who practiced judicial restraint (that is, accepted the legislature's intent even when disagreeing with the statute). To replace Earl Warren as chief justice, Nixon nominated Warren E. Burger, who easily won Senate confirmation. However, under Burger's leadership, the Supreme Court did not become the bellwether of conservatism that Nixon had hoped. The Burger Court engaged in brokerage decision-making (in which the decision maker seeks to satisfy all parties); that is, both the proponents and opponents of the expansion of the legal and constitutional rights of African Americans received some support from the Court (e.g., *University of California Regents v. Bakke* 438 U.S. 265 [1978]). Nixon also appointed Lewis Powell, William Rehnquist, and Harry Blackmun. On racial issues, neither Powell nor Blackmun consistently voted conservatively. Powell tended to take the centrist position, writing opinions that supported both the interests of blacks and countervailing interests. Over time, Blackmun became increasingly more liberal. By the 1980s, Blackmun, Brennan, and Marshall constituted the liberal bloc on the Court. William Rehnquist, however, fulfilled the expectations of the president who appointed him, seldom voting to expand blacks' rights. On becoming chief justice in 1987, Rehnquist had the leadership qualities, the necessary votes, and the judicial doctrine to modify, alter, or even overturn the precedents of the Warren and Burger Courts.

From 1981 to 1991, Republican presidents appointed five justices (Sandra Day O'Connor, Antonin Scalia, Anthony Kennedy, David Souter, and Clarence Thomas), replacing Stewart, Burger, Rehnquist, Brennan, and Marshall, respectively. Fulfilling campaign promises, Republican presidents nominated these individuals because of their conservative credentials. O'Connor, nominated by President Ronald Reagan, is the first woman to be appointed to the Supreme Court, so her appointment represents a significant development in American politics. Her appointment underscores, first, the growing importance of women in the body politic and, second, the increased visibility of women's issues on the national agenda. Throughout much of O'Connor's tenure on the Court, supporters of blacks' policy preferences and constitutional rights have hoped that the fragile political coalition between blacks and women and the similarity between their constitutional needs would influence O'Connor to be more liberal on race issues. Although she has not voted consistently with the conservative bloc, Justice O'Connor has increasingly opposed the expansion of the constitutional rights for blacks, particularly in the area of affirmative action.[9]

Scalia and Kennedy, both appointed by Reagan, and David Souter, appointed by President George Bush, have not disappointed conservatives. Justice Souter, however, is demonstrating centrist tendencies. In

Shaw v. Reno (1993), he wrote a sharp dissenting opinion rejecting O'Connor's assertion that race-conscious measures harm the Constitution. Justice Clarence Thomas is performing as his appointing president, Bush, had hoped in that he consistently takes positions opposed to an expansion of the interests and rights of African Americans and the role of the federal government in racial matters.

Shortly after Bill Clinton assumed the presidency, Justice Byron White informed President Clinton of his intention to resign from the Court. At the conclusion of the Court's 1993 summer term, White officially resigned from the Supreme Court and President Clinton nominated Ruth Ginsburg, who easily won Senate confirmation. The present ideological tendencies and policy preferences of the majority of the justices assure conservative Chief Justice Rehnquist of a majority. Thus just as the Warren Court expanded the constitutional and legal rights of African Americans and the role of the federal government, so may the Rehnquist Court contract them.[10] However, with the resignation of Blackmun and the subsequent nomination and confirmation of Stephen Breyer to fill the vacancy, the calculus might change. Breyer might follow a more centrist direction, not unlike the political tendencies of his appointing president, Clinton.

This overview has summarized how personnel changes on the Court bring about policy changes. Judicial appointments reflect the maturation and decomposition of issues in the body politic. Nominations to the Supreme Court are also affected by partisan and policy objectives as well as gender and race considerations; of these, the recent nominations to the Court have been dominated by policy considerations.

Race and Supreme Court: Forty Years of Policy-Making

Over the past four decades, the Supreme Court has assumed the lion's share of the responsibility for the establishment of national policy on racial matters. This involvement has included the pathbreaking pronouncements of the Warren Court, the brokerage decision-making of the Burger Court, and the majoritarian propensities of the Rehnquist Court (that is, its tendency to require the legislature to resolve or to participate in the resolution of issues). At times, the Supreme Court received support from Congress and the president for its race-related pronouncements, but at other times, its statements made the Court the object of criticism from those same quarters.

The Supreme Court continues to be a major force in the development of racial policy, and its salience in articulating racial policy is not likely to abate in the near future.

The First Twenty Years: *Brown v. Board of Education*

The first twenty years witnessed a great expansion in the rights of African Americans. Seldom did the Supreme Court decide against the claims of African Americans. *Brown v. Board of Education* (1954) reflects the consummation of attempts to overcome judicial interpretations of the Constitution that denied blacks their constitutional rights.[11] Before the historic *Brown* decision, the Constitution was basically a document that legitimated and sanctioned the second-class status of African Americans. This is not to suggest that the Supreme Court did not occasionally rule in favor of blacks but, rather, that the larger constitutional doctrine governing case law severely limited the African Americans' rights. In the infamous *Dred Scott v. Sanford* (1857) decision, for example, the Supreme Court held that African Americans, whether slave or free, were not members of the political community of the United States, and thus possessed no rights secured by the United States.[12] In the Court's opinion, Chief Justice Taney concluded with the chilling contention that blacks "had no rights which the white man was bound to respect."[13] Constitutionally, this was the law of the land until the enactment of the Fourteenth Amendment of the Constitution in 1867.

After the Civil War, Congress enacted several civil rights acts and constitutional amendments favoring blacks during the Reconstruction period. However, the hopes these legal measures engendered for African Americans were short-lived. The status of African Americans, Reconstruction legislation, and the meaning of the constitutional amendments were contested in the Supreme Court. Through statutory and constitutional interpretation, the Court dismantled Reconstruction policies. In the *Civil Rights Cases of 1883,* the Supreme Court held that because the Civil Rights Act of 1875 made no reference to violation of the Fourteenth Amendment on the part of the state the contested sections were not "appropriate legislation" to enforce the Fourteenth Amendment.[14] The majority concluded that the intent of the Fourteenth Amendment was the protection of U.S. citizens from state action and not from "individual invasion of individual rights." Here the Supreme Court established in crystallized form the state action doctrine: this doctrine required proof that state officials or individuals were acting under state law before the Fourteenth Amendment could be invoked. One of the consequences of this doctrine was the victimization of African Americans by private individuals with the tacit approval of state officials. In addition, the Supreme Court refused to uphold the constitutionality of the statutes when it was quite apparent that state officials had engaged in activities that clearly discriminated against African Americans.

In *Plessy v. Ferguson* (1896), the Supreme Court wove into the constitutional tapestry the separate but equal doctrine, which informed the decisions of the Supreme Court until it was overruled in *Brown v. Board of Education.*[15] At issue was whether or not the Louisiana statute that provided separate accommodations for white and black citizens contravened the Thirteenth and Fourteenth Amendments of the Constitution. The Court took judicial notice that several states had established precedents in which the two races were separated, such as in schools and public accommodations. The majority concluded that this legislation was within the police power of the state legislatures. Moreover, the Court argued that separation of the races by the Louisiana statute did not place an undue burden on interstate commerce; and that it did not abridge the privileges and immunities of blacks or deny them equal protection of the law within the meaning of the Fourteenth Amendment. The Court also reasoned that separation of the races by the statute was not a badge of inferiority stamped on blacks. According to the Court, social prejudices could not be eradicated by legislation.

Plessy and its "separate but equal" doctrine legitimated the tremendous shift in political power in the South and the systematic exclusion of blacks in various political, social, and legal contexts throughout the United States.[16] At the state and local level and, eventually, at the national level as well, the "separate" portion and not the "equal" component of the doctrine received the greater popular and legal support. For example, in *Cumming v. Richmond County Board of Education* (1899), the Supreme Court permitted the closing of the African American high school in Richmond County, while the white high school remained open.[17] The Court also refused to require the Richmond County Board of Education to enroll African American students in the white high school. The justices accepted the argument of the county that the black school had been closed because of a shortage of funds. In *Berea v. Kentucky* (1908), the separate but equal doctrine was invoked to prohibit the instruction of African Americans and whites at the same time and place.[18]

As noted earlier, the separate but equal doctrine governed the legal, political, social, and economic interactions of African Americans and whites. The forces that brought about the *Plessy* doctrine also instituted discriminatory policies and practices in every facet of American life. The supporters of the protection and advancement of the constitutional rights of blacks increasingly turned to the Supreme Court. This strategy produced some judicial victories. In *Guinn v. United States* (1939),[19] and *Lone v. Wilson* (1939),[20] the Court voided grandfather clauses (which allowed persons to vote whose ancestors had voted on or before January 1, 1866). In a series of white primary cases, the strategy yielded mixed results.[21] The "cat and mouse" game finally ended in *United States v. Classic* (1941)[22] and *Smith v. Allwright* (1944).[23] Both *Classic* and *Allwright* demonstrate how personnel changes on the Supreme Court often lead to policy transformations. Roosevelt appointed justices that he thought would support his New Deal. Most of these justices embraced an expansion of the powers of the federal government and sympathy for the equal rights of blacks. In *Classic,* the Court concluded that the right to vote in primary elections was secured by the Constitution, since the primary election had a signal impact on the general elections and the winner in the Democratic primary effectively determined the chain of elected representatives. Employing similar reasoning, the *Allwright* Court overturned the Texas white primary statute. The Court adjudged that state action existed because the state was intimately involved in the structure and conduction of the primary.

During the last twenty years of the Jim Crow era, a legal campaign was launched to end the systematic exclusion of blacks from graduate and legal education as well as to end the use of restrictive housing covenants. Under Thurgood Marshall's leadership, the NAACP Legal Defense and Educational Fund successfully attacked the legal and constitutional underpinnings of the separate but equal doctrine and the state action concept. In one of the first cases in this regard, *Missouri ex rel. Gaines v. Canada* (1938), the Court showed sensitivity to the educational needs of African Americans as well as placed greater emphasis on the quality of education provided by African American schools that operated in conformity with the separate but equal doctrine.[24] The Court noted that out-of-state legal fellowships for blacks did not remove the state's obligation under the Constitution to provide legal education to blacks within its boundaries.

In *Sipuel v. Board of Education Regents of the University of Oklahoma* (1948), the Supreme Court required Oklahoma to offer an African American law student a legal education in conformity with the equal protection clause of the Fourteenth Amendment, just as it did for white law students.[25] In *Sweatt v. Painter* (1950), the Court took judicial notice of the quality of education received in black and white law schools in Texas.[26] The Court held that not only was the black law school inferior because of such tangible factors as the number of volumes in the school's library and of faculty members, but also because of intangible factors as well (e.g., the reputation of the faculty, experience of the administration, position and influence of the alumni, standing in the community, traditions, and prestige).

While the Supreme Court manifested some recognition of the constitutional deficiencies of the separate but equal doctrine, the Court did not overturn the doctrine, but rather narrowed its scope. The *Plessy* doctrine governed the Court's interpretation and application of the equal protection clause of the Fourteenth Amendment. Moreover, the separate but equal doctrine formed the basis of countless interactions between African Americans and whites as well as the delivery or the failure of the delivery of governmental services to African Americans.

In *Brown v. Board of Education,* the NAACP petitioned the Supreme Court to rewrite its interpretation and application of the Fourteenth Amendment. A unanimous Court agreed. Because of the discrimination and inequalities under the separate but equal doctrine, the Supreme Court held that the public policy of the United States would be antidiscrimination and equality. The *Brown* Court declared that the treatment of children is not isolated from their perception of themselves and the total community. The Court argued that the segregation of African American children "may affect their hearts and minds in a way unlikely ever to be undone." Then the Court concluded that the separate but equal doctrine "has no place in American education" because such "facilities are inherently unequal."[27]

The symbolic importance of *Brown* held deeper significance than the words of the Court, and the impact extended beyond the "halls" of education. The *Brown* decision symbolized the establishment of the principle of racial equality on all fronts. The *Brown* decision placed the force of law and the Constitution on the side of blacks, antidiscrimination, and equality.[28] It functioned as a catalyst—a mechanism of support in the efforts to remove segregation and discrimination in housing, voting, employment, and other policy areas. The *Brown* decision also dislodged the race question from the confines of state and local decision-makers, placed it on the national agenda, and facilitated action by Congress and the president.

For a decade after *Brown,* the Supreme Court was the principal authoritative voice that sought to mitigate the impact of discrimination in the United States. Within civil rights policy, the Court played a more signal role in policy-making areas with regional ramifications (i.e., education and voting rights) than those with national ramifications (i.e., housing and employment). As issues, education and voting were similar: (1) They were initially perceived as regional issues, which required elevating the standards of the South to those of the rest of the nation; (2) they involved mostly instances of overt racism; (3) they involved determining the constitutionality of state and local laws; and (4) they were areas in which blacks and their supporters concentrated and devoted the bulk of their political resources. By contrast, the Court was not as active in housing and employment, which were not regional issues. Such discrimination was found throughout the United States.[29]

To deflect its principal leadership role in civil rights for African Americans, the Court pursued the implementation policy of "all deliberate speed."[30] This permitted states to adjust on an incremental basis to a unitary school system, allowing state officials to move with caution and a great deal of calculation. Some state and local officials, however, interpreted "with all deliberate speed" to mean no speed at all. In *Cooper v. Aaron* (1958), however, the Supreme Court warned state officials that violence or the threat of violence did not justify denying black youths their constitutional rights.[31] In *Griffin v. Prince Edward County* (1964), the Court prohibited Prince Edward County, Virginia, from closing its public schools in order to evade desegregation.[32] Still further, in *Green v. County Board of New Kent County, Virginia* (1968), the Court held that the school board's freedom-of-choice plan was an inadequate compliance in its efforts to achieve desegregation.[33] By 1969,

fifteen years after *Brown,* the justices of the Supreme Court had concluded that the states employed more deliberation than speed, which
had the effect of perpetuating dual schools. Thus in *Alexander v. Holmes
County [Mississippi] Board of Education* (1969), the Supreme Court
abandoned the doctrine of all deliberate speed.[34]

In the early 1970s (and through the mid-1980s), Warren Burger was
chief justice. The locus of school desegregation litigation shifted to the
federal courts, and the cases focused on the standard federal judges
should apply to determine whether or not unconstitutional segregated
schooling had been maintained or perpetuated and the remedies that
federal courts should use to end it. In *Swann v. Charlotte-Mecklenburg
County Board of Education* (1971), the Supreme Court gave the green
light for court-ordered busing.[35] The Court noted that the remedial
powers of federal courts were limited to state-imposed segregation and
not to de facto segregation. That is, federal courts could design remedies
to eliminate only segregated conditions created by state officials. The
Swann Court's reference to de jure segregation was a prelude to the
controversy over what constituted unconstitutional segregated schooling
in the North, where state statute had not dictated segregation.

The *Keyes v. Denver* (1973) ruling hinged on the distinction between
de jure and de facto segregation.[36] In *Keyes,* the Supreme Court held
"that the differentiating factor between de jure segregation and so-called
de facto segregation . . . is purpose or intent to segregate."[37] The *Keyes*
Court also declared that a finding of intentional discrimination in a
portion of the school system presumed such discrimination in other
parts of the district. The burden of proof was then placed on school
authorities. The de jure/de facto distinction, in a real sense, limited the
powers of lower federal courts, while allowing the northern cases to
proceed. The powers of federal courts could be invoked only when
purposeful segregated schooling occurred, was maintained, or was perpetuated.

Voting, Employment, and Housing

Although the Supreme Court may not have played as significant a role
in the area of voting rights as it did in education, employment, and
housing, in voting rights the Court was more active and assertive. Congress and presidents took action to eliminate racial discrimination in

these areas: (1) voting rights—the Civil Rights Act of 1957,[38] the Civil Rights Act of 1960,[39] Title I of the Civil Rights Act of 1964,[40] and the Voting Rights Act of 1965;[41] (2) employment—Title VII of the Civil Rights Act of 1964;[42] and (3) housing—Title VI of the Civil Rights Act of 1964[43] and the Fair Housing Act of 1968.[44] Eventually, the Supreme Court was asked to determine the constitutionality of these enactments as well as to provide guidance on the meaning and scope of these congressional enactments. In affirming the constitutionality of all these statutes, the Supreme Court often expanded the powers of the federal government in protecting the rights and interests of blacks.

Voting Rights

In the area of voting rights, the Supreme Court assumed a substantial role. In *South Carolina v. Katzenbach* (1966), the Court held that the Voting Rights Act of 1965 was a legitimate exercise of congressional power to rid the nation of racial discrimination in voting.[45] In *Gaston v. United States* (1969), the Supreme Court prohibited the usage of literacy tests in any state or political subdivision covered by the Voting Rights Act of 1965.[46] In *Allen v. Board of Education* (1968), the Court sustained the constitutionality of the provision of the Voting Rights Act of 1965 that prohibited covered states and jurisdictions from changing voting laws before obtaining clearance from the Justice Department or a declarative judgment from the District Court in the District of Columbia.[47] The effort was to prevent the dilution of the voting strength of blacks.

The Supreme Court is not always willing to prevent the dilution of the black voting strength in states or jurisdictions that were not covered by the 1965 Voting Rights Act. In *Whitcomb v. Chavis* (1971), for example, the Supreme Court was petitioned to determine whether Indiana's establishment of multimember districts for the election of state senators and representatives unconstitutionally diluted the voting power of African Americans.[48] The Supreme Court argued that the evidence did not demonstrate "an invidious discrimination against blacks." According to the Court, the absence of blacks in elective positions in the county is not a reflection of a purposeful attempt to discriminate against blacks, but rather, "a function of losing elections." The majority employed "invidious" intent as the sole touchstone in determining whether the Indiana statute should be outlawed. The disproportionate number of defeats suffered by African American candidates was not sufficient evidence. For the Court, "multi-member districts were not inherently invidious and violative of the Fourteenth Amendment."[49]

Employment

In employment, the Supreme Court's role in shaping public policy has stemmed from interpreting and applying Title VII rather than from constitutional interpretation. Employment discrimination was not a peculiarly southern or regional problem, nor was it a state and local problem; rather, it was interwoven throughout all public and private employment. It was generally believed that employers had enormous discretion in the hiring, retention, and promotion of employees. However, the passage of Title VII established a policy that was national in its coverage. It prohibited employers and labor organizations from racial discrimination in hiring, wages, retention, promotion, and in terms and conditions of employment. Title VII also compelled employers and labor organizations to take positive steps to prevent discrimination within their businesses.

Because the Court has been called on to interpret the meaning and scope of Title VII, it has participated in shaping the contours of employment policy. In *Griggs v. Duke Power Co.* (1971), for example, the Supreme Court ruled on whether Title VII forbade an employer from requiring a high school diploma or standardized intelligence test as a condition of employment or promotion when the devices are not job-related and functioned to exclude blacks.[50] The Court held that Title VII did not permit such devices when they are not geared to measure one's "ability to learn to perform a particular job or category of jobs." In order for an employment practice that operated to disqualify blacks to meet Title VII standards, the practice (or device) must be job-related.[51]

Housing

Between 1955 and 1966, the Supreme Court made no major policy pronouncements in the area of housing discrimination. However, in 1967, the Court became involved in the formation of housing policies. In *Reitman v. Mulkey* (1967), the Supreme Court voided Proposition Fourteen of the California constitution, which repealed the state's fair housing statutes.[52] The majority held that the state of California could not sanction racial discrimination in the disposal of property by the owner. In short, the Court concluded that Proposition Fourteen encouraged racial discrimination in the disposal of property because "those practicing racial discrimination need no longer rely on their personal choice."[53]

In 1968, the Supreme Court pronounced its most far-reaching decision on housing. Based on a Reconstruction statute enacted in 1866, the Court removed all discrimination in the sale, leasing, or rental of private property.[54] The Court's decision in *Jones v. Mayer* came less than three months after Congress enacted the "Fair Housing" Provision of the Civil Rights Act of 1968. Largely because of this concern, the Supreme Court was strongly criticized for the decision. Critics contended that the *Jones* decision had no constitutional or policy significance. However, the "Fair Housing" Provision of the Civil Rights Act of 1968 covered only 80 percent of housing.

In *Jones,* the Supreme Court held that the Civil Rights Act of 1866 prevents all racial discrimination in the sale or rental of public or private property. The Court declared that the Thirteenth Amendment permits Congress to pass legislation to remove the "badges of slavery." According to the Court, the exclusion of blacks from white residential areas was the same as the "black codes" enacted immediately after the Civil War. As interpreted in *Jones,* the 1866 statute provides a much broader base of civil rights protection than that provided by the more recently enacted 1968 law.

The establishment of the antidiscrimination policy, the expansion of the federal government, and the active effort of the federal government to bring about an egalitarian society seemed to be the focus of public policy during this period. Through both constitutional and statutory construction, the Supreme Court assumed a leadership role. During this period, especially under Chief Justice Warren and, to lesser extent, under Chief Justice Burger, the Court set the moral tone for the nation, breaking with the separate but equal doctrine and policies. The Supreme Court came to represent the interests of the underrepresented, the unrepresented, and the politically impoverished; though it has neither the purse nor the power of the sword, particular decisions of the Court hold both substantive as well as symbolic force in the policy-making process.

Because of the Supreme Court's policy position, Congress and the president joined the political struggle to remove some of the exclusionary barriers against blacks. It should be noted, however, that at the end of this period, Congress and the president enacted legislation that curbed the remedial powers of lower federal courts, especially in the area of school desegregation (e.g., the Equal Educational Opportunity Act of 1974).[55] The Equal Educational Opportunity Act, for example, was amended to the Extension of the Elementary and Secondary Education Act of 1965. The Act (1) prohibited federal courts from making annual readjustments in school desegregation plans on the account of population shifts; (2) prohibited federal courts from imposing an interdistrict remedy unless segregative intent was proved; and (3) concluded that the assignment of students to neighborhood schools did not contravene the Constitution.

The Second Twenty Years: *Milliken v. Bradley*

During the second twenty years, the Supreme Court announced decisions and established precedents that might be employed to build a new constitutional order that would depart significantly from and endanger the antidiscrimination and egalitarian principles of *Brown* as well as reduce the role of the federal government in eradicating racial discrimination and its consequences. The Burger court slowed down from the Warren Court's pace, and the Rehnquist Court has been judicially active in contracting the rights of African Americans. On balance, this trend is manifested in every major area of civil rights (e.g., education, employment, housing, and voting).

Education

In *Milliken v. Bradley* (1974), Justice Marshall argued that the Supreme Court "[took] a giant step backward."[56] The Court was asked in *Milliken* to decide whether the lower courts had superseded their remedial powers in imposing a metropolitan desegregation plan to integrate the schools of Detroit. In addition to Detroit, the plan would have included fifty-three outlying school districts. The Supreme Court disallowed the metropolitan plan. The major thrust of the Court's holding was the intent doctrine. Before an interdistrict plan can be put into place, the Court argued in *Milliken,* the Constitution requires the finding of a purposeful segregative effect. The Supreme Court also held that the Constitution requires the Detroit school board to produce the best level of racial balance possible with "within district busing" and that the Detroit school was a "self-contained" unit. To support its holding, the Supreme Court turned to the desirability and necessity of local autonomy in public schools. According to the *Milliken* decision, the metropolitan plan would create a "super-school" district, and that, without the restructuring of local laws, the district court would become both a "de facto legislative authority" and the "school superintendent" for the entire metropolitan area. The Supreme Court argued that such competence was beyond district court judges.[57]

In a dissenting opinion, Justice Marshall challenged the judicial courage of the majority. According to Marshall, the majority significantly diverted "from its appointed task of making 'a living truth' of our constitutional ideal of equal justice under law." Next, Marshall provided a detailed refutation of the majority's denial of an interdistrict remedy. "[The] inter-district relief," insisted Marshall, "was . . . a necessary part of any meaningful remedy to the state caused segregation within the city of Detroit." He went on to argue that the state of Michigan, and not the city of Detroit, shouldered the responsibility for eliminating all vestiges of state-imposed segregation within Detroit. A Detroit-only remedy failed to do so. Marshall argued that the laws of the state of Michigan permitted the state to impose a metropolitan remedy. Marshall also focused on the practicalities of a Detroit-only remedy. For Marshall, the Detroit-only remedy would increase white flight to the suburbs, which would serve to "perpetuate or re-establish segregation in Detroit." Finally, Marshall insightfully placed the majority's position in the context of public and congressional opposition to busing for the remediation of segregated schools in the North. "Today's holding, I fear," insisted Marshall, "is more a reflection of a perceived public mood that we have gone far enough in enforcing the Constitution's guarantee of equal justice than it is the product of neutral principles of law."[58]

The intent doctrine also formed the basis for other decisions that retreated from the principles of *Brown*. As new school desegregation cases and other cases came before the Court, the intent doctrine received increased constitutional footing. In *Columbus Board of Education v. Penick* (1979)[59] and *Dayton Board of Education v. Brinkman, II* (1979),[60] the Court seemed to halt its decisional trend of restricting the remedial power of federal courts to create effective remedies, but not necessarily its doctrinal march away from the principles of *Brown*. In these two cases, the Supreme Court removed the ambiguity of its position on the interrelatedness of past and present discrimination. In *Columbus*, the Court held that "proof of purposeful and effective maintenance of a body of separate black schools in a substantial part of the system itself is prima facie proof of a dual school system and supports finding to this effect absent sufficient contrary proof by the Board." Since *Brown*, the Court noted that school officials continued to engage in decisions and acts that increased the segregation in the Columbus school district. The Court in *Dayton II* pointed more directly to the connection between past and present discrimination. The Supreme Court argued that "the measure of the post *Brown* conduct of a school board under an unsatisfied duty to liquidate a dual school system is the effectiveness, not the purpose, of the actions in decreasing or increasing the segregation caused by the dual system." The affirmative duty requirement necessitated school officials "to do more than abandon [their] prior discriminatory purpose."

In both *Columbus* and *Dayton II*, the Supreme Court reminded school officials that a desegregated school system was one in which affirmative steps had been taken by school officials to remove discriminatory barriers. Moreover, while the Court did not discontinue the usage of the intent doctrine, approval was given to the employment of the "foreseeable consequence" standard to determine intent: lower courts do not focus on the motivation of the actors' decision but, rather, presume that the decision-makers intended the probable and foreseeable consequences of their action and thus are blameworthy.[61]

In *Missouri v. Jenkins* (1990), the controversy over school desegregation centered on the scope of the remedial powers of federal courts to implement the principles of *Brown*. The Supreme Court disallowed the authority of the district court judge to impose a tax increase to ensure adequate funding of desegregation in the city of Kansas City, Missouri. Speaking for the Court, Justice White argued that by imposing a tax increase the district court had violated the integrity and function of local governmental institutions. According to the Court, the district court could have *authorized* the Kansas City, Missouri, School District (KCMSD) to levy property taxes at a rate adequate to fund the desegregation remedy and could have enjoined the operation of state laws that would have prevented KCMSD from exercising this power.[62] Local authorities were primarily responsible for solving the problems of financing desegregation.

In *Board of Education of Oklahoma City Public Schools v. Dowell* (1991), the Rehnquist Court was given the opportunity to establish the constitutional standards and requirements for terminating federal courts' involvement in school desegregation.[63] The Board of Education of Oklahoma City sought dissolution of a decree, entered by the district court in the 1970s, which mandated a school desegregation plan for the Oklahoma City public schools. The district court granted the dissolution relief; however, it was disallowed by the Court of Appeals for the Tenth Circuit. Moreover, the appellate court put forth a very exacting standard: the school board "would be entitled to such relief only upon nothing less than a clear showing of grievous wrong evoked by new and unforeseen conditions." Moreover, the Court of Appeals held that the school board possessed an "affirmative duty . . . not to take any action that would impede the process of disestablishing the dual system and its effects."

Writing for the majority, Chief Justice Rehnquist chided the Court of Appeals for applying a standard that "is more stringent than is required either by [the Supreme Court Cases] dealing with injunctions or by the Equal Protection Clause."[64] Looking at the school desegregation cases, Rehnquist argued that "federal supervision of local systems was intended as a temporary measure to remedy past discriminations."[65] Rehnquist further contended that the Court of Appeals misinterpreted the proper precedent. According to Rehnquist, the standard advocated by the appellate court "would condemn a school district, once governed by a board which intentionally discriminated, to judicial tutelage for the indefinite future."[66] Calling the standard draconian, Rehnquist remanded the case to the district with a two-pronged standard: "Whether the Board had complied in good faith with the desegregation decree since it was entered, and whether the vestiges of past discrimination had been eliminated to the extent practicable."[67] Rehnquist conspicuously did not note the recalcitrant behavior of the Oklahoma system, nor did he note the past involvement of the government in bringing about and fostering residential segregation. Moreover, Rehnquist seemed to favor the good faith of the school board over whether or not the vestiges of segregation had been removed from the school system and did not deal with the stigmatic injury of segregative schools.

In a dissenting opinion, Marshall, joined by Blackmun and Stevens, presented evidence that revealed the weaknesses of the majority's argument. First, Marshall underscored the intransigence of the Oklahoma School Board. Second, Marshall insisted that the threatened emergence of single-race schools illustrated a relevant vestige of de jure segregation. Third, Marshall argued that the majority's standard does not "reflect the central aim of the Court's school desegregation precedents." Remediating the evils of segregation to prevent its recurrence are "the motivations animating [the Court's] requirement that formerly de jure segregated school districts take all feasible steps to eliminate racially identifiable schools." Fourth, Marshall contended that eradicating stigmatic injury required "a formerly de jure segregated school district to provide its victims a 'make whole' relief." Fifth, Marshall asserted that the stigmatic injury must be associated with the standard for disallowing a judicial decree. Sixth, Marshall wrote that the judicial decrees must continue until the effects of past discrimination have been fully eliminated. Seventh, Marshall stated that the Supreme Court cases "have imposed on school districts an unconditional duty to eliminate any condition that perpetuates the messages of racial inferiority inherent in the policy of state sponsored segregation."[68]

At issue in *Freeman v. Pitts* (1992) is whether or not a district court is permitted to relinquish control over some areas of the school district even though a unitary (completely integrated) status does not exist in all areas of the school district.[69] Speaking for the majority, Justice Kennedy argued that a district court could maintain partial control over a school administration; it could relinquish control in those areas where a school district had achieved unitary status. According to Kennedy, partial relinquishment did not countermand the court's precedents. For Kennedy, the good faith standard of *Dowell* was very important. He suggested that judicial control of school districts was a temporary measure, and the ultimate purpose was to return the school districts to local control.

Housing

The holdings of the Supreme Court on housing mirror the uneven pattern found in education. In *Hills v. Gautreaux* (1976), the Court approved a metropolitan remedy for housing discrimination for Chicago and its suburban areas.[70] It was alleged that the actions of the Chicago Housing

Authority and the U.S. Department of Housing and Urban Development (HUD) perpetuated the concentration of public housing in black urban areas of Chicago, and not the suburban areas, violating federal statutes and the equal protection clause of the Fourteenth Amendment. The Court declared that both the Chicago Housing Authority and HUD had authority to operate public housing in the suburban areas. The housing options available to the tenants included the entire Chicago Market, which is not confined to the city limits.

In *Village of Arlington Heights, Ill. v. Metropolitan Housing Development* (1977), however, the Supreme Court decided in favor of supporters of local autonomy.[71] The defendants had requested the city of Arlington Heights to rezone a fifteen-acre parcel of land from a single-family to a multifamily classification. The municipality rejected the request. The defendants argued that the rejection of the request violated the Fourteenth Amendment and the Fair Housing Act of 1968. The Supreme Court adjudged that the municipality had not violated the Fourteenth Amendment and remanded the issue of fair housing provision to the lower court. The Court held that establishing a violation of the Fourteenth Amendment required more than a showing of disproportionate impact on African Americans. To prevail, the defendants had to show proof that the action or the law was racially inspired—the proof of discriminatory intent. Here again, the intent doctrine was imposed and the Court gave greater weight to the interests of local decision-makers than to those of blacks.

The attempt to eradicate housing discrimination brought federal courts into conflict with local and state officials. At issue in *Spallone v. United States* (1990), for example, was whether or not the district court properly exercised judicial power when it held four Yonkers city council members in contempt for refusing to vote in favor of legislation implementing a consent decree approved earlier by the city.[72] The Rehnquist Court concluded that the district court had abused its powers.

As it did in *Board of Education of Oklahoma City v. Dowell*, the Rehnquist court in *Spallone* gave short shrift to the intransigence of the four city council members. According to the majority, the city council members had never been made parties to the case and the liability was limited to the city of Yonkers and the Community Development Agency. This means that the imposition of the contempt sanctions against individual city council members was impermissible. The majority adjudged that case law and federal common law of immunity prohibit restriction on legislators' freedom that undermines the " 'public good' by interfering with the rights of the people to representation in the democratic process." Speaking for the majority, Rehnquist argued that the imposition of the contempt sanctions "is designed to cause them to vote, not with a view to the interest of their constituents or of the city, but with a view solely to their own personal interest." For Rehnquist, the motivation for compliance is of utmost importance. He insisted that the district court should have imposed such sanctions against the city alone, and only if that approach failed to bring about "compliance within a reasonable time should the question of imposing contempt sanctions against [city council members] even have been considered." According to the majority, a district court "must exercise [t]he least possible power adequate to the end proposed."

In dissent, Justice Brennan challenged the majority's conclusion on several grounds, only two of which will be presented here. First, Brennan insisted that the district court judge's "intimate contact for many years with the recalcitrant council members and his familiarity with the city's political climate gave him special insights into the best way to coerce compliance when all cooperative efforts had failed." Second, Brennan strongly disagreed with the majority's posture that the sanction undermined legitimate legislative activity. "Once a federal court has a valid order to remedy the effects of a prior, specific constitutional violation," asserts Brennan, "the representatives are no longer 'acting in a field where legislators traditionally have power to act.' " Brennan argued that once the remedial order is issued the "Constitution itself imposes an overriding definition of the 'public good.' " In fact, for Brennan, defiance at this stage "results . . . in a perpetuation of the very constitutional violation at which the remedy is aimed." Brennan concluded that the "Court's message will have the unintended effect of emboldening recalcitrant officials . . . to test the ultimate reach of the remedial authority of the federal courts."[73]

Job Discrimination and Affirmative Action

Since the mid-1970s, the scope and meaning of Title VII of the Civil Rights Act of 1964 and the Fourteenth Amendment have frequently been tested before the Supreme Court. At first, the Court balanced the interests of blacks against those of competing claims (e.g., the seniority of white employees and the discretion of the employer), employing a brokerage approach. Even so, over time, the Court became less sympathetic to the interests of African Americans. In *Washington v. Davis* (1976), the Court concluded that disproportionate impact was "not the sole touchstone of an invidious racial discrimination forbidden by the Constitution. Standing alone, it did not trigger the rule."[74] The District of Columbia used employment tests that had an adverse impact on black applicants. The Court held that Title VII's standard for job-relatedness of the test was too rigorous for the "purpose of applying the Fifth and Fourteenth Amendments in cases such as this." After *Washington v. Davis,* the intent doctrine became the constitutional standard, in contrast to *Griggs's* statutory impact doctrine in Title VII cases.

In *International Brotherhood of Teamsters v. United States* (1977), the issue of seniority and pre–Title VII discrimination reached the Supreme Court.[75] The federal government successfully proved that before Title VII the employer had indeed practiced unlawful and intentional discrimination. The Court, however, concluded that Title VII distinguishes pre-act and post-act discrimination. Pre-act systems of seniority, argued the Court, are immune. That is, Title VII prohibits only post-act discrimination in seniority plans.

In the late 1970s and the 1980s, the focus of litigation before the Supreme Court was on the permissibility of affirmative action under Title VII and the Fourteenth Amendment. In *University of California Regents v. Bakke* (1978), the Supreme Court held that raw quotas, under normal circumstances, contravened the Constitution.[76] The Court also ordered the admission of Bakke to the University of California-Davis Medical School because the school's affirmative action plan failed to provide for the individual consideration of each applicant and because white applicants were barred from competing for the sixteen positions reserved for minority applicants. But the majority agreed that race could be a "plus in admission decisions." On balance, the majority argued that the Fourteenth Amendment provides rights to individuals, not groups.

In Marshall's most-noted dissent, he took exception to the conclusions reached by the Court in *University of California v. Bakke,* except the one permitting consideration of the race of the applicant in admission decisions. Marshall strongly contested the argument that the Constitution protects only the rights of the individual. To refute this conclusion, he demonstrated the historical linkage between law and the denial of both legal and eventually constitutional rights of African Americans. With the care of a legal historian, Marshall sieved through colonial statutes and documents, the Declaration of Independence, and even the Constitution to establish that African Americans were denied human rights not on the basis of individual consideration, but instead on the basis of group considerations. Regarding the Declaration of Independence, Marshall underscored that the "self-evident truths and unalienable rights were intended . . . to apply to white men." Then Marshall noted that the Constitution itself treated blacks not as individuals but as a group. That is, the Constitution codified African Americans as three-fifths of a person and permitted the importation of blacks until 1808. He also pointed to the *Dred Scott* decision. For Marshall, "the legacy of years of slavery and of years of second-class citizenship in the wake of emancipation could not be . . . eliminated."[77] Marshall concluded:

> I fear that we have come full circle. After the Civil War our Government started several "Affirmative Action" programs. This Court in the *Civil Rights Cases* and *Plessy v. Ferguson* destroyed the movement toward complete equality. For almost a century no action was taken, and this nonaction was with the tacit approval of the Courts. Then we had *Brown v. Board of Education* and the Civil Rights Act of Congress, followed by numerous affirmative-action programs. Now, we have this Court again stepping in, this time to stop affirmative-action programs of the type used by the University of California.[78]

Through historical analysis, Marshall sought to establish that African Americans had been denied rights as a group, thus the remedy must also be on a group basis. Moreover, Marshall indicated that governmental officials participated in and supported the discrimination against blacks as a group.

In *United Steel Workers of America v. Weber* (1979), the Supreme Court concluded that Title VII allowed the establishment of voluntary affirmative action programs by private sector companies provided that the measures are temporary and that the programs do not unnecessarily trammel the rights of innocent persons.[79] In *Fullilove v. Klutznick*

(1980), the Court upheld the constitutionality of a congressional statute that set aside 10 percent of a $4 billion public works program for "minority business enterprises" to benefit companies in which blacks, Latinos, Asian Americans, Native Americans, Eskimos, or Aleuts controlled at least 50 percent of the companies.[80] The Court argued that the administrative apparatus of the set-aside programs provided for the individual consideration of each company that sought to take part in the program. Each company had to establish that it was an actual victim of discrimination in construction.

The actual victimization precedent became a rallying cry for the opponents of the rights and interests of African Americans. In *Firefighters v. Stotts* (1984), the Supreme Court's language gave tacit approval to the actual victimization requirement.[81] "Each individual must prove," the Court argued, "that the discriminatory practice had an impact on him."[82] The actual victimization standard, however, received a rebuff in *Firefighters v. Cleveland* (1986), in which the Court concluded that Title VII did not prohibit the "voluntary adoption [in a consent decree] of race conscious relief that may benefit non-victims" of discriminatory practices.[83] In *Sheet Metal Workers v. Equal Employment Opportunity Commission* (1986), the Supreme Court held that Title VII did not require district courts to limit remediation to actual victims.[84] It makes illegal acts of egregious discrimination. Speaking for the Court, Brennan stated that "the purpose of affirmative action is not to make identified victims whole but rather to dismantle prior patterns of employment discrimination and to prevent discrimination in the future." "Such relief," insisted Brennan, "is provided to the class as a whole rather than to individual members; no individual is entitled to relief and beneficiaries need not show themselves victims of discrimination." In his language, Brennan supported the contention that the "group provides the moral and legal motivations or basis for affirmative action rather than the exoneration of the specific rights of specific individuals, [and] at the same time the [Supreme] Court accepted the district court's use of numerical goals and its directive that the necessary funds be provided to finance portions of the affirmative action program."[85]

In *United States v. Paradise* (1987), the Supreme Court was petitioned to determine whether or not a district court could impose a "one black for one white promotion" relief on an interim basis. The district court found that the Alabama Department of Public Safety had engaged in racially discriminatory practices in the state police force. The Supreme Court, however, upheld the "one black for one white promotion" scheme, explaining that the strict scrutiny standard should not be applied because the relief was "narrowly tailored" to serve a "compelling governmental interest."[86] According to the Court, the unwillingness of the department to discontinue and disestablish the discriminatory practices made the remedial decrees of the district court necessary. The Court also noted (1) that the measure was "effective, temporary and flexible"; (2) that the measure applied "only if qualified blacks are available"; and (3) that the measure applies "only if the Department fails to implement a promotion procedure that does not have an adverse impact on blacks."

After the *Paradise* ruling, the Supreme Court became increasingly less willing to advance or protect the interests of African Americans. The result, on the whole, has been the establishment of precedents that may ultimately revert to the constitutional order predating *Brown*. In *Richmond v. Croson* (1989), for example, the Supreme Court voided a set-aside program put in place by the City of Richmond.[87] The city council modeled its program using *Fullilove v. Klutznick* as a guide. Writing for the majority, Justice O'Connor found the Richmond set-aside program deficient on several grounds. First, she argued that there was "no direct evidence of race discrimination on the part of the city in letting contracts or any evidence that the city's prime contractors had discriminated against minority owned subcontractors." Second, O'Connor objected to Richmond's employment of national statistics of racial discrimination in the construction industry as a basis for establishing the set-aside program. Third, O'Connor stated that because "Congress may identify and redress the effects of society-wide discrimination does not mean that, a fortiori, the States and their political subdivisions are free to decide that such remedies are appropriate." Fourth, O'Connor insisted that the set-aside program operated on group rights rather than individual rights. Fifth, because African Americans constitute the majority in Richmond, O'Connor employed the strict scrutiny standard.

O'Connor insisted that "a generalized assertion that there has been past discrimination in an entire industry provides no guidance for a legislative body to determine the precise scope of the injury it seeks to remedy." She asserted that the general lack of opportunities for "black entrepreneurs," standing alone, "cannot justify a rigid racial quota in the awarding of public contracts in Richmond, Virginia." According to O'Connor, "There is nothing approaching a prima facie case of a constitutional or statutory violation by anyone in the Richmond construction industry." For O'Connor, the paucity of "black membership in . . . trade organizations, standing alone, cannot establish a prima facie case of discrimination." Finally, O'Connor found that Richmond failed "to demonstrate a compelling interest in apportioning public contracting opportunities on the basis of race."

In a dissenting opinion, Marshall argued that Richmond's set-aside program was indistinguishable in all meaningful aspects from—and in fact was patterned after—the federal set-aside plan upheld by the Supreme Court in *Fullilove v. Klutznick*. Marshall accused the majority of taking "an exceeding myopic view of the factual predicate on which the Richmond City Council relied when it passed the Minority Business Utilization Plan." Marshall insisted that "it is only against . . . [the] backdrop of documented national discrimination, . . . that the local evidence adduced by Richmond can be properly understood." Second, Marshall strongly denounced the majority's usage of the strict scrutiny standard. When racial classifications are designed to further remedial goals, Marshall adjudged that the intermediate standard should be invoked. That is, the racial classification "must serve important governmental objectives and must be substantially related to achievement of these objectives in order to withstand constitutional scrutiny." Under the two-pronged or intermediate standard, Marshall insisted that Richmond's set-aside program passed constitutional muster. Marshall concluded: "I . . . profoundly disagree with the cramped vision of the Equal Protection clause which the majority offers today and with its application of that vision to Richmond, Virginia's laudable set aside plan. The battle against pernicious racial discrimination or its effects is nowhere near won."[88]

In 1989, the Court nearly established a new order in employment discrimination law. In *Wards Cove Packing Company, Inc. v. Frank Antonio*, minority employees contended that various hiring and promotion practices were responsible for their disadvantaged or disparate positions in relation to white employees.[89] The Supreme Court rejected the statistics advanced by the minority employees. In language that overturns *Griggs v. Duke Power Co.*, the Rehnquist Court held that under Title VII proof of disparate impact required more than a showing of racial imbalance in the work force. According to the Court, the plaintiffs have to demonstrate that "the disparity they complain of is the result of one or more of the employment practices that they are attacking . . . , specifically showing that each challenged practice has a significantly disparate impact on employment opportunities for whites and non-whites."

The Court also indicated that the burden of proof does not shift to the employer, who only "carries the burden of producing evidence of a business justification for his employment practice." The Court provided little or no guidance as to what constitutes a business justification, leaving the employer considerable discretion to engage in practices that have a disparate impact on blacks and other minorities. The aggrieved plaintiff shoulders the burden of establishing that the business practice is not neutral. One of the consequences of this burden of proof is a further taxation of the resources of the African American or minority community. The Court warned lower courts to be very cautious in "mandating that an employer must adopt a plaintiff's alternate selection or hiring practice in response to a Title VII suit."[90] The Supreme Court ignored the issue of the separate accommodations for nonwhite and white employees. The tenor of *Wards* is strikingly reminiscent of *Plessy*. The Court did not consider the overall impact of the decision on the principles of antidiscrimination and equality or the eradication of racism.

In *Martin v. Wilks* (1989), the Supreme Court continued its assault on those principles, denying the existence of racial discrimination in the country while putting forth its own definition.[91] In *Martin,* the Court permitted white firefighters to challenge employment decisions made by a city and a county personnel board in accordance with a consent decree, which, the firefighters alleged, denied them promotions in favor of less qualified black firefighters. The Court held that the white firefighters were not bound by a judgment in litigation "in which [they were] not designated as a party or to which [they have] not been made a party service of process." The dissenters argued that the Court has made it increasingly easy for disgruntled employees to initiate "vexatious litigation against voluntary affirmative action programs." As the dissenters suggest, this decision might also make employers unwilling to establish or maintain affirmative action programs. The *Martin* holding will "bleed upon" (affect) the judiciary itself. Moreover, consent decrees reached before one district court judge can be challenged before another. Affirmative action cases may become interminable.

In *Patterson v. McLean Credit Union* (1989),[92] the Supreme Court refused to overturn its construction of the Civil Rights Act of 1866 established earlier in *Runyon v. McCrary* (1976).[93] But in *Patterson* the Court was unwilling to expand the protection of African Americans under the Civil Rights Act of 1866 so as to include racial harassment on the job. According to the Court, the Civil Rights Act of 1866 "prohibits, when based on race, the refusal to enter into a contract with someone, as well as the offer to make a contract only on discriminatory terms." As such, the Court held that racial harassment once the person is on the job is not actionable under the Civil Rights Act of 1866. Victims of racial harassment on the job can seek relief under Title VII of the Civil Rights Act of 1964. The majority concluded that the Civil Rights Act of 1866 provided protection only for entering into a contract and not for fulfillment of the terms of a contract.

In dissent, Justice Brennan insisted that the scope of section 1981 of the Civil Rights Act of 1866 was broader than Title VII.[94] The Civil Rights Act of 1866 covered all contracts, not just employment; Brennan distinguished Section 1981 from Title VII: (1) unlike Title VII, Section 1981's coverage is not limited to businesses with fifteen or more employees; (2) unlike Title VII, Section 1981's back pay award is not limited to two years; (3) unlike Title VII, Section 1981's plaintiffs may recover back pay and obtain damages, including punitive damages; and (4) unlike Title VII, Section 1981's plaintiffs have a right to a jury trial. Brennan concluded that "proof that an employee was not promoted because she is black—while all around [her] white peers are advanced—shows that the black employee has in substance been denied the opportunity to contract on the equal terms that Section 1981 guarantees."

As noted above, the Civil Rights Act of 1991 reverses many of the decisions of the Rehnquist Court, e.g., *Wards Cove Packing Company, Inc. v. Antonio*, *Martin v. Wilks*, and *Patterson v. McLean Credit Union*. The Civil Rights Act of 1991 also constitutes congressional efforts to curb the Rehnquist Court. Specifically, the Act: (1) requires the employer to "demonstrate that the challenged practice is job related for the position in question and consistent with business necessity"; (2) provides that a "demonstration that an employment practice is required by business necessity may not be used as a defense against claims of intentional discrimination"; (3) prohibits challenges to consent decrees, by persons who had a reasonable opportunity to present objections or whose interests were adequately represented by another person who had previously challenged the contested consent decree; and (4) prohibits all forms of racial bias in employment, both the making and enforcement of contracts. More generally, the Civil Rights Act of 1991 expands the right to challenge discriminatory seniority systems; the coverage of the House of Representatives and the Senate, which had not been covered in the Civil Rights Act of 1964; and the establishment of the Glass Ceiling Commission.[95]

Metro Broadcasting v. Federal Communications Commission (1990) revealed that the Rehnquist Court is not consistently opposed to the constitutional rights of African Americans.[96] Here the Court was asked to determine whether the Federal Communications Commission's (FCC's) policies seeking to enhance minority ownership of radio and television stations violates the equal protection clause of the Fourteenth Amendment. Brennan delivered the majority's opinion, in which he took judicial notice of the desire of Congress and the FCC to bring cultural diversity to the broadcast industry. In fact, Brennan refused to apply strict scrutiny, but rather opted for the two-pronged standard. Aware of establishing a strong precedent for the future, Brennan stated, "We hold that benign race conscious measures mandated by Congress—even if those measures are not remedial in the sense of being designed to compensate victims of past discrimination—are constitutionally permissible to the extent that they serve important governmental objectives within the power of Congress and are substantially related to the achievement of those objectives."[97]

Brennan distinguished *Metro Broadcasting* from *Croson*. Unlike *Croson*, *Metro Broadcasting* was conceived with a "benign racial classification employed by Congress." Because Congress employed the benign racial classification, the proper test was the intermediate or two-pronged standard. Using Powell's conclusion in *Bakke*, Brennan argued that diversity pays dividends for all of society. That is, "the benefits of such diversity," argued Brennan, "are not limited to the members of minority groups who gain access to the broadcasting industry, rather the benefits redound to all members of the viewing and listening audience."[98]

Voting Rights

The Supreme Court applied the intent/purposeful discrimination standard in the construction of the Voting Rights Act of 1965. In *City of Richmond v. United States* (1975), a three-judge panel had ruled that the city's annexation of an area consisting of an overwhelming white population diluted black voting strength.[99] Overturning the district court, the Supreme Court reasoned that Richmond's single-member ward system would prevent the abridgment of black voting strength. The Court did not find purposeful discrimination, but rather that the adjacent area was annexed because of economic considerations. Because purposeful discrimination was absent, according to the Supreme Court, the annexation did not violate the Voting Rights Act of 1965.

In *City of Mobile v. Bolden* (1980), African Americans alleged that the practice of electing the city commissioners at large unfairly diluted black voting strength in violation of the Voting Rights Act of 1965, of the Fourteenth Amendment, and of the Fifteenth Amendment.[100] The Supreme Court rejected this allegation, concluding that proof of purposeful discrimination is necessary to establish a violation in voter dilution cases. It should be noted in the 1982 extension of the Voting Rights Act of 1965 Congress rejected this more exacting standard of proof to establish a violation of the Voting Rights Act and enacted the less exacting standard of discriminatory effect.

In *Thornburg v. Gingles* (1986), black voters in North Carolina challenged the redistricting plan for the state's senate and house of representatives, contending that one single-member district and six multimember districts impaired black citizens' ability to elect representatives of their choice in violation of section 2 of the Voting Rights Act of 1965.[101] The Supreme Court supported the contention of the African American voters. The Court made it clear, however, that "[m]ulti-member district and at large election schemes . . . are not per se violative of minority voters' rights." "Minority voters," said the Court, "who contend that the use of a multi-member form of districting violates [the voting rights act] must prove that the use of a multi-member electoral structure operates to minimize or cancel out their ability to elect their preferred candidates." The preconditions for multimember voting schemes to impair minority voters' ability to elect candidates of their choice are: (1) "the minority group must be able to demonstrate that it is sufficiently large and geographically compact to constitute a majority in a single-member district"; (2) "the minority group must be able to show that it is politically cohesive"; and (3) "the minority must be able to demonstrate that the white majority votes sufficiently as a bloc to enable it . . . usually to defeat the minority's preferred candidate." The Court rejected the intent standard: "plaintiffs need not prove causation or intent in order to prove a prima facie case of racial bloc voting and defendants may not rebut that case with evidence of causation or intent."

Litigation that focuses on the Voting Rights Act of 1965 and its 1982 amended extension increasingly came before the Supreme Court. In *Chison v. Roemer* (1991), the court held that the result tests protected the right to vote in judicial elections.[102] However, in *Presley v. Etowah County Commission* (1992), the justices refused to hold that the Voting Rights Act of 1965 prohibits an elected body or commission from changing the distribution of authority among the members.[103] In *Presley,* the Etowah County Commission voted 4 to 2 to reconfigure the administrative authority. The enacted law or resolution provided for the four holdover commissioners who are all white to possess authority over the major duties of the commission. The two new members—one black and the other white—were assigned minor responsibilities. The majority argued that the Voting Rights Act does not cover the allocation of power among governmental officials. Moreover, speaking for the majority, Justice Kennedy limited the application of the preclearance section of the Voting Rights Act to voting itself.

In *Shaw v. Reno* (1993), the Supreme Court rejected an irregularly shaped, majority-black congressional district drawn by the North Carolina General Assembly.[104] Speaking for the 5-4 majority, Justice O'Connor argued that the "appellants have stated a claim under the Equal Protection clause by alleging that the North Carolina General Assembly adopted a reapportionment scheme so irrational on its face that it can be understood only as an effort to segregate voters into separate voting districts because of their race, and that the separation lacks sufficient justification."[105] For O'Connor, the remedial nature of the reapportionment effort held little importance. "Racial classifications," she insisted, "reinforce the belief, held by too many for too much of our history, that individuals should be judged by the color of their skin."[106]

The dissenters raised strong objections. Justice White contended that the "appellants have not presented a cognizable claim, because they have not alleged a cognizable injury."[107] Justice Blackmun argued, "The difference between constitutional and unconstitutional gerrymanders [is] whether their purpose is to enhance the power of the groups in control of the districting process at the expense of any minority group, and thereby to strengthen the unequal distribution of electoral power."[108] And Justice Souter claimed, "The court offers no adequate justification for treating the narrow category of bizarrely shaped district claims different from other district claims."[109]

Summary and Conclusions

After the *Milliken* decision, the Supreme Court became increasingly less responsive to the interests and rights of blacks and more inclined to rule in favor of state and local decision-makers and employers. The intent doctrine and precedents may prove to be the building blocks for a counterrevolution that seriously undermines (even overturns) *Brown*. Moreover, given the legal philosophy of the Rehnquist Court, the intent doctrine and the case law since *Milliken* will certainly be employed to retreat from the *Brown* decision and its symbolism. This is also reflected in the affirmative action case law. The Supreme Court has distinguished between benign race-conscious measures mandated by Congress and those mandated by the states and their political subdivisions. The less exacting two-pronged standard is applied to congressional enactments, while the more exacting strict scrutiny standard is used to determine the permissibility of state and local enactments. In *Croson*, for example, the Rehnquist Court castigated the City of Richmond for enacting a set-aside program modeled after the congressional one upheld in *Fullilove*. All these developments provide little constitutional comfort for black Americans and their supporters.

For more than forty years, the Supreme Court has been the primary forum in which African Americans have tried to protect their rights and advance their interests. In this regard the court's performance during this period is consistent with pluralist theory. *Brown v. Board of Education* represented an attempt to overcome adverse constitutional interpretation and launch a new legal order. In the American political system, the nexus between a group or individual with the constitution is of utmost importance. *Brown* sought to undo what the Supreme Court had done in the *Civil Rights Cases of 1883* and in *Plessy v. Ferguson*.

The *Civil Rights Cases* and *Plessy* effectively placed the Constitution on the side of forces and interests that were opposed to the full citizenship of African Americans. In *Brown*, the Supreme Court ushered in a new constitutional order that continues to be the dominant constitutional paradigm in American equality and antidiscrimination. Moreover, the *Brown* decision and the consistent decisions of the Warren Court inspired many blacks to take a positive view of the Supreme Court as an institution.[110]

However, the Rehnquist Court, as did the Burger Court, is putting into place precedents and doctrines that might easily be employed to overturn or significantly modify the equality and antidiscrimination principles of *Brown*—principles that are not etched in concrete. The Rehnquist Court appears to have the will, the judicial philosophy, and the votes to create a new constitutional order, one that seems to be favored by the current political climate. This is illustrated by the judicial appointments made by presidents in the late 1960s, 1970s, 1980s, and in the early 1990s. For example, President Reagan deliberately appointed justices who were inclined not to maintain or expand the existing constitutional order but instead to retreat from the existing constitutional order and contract the constitutional rights of blacks. In his nominations of Justices David Souter and Clarence Thomas, President Bush pursued the same course. This trend may be mitigated by President Clinton's appointment of Ruth Ginsburg and Stephen Breyer, who seem to reflect his centrist, or moderate, position.

Personnel changes often lead to changes in the decisions of the Supreme Court, and presidents often make appointments to the Court with policy implications in mind. But not always: Eisenhower, for example, recruited Earl Warren to the Supreme Court and the chief justiceship more because of partisan than policy considerations. Johnson seemed to have been influenced by race and policy considerations when he appointed Thurgood Marshall to the Court. Furthermore, Nixon, Reagan, and Bush were guided extensively by judicial philosophy, policy ramifications, and race. It should be noted that judicial philosophy and policy ramifications can be a surrogate for race. Moreover, in his first appointment, Reagan reflected concern for gender and the increased salience of women's issues in national politics. In short, personnel transformations reveal the connection that exists between the Supreme Court and electoral politics. From the late 1960s to 1992, moderate-to-conservative Republican presidents won presidential elections, except in 1976. In turn, these presidents made appointments to the Supreme Court mindful of judicial philosophy and policy goals.

Finally, the justices of the Court are aware of the impact of Court personnel changes on the development of precedents and doctrines. Brennan and Marshall wrote opinions quite conscious of that potential impact. Brennan penned exceptionally strong opinions on affirmative action, establishing clear precedents that would be difficult for later Courts to overturn. Marshall employed dissenting opinions to put in place constitutional arguments and reasoning that might be used by legal scholars and even future justices to refute the arguments of the Rehnquist-led Supreme Court. Overall, however, the Supreme Court and its policies reflect and are a part of the changes and transformations that prevail in the American political system.

Notes

1. See, generally, Paul Sniderman, *Race and Inequality: A Study in American Values* (Chatham, N.J.: Chatham House, 1985).

2. See, generally, E. E. Schattschneider, *The Semi-Sovereign People: A Realist's View of Democracy in America* (Hinsdale, Ill.: Dryden Press, 1960); Murray Edelman, *The Symbolic Uses of Politics* (Urbana: University of Illinois Press, 1964); and Lucius J. Barker, *Our Time Has Come* (Urbana: University of Illinois Press, 1988).

3. Robert A. Dahl, "Decision-Making in a Democracy: The Supreme Court as a National Policy-Maker," *Journal of Public Law* 6 (fall 1957): 279; Martin Shapiro, *Freedom of Speech: The Supreme Court and Judicial Review* (Englewood Cliffs, N.J.: Prentice Hall, 1966); Lucius J. Barker, "Black Americans and the Burger Court: Implications for the Political System," *Washington University Law Quarterly* (fall 1973): 747; Jonathan D. Casper, "The Supreme Court and National Policy Making," *American Political Science Review* 70 (March 1976): 50–63; John Hart Ely, *Democracy and Distrust: A Theory of Judicial Review* (Cambridge: Harvard University Press, 1980); Michael W. Combs, "The Policy-Making Role of Courts of Appeals in Northern School Desegregation: Ambiguity and Judicial Policy-Making," *Western Political Quarterly* 35 (September 1982): 359.

4. Walter Murphy, *Congress and the Court* (Chicago: University of Chicago Press, 1962), 53–62.

5. Ibid., 78.

6. See *Brown v. Board of Education*, 347 U.S. 483 (1954), *Brown v. Board*

of Education, 349 U.S. 294 (1955); *Bolling v. Sharpe,* 347 U.S. 497 (1954); *Cooper v. Aaron,* 358 U.S. 1 (1958); *Griffin v. Prince Edward County,* 377 U.S. 218 (1964); *Gomillion v. Lightfoot,* 364 U.S. 339 (1960); *Harper v. Virginia,* 383 U.S. 663 (1966); *Katzenbach v. Morgan,* 384 U.S. 641 (1966); *South Carolina v. Katzenbach,* 384 U.S. 301 (1966); and *Jones v. Mayer,* 392 U.S. 409 (1968).

7. See, for example, *Sheet Metal Workers v. Equal Employment Opportunity Commission,* 106 S.Ct. 3014 (1986) and *Johnson v. Transportation Agency,* 107 S.Ct. 1442 (1987). "Actual victimization" refers to the requirement that potential beneficiaries of affirmative action prove that they have been affected by discriminatory practices.

8. See Twiley W. Barker and Michael W. Combs, "Civil Rights and Liberties in the First Term of the Rehnquist Court: The Quest for Doctrines and Votes," *National Political Science Review* 1 (1989): 31–34.

9. Ibid., 31–34.

10. See Barker and Combs, "Civil Rights and Liberties in the First Term of the Rehnquist Court."

11. 347 U.S. 483 (1954) and 349 U.S. 294 (1955).

12. 19 Howard 303 (1857).

13. Ibid.

14. *Civil Rights Cases of 1883,* 109 U.S. 3 (1883).

15. 163 U.S. 532 (1896).

16. See Schattschneider, *The Semi-Sovereign People;* Paul Lewinson, *Race, Class, and Party* (New York: Russel and Russel, 1963); and C. Vann Woodward, *The Strange Career of Jim Crow,* 3rd rev. ed. (New York: Oxford University Press, 1966).

17. 175 U.S. 528 (1899).

18. 211 U.S. 45 (1908).

19. 238 U.S. 268 (1939).

20. 307 U. S. 268 (1939). Although they occurred in various forms, most grandfather clauses allowed persons to vote whose ancestors had voted on or before January 1, 1866. This obviously excluded most blacks.

21. See *Nixon v. Herndon,* 273 U.S. 536 (1927) and *Nixon v. Condon,* 286 U.S. 73 (1936).

22. 313 U.S. 299 (1941).

23. 321 U.S. 649 (1944).

24. 305 U.S. 337 (1938).

25. 332 U.S. 631 (1948).

26. 339 U.S. 629 (1950).

27. See note 7.

28. See Lucius J. Barker and Jesse McCorry, *Black Americans and the Political System* (Cambridge, Mass.: Winthrop Publishers, 1976).

29. See Michael Warren Combs, "Courts, Minorities, and the Dominant

Coalition: Racial Policies in Modern America" (Ph.D. dissertation, Washington University, 1973).

30. *Brown v. Board of Education,* 349 U.S., at 294 (1955).

31. 358 U.S. 1 (1958).

32. 377 U.S. 218 (1964).

33. 391 U.S. 430 (1968).

34. 396 U.S. 19 (1969).

35. 402 U.S. 1 (1971).

36. 413 U.S. 189 (1973).

37. Ibid., at 208.

38. 71 Stat. 633 (1957).

39. 74 Stat. 86 (1960).

40. 78 Stat. 241 (1964).

41. 79 Stat. 437 (1965).

42. 78 Stat. 241 (1964).

43. Ibid.

44. 82 Stat. 81 (1968).

45. 383 U.S. 301 (1966).

46. 395 U.S. 285 (1969).

47. 393 U.S. 544 (1968).

48. 403 U.S. 124 (1971).

49. Ibid., at 160.

50. 401 U.S. 424 (1971).

51. Ibid.

52. 387 U.S. 369 (1967).

53. Ibid.

54. Civil Rights Act of 1866, 14 Stat. 27 (1866).

55. Michael W. Combs, "The Supreme Court as a National Policy Maker: A Historical-Legal Analysis of School Desegregation," *Southern University Law Review* 8 (spring 1982): 221–27.

56. Marshall, dissenting, *Milliken v. Bradley,* 418 U.S. 717, 782 (1974).

57. Ibid., at 717.

58. Marshall dissenting, ibid., at 789, 814.

59. 443 U.S. 526, 538 (1979).

60. 443 U.S. 526 (1979).

61. Combs, "The Policy-Making Role of Courts of Appeals in Northern School Desegregation," 359.

62. *Missouri v. Jenkins,* 50 CCH S.Ct. Bull. 2033, 2043, 2051 (1990). (Cf. *Spallone v. United States,* 493 U.S. 265 [1990].)

63. 498 U.S. 237 (1991).

64. *Board of Education v. Dowell,* 112 L.Ed. 2D 715 (1991).

65. Ibid., at 723.

66. Ibid., at 729.

67. Ibid.

68. Ibid.

69. *Freeman v. Pitts,* 112 S.Ct. 1430 (1992).

70. 425 U.S. 284 (1976).

71. 429 U.S. 254 (1977).

72. 493 U.S. 265 (1990).

73. Ibid.

74. 426 U.S. 229, 242 (1976).

75. 431 U.S. 324 (1977).

76. 438 U.S. 265 (1978).

77. Marshall dissenting, ibid., at 387, 390.

78. Ibid., at 402.

79. 443 U.S. 193 (1979).

80. 448 U.S. 448 (1980).

81. 467 U.S. 561 (1984).

82. Ibid., at 574.

83. 106 S.Ct. 3063 (1986).

84. 106 S.Ct. at 3049.

85. Barker and Combs, "Civil Rights and Liberties in the First Term of the Rehnquist Court," 47.

86. 107 S.Ct. 1053 (1987). The strict scrutiny standard of review is triggered when a classification impacts a suspect class (such as race) or when a classification (or legislation) is claimed to violate a fundamental right (such as freedom of speech or right to travel). The classification is presumed unconstitutional unless the maker of the classification proves that the classification is necessary to promote a compelling state interest and that less intrusive means are not available.

87. 488 U.S. 469, 480, 490, 498, 499, 505 (1989).

88. Marshall dissenting, ibid., at 528, 530, 535, 561.

89. 57 U.S.L.W. 4583, 4587, 4588 (1989).

90. Ibid., at 4588.

91. 49 CCH S.Ct. Bull. 2999, 3005 (1989).

92. 57 U.S.L.W. 4705, 4708 (1989).

93. 427 U.S. 160 (1976).

94. Brennan dissenting, 57 U.S.L.W., at 4711, 4719.

95. Civil Rights Act of 1991, 105 Stat. 1071 (1991).

96. 50 CCH S.Ct. Bull. at, 4500, 4517, 4518, 4521 (1990).

97. Ibid.

98. Ibid.

99. 422 U.S. 387 (1975).

100. 446 U.S. 55 (1980).

101. 92 L.Ed. 2D 21, 25, 45, 46, 47 (1986).

102. *Chisom v. Roemer,* 111 S.Ct. 2354 (1991).

103. *Presley v. Etowah County Commission,* 112 S.Ct. 820 (1992).

104. *Shaw v. Reno,* 113 S.Ct. 2816 (1993).

105. 113 S.Ct. 2832.

106. Ibid., at 2832.

107. Ibid., at 2834.

108. Ibid., at 2844.

109. Ibid., at 2848.

110. James L. Gibson and Gregory A. Caldeira, "Blacks and the United States Supreme Court: Models of Diffuse Support," *Journal of Politics* 54 (November 1992): 1120–45.

Part IV

Blacks and National Public Policy

Chapter 9

Black Interest Groups and the 1982 Extension of the Voting Rights Act

Dianne M. Pinderhughes

Black interest groups that participated in the 1982 campaign to extend the 1965 Voting Rights Act rarely acted in isolation, choosing instead to form coalitions with various other civil rights interest groups. The focus in this chapter is on the organizations that helped define the parameters of and create the support for that extension. The chapter discusses the impact these organizations had on the formulation of the 1982 Voting Rights Act and shows how these organizations were affected by their lobbying campaign to enact the 1982 voting rights legislation.

The general purpose of this chapter is to provide insight into the contribution of black interest groups to the policy formulation and implementation process at the national level. Mancur Olson suggests that economic interests are a powerful motivating, unifying, and resource-generating force in the process of shaping organizations. Within that context, it is expected that collective organizations representing heterogeneous associations like racial groups would have an especially difficult time organizing, developing resources, and identifying, sorting, resolving, and shaping ideological demands in a consistently coherent fashion.[1]

Previous research hypothesized that small, economically homogeneous racial groups operating in competitive (that is, unregulated) arenas would have the strongest opportunity to influence public policy.[2] Groups operating in regulated areas would have difficulty competing with other economic groups already relatively well integrated into the political process, and large heterogeneous groups would face a highly complex task sorting through the competing economic and political issues raised by the universe of political ideas in the black population.[3] Such groups would therefore also have difficulty penetrating the legislative and administrative arenas or environments in which policy is made and would find it difficult to define political issues in a form that would be acceptable to policy-makers in relatively established arenas.

These informal Olson-derived hypotheses challenge interest group pluralism, which suggests, based both on access and ideology, that political influence is a routine, nonproblematic set of processes requiring only that interests organize to develop control over policy formulation. At the local level, James Q. Wilson criticized black organizations for failing to formulate their political demands in a nonracial framework, or in a way that would be able to permeate the existing policy institutions.[4] Robert Dahl predicted that blacks would penetrate political institutions, like other groups before them, within a specified period of time.[5] Huey Perry's summation of propositions that outline a pluralist character to political institutions also offers a strategy for evaluating whether black politics fits comfortably within the pluralist theory.

This chapter reports the results of interviews designed to investigate the above hypotheses through an examination of the organization and operations of black and other civil rights interest groups that participated in the campaign to extend the Voting Rights Act of 1965 in 1981 and 1982. The results of the interviews show that the voting rights campaign was run by a complex, interracial, broad civil rights coalition of heterogeneous organizations.[6]

The chapter has four overarching objectives. First, it describes how the coalition was originally formed and how it functioned, identifies the dominant organizations within the coalition, and shows that the coalition was supplemented by the activities of other black, regional, and civil rights organizations. Second, the chapter identifies the sources of political and ideological conflict within the coalition and shows how they were related to the composition of specific groups and to the varying types of organizations within the coalition. The major divisions were race, ethnicity, adherence to procedural norms, and economic-professional differentiation. Third, the chapter identifies the major issues in the campaign and shows that they relate fairly consistently to these ideological faults within the coalition. One such issue is discussed in considerable detail: the decision to push to overturn the *Mobile v.*

Bolden (1980) decision[7] and to ask for legislative support for the section 2 results test. Finally, the chapter discusses how the campaign to win passage of the 1982 Voting Rights Act shaped and reshaped the composition, behavior, and ideological position of the coalition and individual organizational members within the coalition.

The Voting Rights Coalition

William Gamson has defined a coalition as "the joint use of resources to determine the outcome of a mixed-motive situation involving more than two units."[8] Barbara Hinckley notes the involvement of three components in coalitions: an application of power, a combination of conflict and coordination, and a collective activity. According to Hinckley, " . . . people confront, with others, a particular kind of situation in which an outcome must be determined. As rational individuals, they seek to maximize their own returns. But to do this, they must work with others who are also trying to maximize their own returns; and the situation provides no outcome that maximizes the returns to everyone."[9] This situation provides the basis of coalition formation.

The word *coalition* is used in two different ways in this chapter: first, as in ordinary language, to indicate organizations that united to push for the Voting Rights Act; and second, as the way in which the ordinary usage of the word intersects with its theoretical definition, to indicate the structured interactions among the organizations lobbying for passage of the 1982 Act. This set of structured interorganizational interactions is more complex than a simple association of interests. Since the voting rights campaign fits neither game theory nor the social-psychological experimental categories for coalitions, but is a real world case in a natural setting,[10] it is a considerably more complex problem because of the difficulty in identifying the variables critical to understanding the outcome of the campaign.

The voting rights coalition in ordinary language actually consisted of interlocking groups, some more closely interactive than others. The coalition was built on the foundation of a long-term peak association, the Leadership Conference on Civil Rights (LCCR).[11] LCCR members planned the campaign to extend the 1965 Voting Rights Act to create a maximum rather than a minimum winning coalition in order to secure the legislative votes to overcome opposition from the Reagan administration. Designing the campaign to create a maximum winning coalition made the campaign more difficult to control, as William Riker, Robert Axelrod, Hinckley, Jerome Chertkoff, Wilson,[12] and others have shown about this strategy in general.

The Major Voting Rights Organizations

The LCCR was the dominant group in the initial planning phase for lobbying for the extension of the 1965 Voting Rights Act. An association of approximately 160 civil rights associations, the LCCR's membership includes the American Federation of Labor and Congress of Industrial Organizations (AFL-CIO), the National Organization for Women (NOW), the United States Catholic Conference, the National Association for the Advancement of Colored People (NAACP) Legal Defense and Educational Fund, and several racial and ethnic organizations. Racial and ethnic groups include the National Urban League, the Japanese-American Citizens' League, the Organization of Chinese Americans, the Anti-Defamation League of B'nai B'rith, and the National Council of La Raza. The LCCR was founded in 1949 as a coalition of fifty groups by A. Philip Randolph, who organized the Brotherhood of Sleeping Car Porters, Roy Wilkins of the NAACP, and Arnold Aronson, an activist in labor and Jewish organizations. While two of the three original founders represented organizations with black constituencies, the racial composition of the coalition itself was not majority black. By the late 1970s, only 30 to 40 percent of the LCCR's membership was black.

The Voting Rights Act Steering Committee directed the 1981–82 campaign. The committee was organized by and its political capital was primarily attributable to the LCCR. Although the committee's membership was not limited to representatives from LCCR organizations, it was dominated by them and by the coalition's norms and values. The LCCR's offices were in the basement of a building otherwise occupied by Jewish organizations, including the American Jewish Committee, the American Jewish Congress, and the Union of American Hebrew Congregations. Ralph Neas, the LCCR's executive director, appointed in early 1981 as the extension campaign picked up speed, is a white Republican who previously worked as a legislative assistant to two U.S. senators, one black and one white.

Several smaller but very important organizations are also active in the civil rights policy domain. These include the Black Leadership Forum, the Congressional Black Caucus, and southern black organizations. The Black Leadership Forum includes the heads of national black political organizations such as the Congressional Black Caucus, the Urban Coalition, the Joint Center for Political Studies,[13] People United to Save Humanity (PUSH), the Southern Christian Leadership Conference, the NAACP, the National Urban League, and the National Business League.

The Congressional Black Caucus, which is thoroughly examined in Chapter 7 of this book, consists of black members of Congress. Marguerite Barnett has shown that the caucus moved back and forth through collective, ethnic, and synthesis stages in carrying out its legislative responsibilities.[14] The collective stage indicates a commitment to represent the entire black nation, the ethnic stage a decision to represent its specific constituency, and the synthesis stage, a combination of the two. By the 1980s, the caucus had largely abandoned a purely collective orientation and was more frequently in a synthesis or ethnic stage. In this stage, members are more likely to focus on serving their own mostly black constituencies and achieving mobility in Congress.[15]

Southern black organizations chose a different strategy from that developed by Washington organizations. These southern organizations were best symbolized by the Southern Christian Leadership Conference (SCLC). Founded in 1957 by Martin Luther King, Jr., Ralph Abernathy, Ella Baker, and others, the SCLC used black organizational and institutional networks directed by black religious leaders during the civil rights movement to organize mass local demonstrations. These demonstrations were directed at undermining the positions of local white leaders and at forcing the national government to intervene in local jurisdictions.[16]

Other black organizations that had helped lead demonstrations in the South include the Student Nonviolent Coordination Committee (SNCC) and the Congress of Racial Equality (CORE). The SNCC is no longer in existence, and CORE is only a remnant of its past. None of the southern black organizations shifted fully from protest to national legislative and administrative politics.[17] Other southern civil rights organizations such as the Southern Regional Council and its offshoot, the Voter Education Project, focused primarily on racial policy issues in the South.[18]

Members from all these organizations created the Voting Rights Act Coalition, but not all of them formally joined the coalition. Those organizations that did formally join the coalition participated in the coalition with varying degrees of enthusiasm.

Sources of Ideological Cohesion and Conflict

The principal unifying force of the coalition was a strong commitment to civil rights, but this commitment did not guarantee that the coalition would hold together. Civil rights and voting rights are issues that would seem to have common appeal to a wide variety of groups; but when the LCCR was founded, American institutions, politics, and social and economic life were highly segregated by race. Labor unions, black organizations, and Jewish organizations formed the core of the early coalition.

As the struggle for legal recognition of blacks' rights produced favorable legislation by the national government, other groups used the black civil rights movement as a model for efforts to combat discrimination against their own group. Women's groups such as the National Women's Political Caucus, NOW, and the Women's Legal Defense Fund, and ethnic groups such as the Mexican-American Legal Defense and Educational Fund and the National Council of La Raza used the formal strategies of the civil rights movement or the analogy of racial discrimination to legitimize their own claim for favorable federal legislation.

After a collective commitment was applied specifically to blacks and blacks won certain rights and benefits, interest representation in the civil rights domain rapidly expanded to include other collective groups subject to discrimination. Groups with status similar or comparable to blacks sought to win support from the federal government equivalent to that received by blacks. Important distinctions in the coalition developed along racial and ethnic lines, and between original and newcomer organizations. These distinctions led to ideological conflict within the coalition.

Racial Conflict

Racial factors are important because organizations such as the NAACP, the National Urban League, and the LCCR, although popularly perceived as black, have frequently been dominated by whites and therefore must deal with racial distinctions between themselves and other organizations as well as with those that exist within their own organizations. Until the mid-1930s many of the top officers, board members, and legal directors of the NAACP were white. While the top posts shifted to blacks in the 1930s, competition over legal responsibilities continued. The NAACP's local cooperating attorneys, who represented NAACP members in cases at the local level, were often white. Black attorneys and the National Bar Association (an organization of black attorneys) were highly critical of the NAACP for these practices.

A version of this sensitive issue resurfaced in the 1950s when the NAACP Legal Defense and Educational Fund (NAACPLDEF), Inc., formally separated from the NAACP, and Jack Greenberg, a white lawyer, was chosen by Thurgood Marshall to head it. The NAACP then sued the NAACPLDEF over the latter's use of "NAACP" in its name. The lawsuit was resolved by the Supreme Court in favor of the NAACP-LDEF. It is an oversimplification to attribute the NAACP-NAACPLDEF troubles entirely to racial conflict since the two competing organizations are not wholly distinguishable by race; however, the conflict cannot be understood without taking race into account.[19]

The National Urban League's executive directors and presidents have long been black, but the chairmen of its Board of Directors have all been white. The LCCR, founded by two blacks and one white, is no longer seen by black organizations as a black coalition, since black groups constitute only about a third of its membership. While its policy-making executive body includes many permanent black groups without whom it could not conduct business, its physical location (in the basement of a building otherwise occupied by Jewish organizations) and white executive director result in its being viewed with some ambivalence and even suspicion by black organizations. The head of one major black organization commented, "I think their agenda [LCCR's] is their agenda and it may not be consistent with what I perceive to be ours."[20]

Ethnic Conflict

The public policy benefits blacks received in the voting rights domain were intended as legislative protections initially applied specifically to southern states where blacks are concentrated. Robert Salisbury discusses the role of the organizational entrepreneur in helping a group become successful in achieving its goals. The organizational entrepreneur is someone who devotes time, develops political resources, makes contacts, and organizes and mobilizes a group to win political support for desired public policies. The role of the organizational entrepreneur is most needed in large, heterogeneous groups whose members are unlikely to organize voluntarily to obtain favorable public policies because of the social and other costs involved inherent in taking such initiative.[21] For such groups, a specialist who can obtain benefits—monetary rewards, personal satisfaction, recognition among public policy elites, or other benefits—for his constituents can serve as a professional organizer to overcome barriers to organizational and political influence. Clarence Mitchell was such an organizational entrepreneur for the NAACP. As the first full-time Washington lobbyist for the organization from 1950 through the late 1970s, Mitchell lobbied persistently on behalf of the NAACP and civil rights issues. He made the personal contacts that helped establish the NAACP's organizational and professional credibility, familiarize members of Congress and their staffs with the details and the framework of racial issues, and reshape the legislative environment in a manner more favorable to blacks' interests. Mitchell's effort in this regard strongly influenced the passage of the Civil Rights Act of 1964, the Voting Rights Act of 1965, and other civil rights legislation. He was known popularly among the civil rights lobby and legislators as the "101st Senator"—symbolizing the extent to which he had become a familiar figure on Capitol Hill.[22]

By the early 1970s, Mexican-American groups recognized the 1965 Voting Rights legislation as a useful resource for protecting Mexican Americans from electoral and language discrimination and sought incorporation into the legislation. Mitchell was concerned about maintaining the stability of the voting rights coalition and preserving the rights of blacks, opposed any expansion of voting rights to new groups, regardless of whether the basis for incorporation was on the grounds of ethnicity or language discrimination. Mitchell's opposition to expanding the 1965 voting rights legislation to include Mexican Americans may be viewed as an attempt to protect blacks from the free-rider problem observed by Olson, that is, having to share benefits with a group that had not helped to achieve them.[23] Coalition theorists such as Riker might cite this as a case for the desirability of a minimum winning coalition, wherein only a number sufficiently large enough to achieve desired benefits is sought in order to avoid sharing the benefits with other groups.

The LCCR is governed by an executive committee that uses a unanimous agreement decision-making mechanism for selecting issues and deciding on the main features of legislative strategy. The executive committee is composed of approximately twenty organizational members who must reach unanimous agreement before the coalition can act as a unit. For example, the LCCR supported the inclusion of Latinos in the coalition in 1975 and 1982, but Mitchell and the NAACP were opposed and vetoed the LCCR's support for including them. Because of the NAACP veto, LCCR members who favored the inclusion of Latinos in the 1975 legislation worked as individuals to achieve this result.[24]

The NAACP's vote in the 1975 campaign created considerable animosity between blacks and Latinos and left a strong residue of bad feelings between the two groups in the years before the expiration of the 1975 legislation in 1982. The question the coalition faced as it entered the planning stages for the 1981 campaign to renew the 1975 legislation was whether black organizations would continue to maintain that blacks held the exclusive privilege of protection against discrimination or whether they would support the minority language provisions. The protection of language minorities was therefore an important and potentially divisive issue entering the 1981 campaign.[25]

Professional Conflict

This category examines conflict engendered as a result of the increase in professional participants—voting rights litigators—who have helped shape, develop, and extend voting rights law since the creation of the Act in 1965. The voting rights litigators during the 1981–82 campaign included Frank Parker and Barbara Phillips, lawyers from the Lawyers' Committee for Civil Rights Under Law's Voting Rights Project; Armand Derfner, an attorney in private practice based at the Joint Center for Political Studies during the campaign; Laughlin McDonald of the American Civil Liberties Union (ACLU); Victor McTeer of the Center for Constitutional Rights; Lani Guinier of the NAACPLDEF; Joachim Avila of the Mexican American Legal Defense and Educational Fund (MALDEF); Margaret Ford of the NAACP; and some individual attorneys in private practice, such as James Blacksher and Larry Minafee. Although all the organizations represented by these attorneys, except the Center for Constitutional Rights, were members of the LCCR, and the ACLU, MALDEF, and the Lawyers' Committee for Civil Rights Under Law representatives testified in the 1975 extension, the 1981–82 campaign was the first time voting rights litigators had chosen as a collectivity to commit their resources directly to a voting rights legislative campaign. The voting rights litigators represent a more specialized and broader spectrum of lawyers than the NAACP and the NAACPLDEF networks of cooperating attorneys who occasionally litigate voting rights cases.

Neither the Center for Constitutional Rights nor the NAACP committed litigators to the 1981–82 Washington lobbying campaign. The NAACP, with its legal office based in New York City, instead used its Washington lobbying office under the direction of Althea Simmons for the day-to-day campaign and used President Benjamin Hooks and a large number of state and local NAACP representatives involved in voting cases to testify at congressional hearings. However, this strategy made the NAACP less than fully competitive with other organizations such as the ACLU, the Lawyers' Committee, NAACPLDEF, and the Joint Center,[26] which committed personnel to the campaign. Simmons, like other Washington lobbyists in the coalition, was not a practicing lawyer; she did not litigate as part of her professional responsibilities.

Some of the professional lobbyists in the civil rights organizations had greater seniority in the civil rights policy community than did the voting rights litigators. Because of their greater seniority, these individuals formed a significant inner leadership core to develop political strategy for the campaign. In the past, when disagreements had occurred, it had been within this group; in the 1981–82 campaign, this group found itself opposed by the litigators.

Differences in professional socialization and experience placed the litigators and the lobbyists on opposing sides on several occasions during the campaign. Representative Henry Hyde's (R-Ill.-6) proposal for a provision in the legislation to permit jurisdictions that had not recently violated the letter or the spirit of the law to avoid coverage. The lobbyists wanted to incorporate a provision into the legislation to accommodate Hyde and to prevent President Ronald Reagan, who supported such a provision, from being opposed to the legislation. The litigators feared Hyde's "bailout" provision would allow jurisdictions that had violated the law to escape coverage and would make their litigative task more difficult. The lobbyists feared that opposition to Hyde's proposal might limit the accumulation of sufficient votes to win the Voting Rights Act extension.

Because civil rights litigators had worked in the open racial hostility of the South, they viewed southern officials and judges as opponents who could be overcome by coercive litigation. In contrast, in order to win legislative victories, civil rights lobbyists sought to expand their base of support within Congress by using personal, logical appeals or by trying to galvanize public support for their position. If the lobbyists thought it was necessary to appeal to southern members of Congress or to try to galvanize favorable public opinion in the South in order to achieve desired legislative victories, they were willing to do so.

In sum, an expanded, more heterogeneous working coalition characterized the civil rights lobby for the 1981–82 campaign. Critical conflicts along racial, ethnic, and professional lines shaped group interaction in the 1980s. In creating massive constituency support, the voting rights steering committee broadened active organizational support for the legislation beyond the traditional civil rights coalition. Thus, the broadened and increasingly complex civil rights organizations incorporated important and potentially powerful divisive interests.

How the Lobby Shaped the Law

The coalition divided in varying ways over three major issues in the campaign, which emerged from the existing ideological faults within the coalition. One issue that precipitated conflict between African Americans and Latinos was the extension of protection for language minorities. A second issue was whether the extension of section 5, the preclearance provision of the act, should allow for a "bailout" by jurisdictions that no longer discriminate against blacks or other protected groups. (Under section 5 of the 1965 act, "preclearance" meant that any new voting law changes initiated by southern jurisdictions had to be examined and cleared by the Civil Rights Division of the Department of Justice, or by the first district of the federal district courts.) The coalition also fought over whether it should compromise on this issue. It had enough votes to pass the bill in the House, without the support of Representative Hyde, who had close ties to President Reagan, or any Republicans. The lobbyists sought to secure broad legislative support in order to maximize the prospects that the legislation would be enacted into law; but the litigators felt such a strategy forced unnecessary compromise and would make their litigative work much more difficult.

The third issue, which will be analyzed in detail, involved the 1980 Supreme Court decision in the *Mobile v. Bolden* case. The Court concluded that proof of discrimination in a suit brought in Mobile, Alabama, against an at-large scheme required evidence of intent to discriminate against blacks. Blacks had sued the city arguing that the at-large electoral system was racially discriminatory because it diluted the black vote and argued as proof that no black had ever been elected to the city council.

The Court ruling—that the plaintiffs had to prove that the change to at-large provisions involved the intent to discriminate—created a more difficult test, not only in the cases of recently enacted legislation but because the Mobile law had been passed in 1911 and all the principals were deceased. While the plaintiff's attorneys returned to court and won the case with new evidence developed by historians about the political and social environment of the era, the human and financial costs were prohibitive: six thousand hours of lawyers' time in addition to seven thousand hours for researchers and expert witnesses; the cost was $120,000, not including attorney fees.[27]

Don Edwards (D-Calif.), chairman of the Subcommittee on Civil and Constitutional Rights of the House Judiciary Committee, called open hearings at which voting rights litigators discussed the problems with the operation of the law, including the intent standard.[28] The litigators discussed the high cost of litigating under the intent standard. Through these hearings, the litigators convinced the traditional civil rights lobbyists—who feared that the civil rights lobby did not have the votes to pass the legislation in Congress and overcome a possible veto by the newly elected Republican president, Ronald Reagan—to use the extension campaign to overturn the *Mobile* decision.

The decision to seek amendment of section 2 of the 1965 Voting Rights Act to overturn the intent standard was very difficult. It simultaneously tapped into the conflict over race and the professional division within the coalition. It took voting rights legislation into the vote dilution area, an area that the litigators had been developing and expanding in the courts but that had not yet come under the explicit protection of congressional legislation as vote denial actions had. Protection of vote dilution suggests that citizenship privileges incorporate not only the right to vote but also include the reasonable right to exercise the franchise and to have an effect on the outcome of its exercise.

Moving from protection against vote denial to prevention of vote dilution was a new and highly aggressive legislative and litigative posture. To do so required litigators to persuade the older civil rights lobbyists in the coalition to take a highly aggressive stance in early 1981. Early in the Reagan administration, the lobbyists were not sure whether they had the votes to extend the Voting Rights Act as it had existed in 1975, let alone expand the definition of discrimination. Not only was this new position a proposal to further extend the legislation, but it was also a specification that the definition of voting discrimination be reshaped considerably. Past extensions in 1970 and 1975 had broadened the populations under coverage and introduced protection of language minorities, but the substance of the discrimination to be controlled was primarily that of vote denial. With more distinctive concerns than the groups that had been more actively involved in the coalition in the previous extension campaigns, the litigators rejected the conventional norms and rules both of the Congress and the coalition that had been accepted in the past.

The lobbyist-litigator conflict also taps into the long history of racial conflict over control of civil rights litigation within civil rights organizations.[29] Voting rights litigators are predominantly white. Part of the reason for the preponderance of white lawyers in voting rights cases is that these cases often take enormous time and require considerable financial resources to pay attorney and expert witness fees. Black attorneys rarely have the financial resources necessary to litigate voting rights cases.

The litigators convinced the rest of the coalition to push for a results test in section 2 of the 1965 Voting Rights Act in which the measure of a law or voting practice is its effect on the voting power of the black electorate rather than proof of officials' intent to discriminate. The Supreme Court had concluded in the *Mobile* case that section 2, because it was modeled after the Fifteenth Amendment, required proof of intent to discriminate. The coalition won relatively easy acceptance on this issue in the House Judiciary Committee and on the House floor where the controversy over the bailout provision in section 5 dominated debate.

In the Senate, Orrin Hatch (R-Utah) , chairman of the Subcommittee on the Constitution of the Judiciary Committee, concentrated on the proposed use of a results test in section 2 to overturn the Supreme Court's decision in *Mobile* and on whether the standard for implementation could create proportional representation. Senator Hatch and others argued that if the courts and the Civil Rights Division of the Justice

Department held that at-large elections discriminated against blacks and others, then the remedy proposed by the courts and the Civil Rights Division of Justice would necessarily create a district system as an alternative.[30] Since the process of redistricting and the shape of districts drawn are subject to section 5 preclearance, creating a nondiscriminatory district system would tend to result in districts drawn so as to elect the proportion of blacks, Mexican Americans, or other minority groups in the population.[31] Hatch argued that this created a system of proportional representation violating the spirit of U.S. law. Conversely, he contended that a finding of lack of proportionality might be interpreted as evidence of discrimination.

Senator Robert Dole (R-Kans.) helped craft a compromise including a nondiscriminatory results test for section 2. The compromise explicitly rejected proportional representation as an implementation standard and extended section 5 preclearance for twenty-five years, rather than the permanent extension agreed to in the House. The provision was passed by the full committee, by the Senate, and by both Houses as part of the final bill.[32]

The language provision was extended for a decade. A "bailout" provision using a standard that made it difficult for jurisdictions to escape coverage was incorporated into the legislation to assuage the concerns of the litigators. Vote dilution was incorporated into law under the effects standard and a compromise achieved in the Senate specifically to exclude proportional representation as a standard of proof.

How the Law Shaped the Lobby

The 1981–82 campaign to extend the Voting Rights Act created a more highly specialized, complex, lobbying organization than had previously existed. Clarence Mitchell, the NAACP, and the LCCR had dominated all previous voting rights campaigns. Mitchell had retired by the time of the campaign in 1981–82 and therefore was not a factor in that effort. Many blacks and black organizations were involved in the 1982 extension, and while every member of the Black Leadership Forum made the extension of the Voting Rights Act a legislative priority, the forum let the more broadly based civil rights coalition (in which many black organizations were active) take the lead on the details of the campaign.[33]

The campaign created a much larger coalition than had previously functioned. Many more participated in the House hearings in 1981 than in previous extensions and in the original legislation, as Table 9-1 shows. The number of individuals and organizations who submitted testimony as witnesses or through statements totaled ninety-four for the 1965 House Judiciary hearings. This number shrank to twenty-four for the 1970 extension, a decrease of 68 percent. The number of individuals and organizations presenting oral and written testimony increased from twenty-four for the 1970 extension to fifty-six for the 1975 extension, representing a 133 percent increase. By 1982, the number of individuals and organizations presenting oral and written testimony had increased to 156, which represented a 179 percent increase over 1975. Overall, from 1965 to 1982, the number of witnesses increased from 74 to 156, which represents an increase of 111 percent over the period. As Table 9-1 also shows, the number of interest groups presenting oral and written testimony decreased from thirty in 1965 to ten in 1970, representing a 67 percent decrease. From 1970 to 1975, the number of interest groups that presented oral and written testimony increased from ten to nineteen, representing a 90 percent increase. By 1982, the number of interest groups which presented oral and written testimony had increased to seventy-five, representing an increase of 295 percent over 1975. Overall, from 1965 to 1982, the number of interest groups presenting oral and written testimony increased from thirty to seventy-five, representing a 150 percent increase over the period.

Organizations also increased the strength of their representation from a maximum of three witnesses by one organization in 1965, 1970, and 1975 (affiliates of the National Council of Churches, the United Auto Workers, and the NAACP, respectively) to nine witnesses by one organization in 1982 (the NAACP, with U.S. Steel and the AFL-CIO following at six and five witnesses, respectively). Overall, the ratio of representatives to organizations was 1.43 in 1965 and 1970, fell to 1.25 in 1975, and rose to 2.00 in 1982. These data support the accounts of representatives of many organizations that the 1981–82 campaign was extraordinarily large and intense.

Summary and Conclusions

The 1982 campaign to extend the Voting Rights Act offers some new perspectives on the hypotheses discussed in the introduction to this

Table 9-1. House Judiciary Subcommittee Witnesses, 1965–1982

Witness Categories	1965 Act		1970 Extension		1975 Extension		1982 Extension	
	#	%	#	%	#	%	#	%
U.S. Congress	29	39.2	8	33.0	11	19.6	7	4.4
Federal	8	10.8	5	20.1	10	17.8	7	4.4
State	3	4.0	1	4.1	11	19.6	27	17.3
Local	2	2.7	0	0	1	1.7	10	6.4
Interest groups	30	40.5	10	41.6	19	33.9	75	47.4
Academics	0	0	0	0	3	5.3	14	8.9
Lawyers*	0	0	0	0	0	0	7	4.4
Private citizens	0	0	0	0	0	0	9	5.7
Other	2	2.7	0	0	2	3.5	0	0
Total	74	100	24	100	57	100	156	100

*Indicates attorneys otherwise unattached to interest groups.

Note: Percentages are correct within 1 percentage point.

Sources: U.S. Congress, House of Representatives, Committee on the Judiciary, "Voting Rights Hearings Before Subcommittee Number 5 on HR 6400," 89th Congress, 1st sess, March 18–April 1, 1956 (Washington, D.C.: U.S. Government Printing Office, 1965); U.S. Congress, House of Representatives, Committee on the Judiciary, "Voting Rights Act Extension: Hearing Before Subcommittee Number 5 on HR 4249, HR 5538, and similar proposals," 91st Congress, 1st sess., May 14–July 1, 1969, Serial no. 3 (Washington, D.C.: U.S. Government Printing Office, 1969); U.S. Congress, House of Representatives, Committee on the Judiciary, "Extension of the Voting Rights Act, Hearings Before the Subcommittee on Civil and Constitutional Rights on HR 939, HR 2148, HR 3247, HR 3501, and other extensions of the Voting Rights Act," 94th Congress, 1st sess., February 25–March 25, 1975, Serial no. 1, part 1 (Washington, D.C.: U.S. Government Printing Office, 1975); and U.S. Congress, House of Representatives, Committee on the Judiciary, "Extension of the Voting Rights Act, Hearings Before the Subcommittee on Civil and Constitutional Rights," 97th Congress, 1st sess, May 6–July 13, 1981, Serial no. 24 (Washington, D.C.: U.S. Government Printing Office, 1982).

chapter. First, for decades collective organizations have played a critical role in introducing and sustaining interest in civil rights issues. They have also integrated broader protest efforts with legislative efforts and have succeeded in shepherding several of those legislative efforts into law. Despite significant economic problems of the populations they serve, black and Latino groups have created sufficient moral resources and have organized in ways that minimize the information costs of mobilizing their constituencies and disseminating information. They have defined a very important role in the policy arena and have played an important role in defining the civil rights coalition and shaping its long-term direction.

Secondly, smaller, homogeneous, and specialized organizations—public interest law groups, the ACLU, the NAACPLDEF, and the Lawyers' Committee, among others—created in response to the political and policy ramifications of the civil rights movement have led in the development of new theories and strategies for voting rights, as well as new directions for the larger coalition. They do not, however, have either the moral weight or the constituency base of the older, more broadly based organizations.

Third, while the larger organizations clearly have difficulty focusing on specific questions arising out of implementation of the 1965 Voting Rights Act and its extensions, they continue to influence the process because of the length of their experience in the arena and because of their breadth in representing large collective groups. Because the voting rights policy area itself is not fundamentally economic, the dynamics of representation in this policy area are distinct from economic policy areas. Within the voting rights policy area, size, homogeneity of interest and specialization matter and give some advantage to the smaller, homogeneous civil rights organizations over the larger, older civil rights organizations. However, the larger, more heterogeneous and the smaller, homogeneous organizations complement each other.

The entrance of litigators into the coalition created a turf problem as the older civil rights lobbyists felt threatened by the litigators. However, the litigators strengthened the coalition and contributed significantly to the scope and passage of the 1982 legislation. They broadened the definition of law to be protected and won through aggressive challenge much of what they wanted.

At the same time, the experienced legislative wing of the lobby legitimized the campaign strategy that created the broad outlines and the major tactics used to win passage of the 1982 legislation. This consisted of the agreement among all organizations that the voting rights extension be made a top legislative priority and the mobilization of a large number of organizations to create the strongest possible support, especially in the House of Representatives. The legitimation of the campaign also consisted of securing the commitment of large numbers of House and Senate members to support the extension of the act, including bipartisan support in both houses.

During the campaign to extend the 1965 Voting Rights Act, the coalition struggled with the question of representation: southern black organizations felt they had paid the initial costs in terms of demonstrations and protests to create the political leverage to pass the original legislation, yet by the early 1980s they felt less in control of the management of the law. The 1981–82 civil rights coalition was never numerically dominated by black organizations.

As the Leadership Conference on Civil Rights broadens its membership to include women, other racial and ethnic groups, homosexuals, and others who may exhibit more competition than cooperation, and as it includes more voting rights litigators whose development of legal strategy is largely divorced from black mass membership organizations, black organizations face a difficult decision as to whether to continue to work within the civil rights lobby or to go their own way. To prevent disintegration of its membership structure, the LCCR not only must manage the resource, mobilization, and ideological complexities within and among black organizations, it must also manage the even more complex interactions among its constituent organizations.

The emphasis in this study rests on relations within the interest group coalition responsible for the 1982 campaign to extend the Voting Rights Act and, to a lesser degree, on their relations with political institutions that play a critical role in policy formulation. When the relationship between these interests and institutions is examined, important elements of Perry's pluralist propositions are compatible with the findings in this study. Clearly the civil rights interests targeted multiple centers of power (P2), and they had multiple opportunities to achieve their goals (P3). The fact that the coalition was able to use Congress to overturn the Supreme Court's interpretation in *Mobile v. Bolden* confirms that proposition. There was considerable give and take between the interest groups and government officials over the form and content of voting rights policy (P4). The extension itself and the strategy used by the coalition were clearly incremental (P5). To an important degree the conflicts between the lobbyists and the litigators reflected incremental and pluralist perspectives used by the lobbyists and the nonincremental rejection of conventional politics used by the litigators. The federal structure and complex organization of political and economic interests in American national politics requires a response by racial and ethnic interests that is at least descriptively pluralist.

As is indicated in the introduction to this chapter, previous pluralist theorists presumed that racial groups, in order to become integrated into the American political system, would lose their racial policy orientation or else were critical of black interests because their approach to policy addressed race at all. The clear implication was that pluralist systems did not allow for racial hierarchy or that racial representation of interests was inappropriate for whites and for blacks. The still unanswered questions associated with pluralism relate to the overall impact of these generic strategies on the political and socioeconomic status of the constituents represented by civil rights interests. These conflicts about the appropriateness of pluralist approaches to political institutions are also clearly reflected within civil rights and racial interest group politics.

Notes

1. Mancur Olson, *The Logic of Collective Action: Public Goods and the Theory of Groups* (New York: Schocken Books, 1988); *The Rise and Decline of Nations* (New Haven: Yale University Press, 1982).

2. Dianne M. Pinderhughes, "Collective Goods and Black Interest Groups," *Review of Black Political Economy* 12 (winter 1983): 219–36.

3. Dianne M. Pinderhughes, *Race and Ethnicity in Chicago Politics: A Reexamination of Pluralist Theory* (Urbana: University of Illinois Press, 1987), chap. 5.

4. James Q. Wilson, *Negro Politics: The Search for Leadership* (New York: Free Press, 1960).

5. Robert A. Dahl, *Who Governs? Democracy and Power in an American City* (New Haven: Yale University Press, 1961), 36.

6. I assured my interviewees of anonymity in order to facilitate their honest appraisal of other participants in the coalition. Some specified that they not be

quoted. Therefore, in these endnotes, I list all my interviewees as anonymous and indicate only the location and date of the interviews.

7. 446 U.S. 55 (1980).

8. William A. Gamson, "Experimental Studies of Coalition Formation," in *Advanced Experimental Social Psychology,* ed. Leonard Berkowitz (New York: Academic Press, 1964).

9. Barbara Hinckley, *Coalitions and Politics* (New York: Harcourt Brace Jovanovich, 1981), 4–5.

10. Ibid., 42–44.

11. W. Douglas Costain and Anne N. Costain, "Interest Groups as Policy Aggregators in the Legislative Process," *Polity* 14 (winter 1981): 269.

12. William H. Riker, *The Theory of Political Coalitions* (New Haven: Yale University Press, 1962); Robert Axelrod, *Conflict of Interest: A Theory of Divergent Goals with Applications to Politics* (Chicago: Markham Publishing Company, 1970); Hinckley, *Coalitions and Politics;* Jerome M. Chertkoff, "Sociopsychological Theories and Research on Coalition Formation," in *The Study of Coalition Behavior, Theoretical Perspectives and Cases from Four Continents,* ed. Sven Groennings, E. W. Kelley, and Michael Leiserson (New York: Holt, Rinehart and Winston, 1970); James Q. Wilson, *Political Organizations* (New York: Basic Books, 1973).

13. The name of this organization has changed to the Joint Center for Political and Economic Studies.

14. Marguerite Ross Barnett, "The Congressional Black Caucus: Illusions and Realities of Power," in *The New Black Politics: The Search for Political Power,* ed. Michael B. Preston, Lenneal J. Henderson, Jr., and Paul Puryear (New York: Longman, 1982).

15. Ibid.

16. David Garrow, *Protest at Selma: Martin Luther King, Jr. and the Voting Rights Act of 1965* (New Haven: Yale University Press, 1978); Doug McAdam, *Political Process and the Development of Black Insurgency, 1930–1970* (Chicago: University of Chicago Press, 1982); Aldon Morris, *The Origins of the Civil Rights Movement: Black Communities Organizing for Change* (New York: Free Press, 1984).

17. Robert Smith, "Black Power and the Transformation from Protest to Politics," *Political Science Quarterly* 96 (fall 1981): 431–43.

18. Anonymous interviews with author, Atlanta, April 22 and 23, 1985.

19. See, for example, August Meier and Elliott Rudwick, "Attorneys Black and White: A Case Study of Race Relations Within the NAACP," *Journal of American History* 62 (March 1976): 913–46; Genna Rae McNeil, *Groundwork: Charles Hamilton Houston and the Struggle for Civil Rights* (Philadelphia: University of Pennsylvania Press, 1983). McNeil's book is about the man who shaped the legal concepts for the NAACP and NAACPLDF's two-decade-long antisegregation campaign. See also Mary White Ovington, *The Walls Came*

Tumbling Down (New York: Harcourt, Brace and World, 1947); Arvarh Strickland, *The History of the Chicago Urban League* (Urbana: University of Illinois Press, 1966); Charles Flint Kellogg, *NAACP: A History of the National Association for the Advancement of Colored People, 1909–1920, Vol. 1* (Baltimore: Johns Hopkins University Press, 1967); Richard Kluger, *Simple Justice: The History of Brown v. Board of Education and Black America's Struggle for Equality* (New York: Vintage Books, 1977); and Stephen L. Wasby, "The NAACP and the NAACP Legal Defense Fund: Preliminary Observations on Conflict Between Allies," unpublished manuscript, n.d.

20. Anonymous interview with author, New York, June 26, 1986.

21. Robert H. Salisbury, "An Exchange Theory of Interest Groups," *Midwest Journal of Political Science* 13 (February 1969): 1–32.

22. Charles Whalen and Barbara Whalen, *The Longest Debate: A Legislative History of the 1964 Civil Rights Act* (New York: New American Library, 1985), 98, 127, 146, 195; Denton L. Watson, *Lion in the Lobby: Clarence Mitchell, Jr.'s Struggle for the Passage of Civil Rights* (New York: William Morrow, 1990).

23. Olson, *The Logic of Collective Action.* Although Olson's discussion of the free-rider concept applies to rational individuals who are members of a group, the logic of the concept applies equally well to intergroup dynamics related to the achievement of group objectives.

24. Anonymous interview with author, Washington, D.C., April 18, 1985. The LCCR is governed by an executive committee that uses a unanimous agreement decision-making mechanism for selecting issues and deciding on the main features of legislative strategy. The executive committee is composed of around twenty organizational members who must reach unanimous agreement before the coalition can act as a unit.

25. Anonymous interviews with author, Washington, D.C., August 4, 1982, and January 25, 1985; San Francisco, May 29, 1985.

26. During the campaign to extend the Voting Rights Act, Armand Derfner, a lawyer active for many years in vote dilution cases under the Voting Rights Act, was on a fellowship at the Joint Center for Political Studies in Washington, D.C., to write a book on the Voting Rights Act. During this time, he also participated in the lobbying campaign to extend the Act. For more information see Chandler Davidson, *Minority Vote Dilution* (Washington, D.C.: Howard University Press, 1984).

27. Chandler Davidson, "Minority Vote Dilution: An Overview," in *Minority Vote Dilution,* ed. Davidson (Washington, D.C.: Howard University Press, 1984), 17.

28. Anonymous interviews with author, Atlanta, April 23, 1985, and June 24, 1986.

29. For a discussion of this history, see Meier and Rudwick, "Race Relations Within the NAACP;" McNeil, *Charles Hamilton Houston;* and Wasby, "The NAACP and the NAACP Legal Defense Fund."

30. Senate Judiciary Committee, Hearings before the Subcommittee on the Constitution of the Committee on the Judiciary, United States Senate, 97th Congress, 2nd sess., vol. 1 (Washington, D.C.: Government Printing Office, 1983).

31. Thomas M. Boyd and Stephen J. Markman, "The 1982 Amendments to the Voting Rights Act: A Legislative History," *Washington and Lee Law Review* 40 (fall 1983): 1347–1428.

32. See Senate Judiciary Committee, *Voting Rights Extension: Report of the Committee on the Judiciary* (Washington, D.C.: Government Printing Office, 15–42.

33. Anonymous interview with author, Washington, D.C., August 30, 1982.

★ *Chapter 10*

Budgets, Taxes, and Politics: Options for African American Politics

Lenneal J. Henderson, Jr.

African Americans have a monumental stake in the politics of government budgets and taxes. Whether by federal, state, or local government, fiscal decision-making often represents fundamental public policy issues and challenges for African American elected officials, public administrators, and most African American institutions. As Charles V. Hamilton indicates, the 1990s will increasingly emphasize struggles over resources "as well as struggles over rights."[1]

A key tenet of pluralist theory is that rights license competing, and often conflicting, interest groups to exert influence on the public policy-making process to affect distributions, or redistributions, of key resources such as education, health care, employment, and business opportunity. Pluralists recognize that rights provide access to resources. The rights to vote, to hold public office, and to mobilize allow African Americans opportunities to influence the allocation of perhaps the principal public resource: tax dollars converted to public budgets. Whether in terms of taxing or spending, public finance is often the public resource sought by African American politicians and advocacy organizations for meeting basic needs of African Americans resulting from poverty, discrimination, and other historical legacies and current trends in the African American experience.

If pluralists argue that government decisions and policies result from collective efforts of various interest groups conveying their preferences to public officials for public resources, African Americans perennially confront a cruel paradox in the web of pluralist theory: how to achieve success in meeting the emergency fiscal needs of African Americans in a pluralist political system that favors incremental over comprehensive public policies and distributive over redistributive choices. There is no better indicator of African American political success than the extent to which African Americans achieve their fiscal preferences. When pluralist theory is applied to African American politics and fiscal policy, two interrelated hypotheses are posited that guide the discussion in this chapter: (1) that African Americans are disproportionately dependent on the public sector for their current social and economic vitality and life chances; and (2) that fiscal policy, the public financial transactions of government, can and do directly and immediately affect the quality of life issues addressed by most African American politicians, interest groups, and institutions.

The economic plan developed by President Bill Clinton, which includes both taxing and spending components, was designed to stimulate economic growth, reduce the federal deficit, and enhance America's global economic competitiveness. Both the short-term stimulus plan to invest nearly $30 billion in an employment-generating program to repair and rebuild roads, bridges, tunnels, highways, airports, and other infrastructure, particularly in cities, could have provided opportunities for millions of African American individuals, households, and businesses experiencing continuing financial and management challenges, particularly in metropolitan areas.

However, the intense congressional politics of budget conflict and compromise, complicated by macroeconomic and political challenges facing the United States, significantly reduced the new president's aspirations for a substantial public investment strategy. The final compromise budget program included less than $4 billion for "empowerment zones" designed to uplift inner-city communities through concentrated investment and development and a retroactive tax provision raising the income tax rate to well over 35 percent for most Americans. Empowerment zones resemble the "enterprise zones" conceptualized by the Reagan and Bush administrations and advocated by former Representative and Housing and Urban Development Secretary Jack Kemp (R-N.Y.). They are designated areas of distress in central cities targeted by the government for intensive and continuous investment, business development, employment development, and infrastructural repair and rebuilding. Tax incentives are used by government to attract investment from businesses in these zones. The intended beneficiaries of the investment are community residents, business owners, and consumers who reside and operate in these zones.

Moreover, many challenges faced by African Americans are increasingly the result of global and national, regional and local macroeconomic developments. Dramatic political and economic changes in the former Soviet Union, Eastern Europe, Central and South America and global economic recession impose substantial pressures on the United States to address its status as a debtor nation with a federal budget deficit of more than $300 billion and a negative balance of payments and trade. The message for African Americans is simple: remain politically active, vigilant about the nation's fiscal decisions and challenges, and attuned to macroeconomic shifts and changes, or risk being disadvantaged in the fiscal policy process.

The task of fiscal vigilance is complex and arduous. John Mikesell, for example, describes fiscal policy as inclusive of the budget cycle, taxes, charges and fees, administration of the government debt, bonds, procurement policy, public enterprise, and the creation and use of various trust accounts earmarked for specific purposes.[2]

The Context of Fiscal Policies and African American Politics

In many respects, fiscal policy combines past, present, and future policy practices and issues. It asks how much of the past allocation patterns should guide present (usually current fiscal year) allocation options. Simultaneously, it ponders and struggles over the short- and long-term consequences of selecting one financial option over another. It debates one method of using budgets and taxes to respond to social priorities over another. Historical, contemporary, and future policies toward blacks are reflected in the nature of fiscal policies adopted by government, whether blacks are explicitly or implicitly the focus of these fiscal policies.[3] This process is further complicated by various equity issues and the national economic and financial woes that undergird budgetary and tax decisions. Such complications imply five interrelated essential points about the relationship between fiscal policies and black economic and political aspirations.

First, blacks continue to be disproportionately dependent on public finance in order to advance their economic and political agenda. This

fiscal dependence takes place at three interrelated levels: macroeconomic, institutional, and household. These three interrelated levels are
shared by other socioeconomically disadvantaged populations in the
United States.[4]

Second, the politics and economics of deficit reduction and tax policies
continue to pose severe challenges for blacks. Deficit reduction is often
employed as a justification for a federal budget rescission (a presidential
decision to withhold funds permanently); a deferral (a presidential decision to withhold funds for a brief period); and reprogramming (taking
money appropriated for one program and diverting it to another that
has emerged as a higher priority). For example, the 1990 budget summit
agreement and eventual deficit reduction package came after one of the
most acrimonious, intense, and difficult budget and tax negotiations
ever to take place. Voters expressed their dismay with both the process
and the product of these negotiations in the 1990 elections, particularly
at the state and local levels.[5]

Third, the continued shifting of financial and public policy responsibility to state and local governments challenge black elected officials who
are more numerous at these levels to maintain existing levels of service
for their constituents with declining revenue. Black mayors and county
officials are particularly vulnerable to fiscal stress in the public sector—
fiscal stress being defined as the "gap between the needs and expectations
of citizens and government employees for government services and benefits and the inability of the economy to generate enough economic
growth to expand (or even sustain, in some places) tax-supported programs without putting unacceptable demands on taxpayers' take-home
pay."[6] Black mayors and county officials are particularly vulnerable to
fiscal stress in the public sector because they frequently use the resources
of government to improve the quality of life for their constituents,
particularly their black constituents (since blacks are often more reliant
than whites on government for their well-being).

Fourth, African Americans have a direct and continuing stake in fiscal
policies because they affect lending institutions, hospitals, local and state
governments, strategic large and small businesses, nonprofit organizations, and other institutions that affect blacks in substantive ways.[7] For
example, President Clinton's proposed investment tax credit, particularly for small businesses, could assist thousands of fledgling African

American businesses challenged by restrictive lending policies and procedures of savings and loan and banking institutions.

Fifth, the impact of fiscal policy on the generic, institutional, and household levels among African Americans simultaneously affects all Americans. African Americans purchase goods and services from non–African American vendors. The continuing socioeconomic struggles of African Americans challenge metropolitan areas, corporations, places of worship, and nonprofit organizations throughout the country to be more attentive to the African American experience. Consequently, the interdependency of African Americans and other Americans is evident in almost any fiscal decision made by a federal, state, or local government.

The Congressional Black Caucus, in its *Quality of Life Fiscal 1991 Alternative Budget,* argues that "a nation's values and concern for social and economic justice are measured by the fiscal priorities established in its national budget."[8] The League of United Latin American Citizens has repeatedly warned tax experts that the failure to incorporate large numbers of unemployed and underemployed Hispanic citizens and aliens represents not only a fiscal failure but also a moral failure. The rapidly rising number of women entering the work force and becoming subject to rising taxes without benefit of adequate child care makes a telling statement about the nation's value priorities as well as its fiscal dynamics.[9]

The Current Dependency of African Americans on Fiscal Policies

To put the relationship of African American public policy interests and fiscal policy in perspective, it is useful to recall the three levels of African American fiscal dependency—macroeconomic, institutional, and household—discussed above. At the macroeconomic level African Americans, like all Americans, depend on the provision of goods and services such as roads, tunnels, schools, hospitals, law enforcement, and defense. However, at the institutional level, community-based organizations, national associations, schools, health care organizations, businesses, and institutions owned, operated, or directed to African Americans depend on public money or are affected by tax policies in far more direct ways than is experienced by most Americans. Local Urban League or Opportunities Industrialization Centers depend on federal employment development funding for significant parts of their budgets and missions. African American business depends on government contracts, including set-aside programs, to remain viable. Hundreds of churches and community-based nonprofit organizations are funded by the Department of Housing and Urban Development or state or local housing programs to provide affordable housing to thousands of African Americans. At the household level, thousands of African American households depend on Aid to Families with Dependent Children (AFDC), food stamps, Low-Income Household Energy Assistance Program (LIHEAP), Section 8 housing certificates, and state and local assistance programs to sustain themselves. Without public support, many households would be at the mercy of charitable institutions.

The term *dependency* is not used pejoratively in this context. Many of America's largest corporate, nonprofit, and educational institutions are substantially, if not predominantly, dependent on public monies or tax credits.[10] Some corporations, particularly defense contractors, receive most of their annual gross sales receipts from the federal government. Many smaller businesses sell solid waste management, transportation, telecommunications, health care, and other services to state and local governments.

However, the absence of diverse and flexible sources of income creates financial vulnerability for any institution or household, particularly given significant fluctuation and change in the public policy environment. Without steady progress in obtaining contracts, employment, and goods and services from the corporate sector, African Americans' dependency on government resources makes them particularly vulnerable to politicians and interest groups advocating reductions in federal, state, or local support for their households and institutions.

For example, of the more than 400,000 businesses owned and operated by African Americans, more than 90 percent supply or provide services directly to government. Less than 50 percent of all other businesses are as dependent on government dollars.[11] In addition, black households are more than twice as dependent on some form of federal, state, or local public assistance, and a black student attending college or university is almost three times as likely as other students to receive government support for tuition or room and board.

African Americans are disproportionately represented in federal, state, and local correctional institutions, and increasing public dollars are devoted to the maintenance and expansion of these institutions. More-over, as Georgia Persons, Hanes Walton, and other experts on black elected officials indicate, black elected officials usually represent congres-sional, state, or local districts or jurisdictions with large numbers of impoverished, poorly housed populations with health care, day care, education, employment, business, and infrastructural needs that severely strain federal, state, and local budgets and taxes.[12] Given increasing rates of poverty, homelessness, health care deficiencies, and other social maladies, the dependency of the needy on government will increase.

Paradoxically, much of the recent dependency of African Americans on public money resulted from the struggles of civil rights, feminist, and other movements of the 1960s, 1970s, and 1980s. These movements insisted on an ethic of social responsiveness by fiscal decision-makers unprecedented even during the Great Depression. For example, through the Great Society programs of the Kennedy and Johnson administra-tions, such as the Manpower Development and Training Act of 1962 (employment training), the Economic Development Act of 1964 (poverty program), and the Cities Demonstration and Metropolitan Development Act of 1966 (model cities), the alleviation of poverty and racism was placed higher on the public policy agenda than ever before in the nation's history. The result was a great redistributive impulse: a desire to reallo-cate the country's financial resources through selected fiscal policies.

Walton argues that federal outlays for civil rights regulatory activities increased from $900,000 in 1969 to $3.5 billion in 1976.[13] In 1968, the Small Business Act of 1953 was amended to create a federal set-aside program for minority businesses. Although challenged in 1989 by the *Richmond v. Croson* Supreme Court decision, many states and localities operate business set-aside programs for minority, particularly African American–owned businesses.[14]

However, although it is common to be concerned primarily about those government programs earmarked specifically for blacks and other "target groups" at the household or institutional levels, the generic, or macro, level of dependency is also critical to African Americans. Three observations are essential about the generic level of dependency. First, like all Americans, African Americans depend on government for "public goods." Support for national defense, the space program, research and development funding, law enforcement, parks and recreation, streets, highways, and bridges represent a generic, or macro, level of funding for goods and services needed by all Americans. Although African Americans may receive inadequate quantities or qualities of these goods or services, they are public in the broadest sense of the word. These public goods are supported by public spending and revenue schemes such as corporate and individual income taxes, property taxes, sales taxes, excise taxes, trust funds, bonds, and user fees.

Generic levels of fiscal policy affect African Americans in particular ways because they depend disproportionately on key components of generic-level spending compared with other citizens. For example, when recommendations are made for overall reductions in military installations, weapons systems, or research and development, African Americans employed as civilians or enlisted personnel in the armed services suffer more than others because they are represented more in employment at military installations than are others.[15] When President Richard Nixon closed or reduced 274 military installations in 1974, many African Americans lost jobs or were transferred to lower-paying employment. Recent recommendations to President Clinton for additional base closings include many installations in, or near, substantial African American communities. Although less than $3 billion dollars of defense reductions are proposed by Congress for fiscal year 1994, many of these reductions will profoundly affect African American institutions and households. Military spending creates jobs: so, conversely, each $1 billion reduction in Pentagon outlays affects thirty-eight thousand U.S. workers.[16]

The peace dividend expected to result from reductions in military outlays because of democratization in Eastern Europe and the former Soviet Union has yet to materialize. Before the Persian Gulf War, Defense Secretary Dick Cheney instructed the services to consider reductions of up to $180 billion for fiscal years 1992–94.[17] But U.S. participation in the war temporarily suspended discussions of major defense reductions. Although Cheney's suggested reductions have not been substantially incorporated in the federal budget, President Clinton has seriously considered defense cuts as part of his deficit reduction strategy and as an opportunity to convert defense spending into domestic human and physical infrastructural investment.

A second observation about the generic level of dependency is its intergovernmental nature. Federal defense, education, space, and infrastructural spending is so inextricably intertwined with fiscal decisions of states, cities, and counties that any political or economic strategy involving public finance must consider its intergovernmental impact. Table 10-1 illustrates the impact of federal defense spending for goods, services, and research and development on selected metropolitan areas.

In addition to defense, infrastructure—the nation's systems of roads, bridges, tunnels, water distribution, transit, highways, airports, gas mains, and other public works—is in terrible disrepair. Estimates for infrastructural restoration range from $50 billion to $3 trillion dollars over the next ten years.[18] While federal leadership is essential, an intergovernmental response is imperative. All Americans, including black Americans, are hindered by poor infrastructural conditions.

Poorer infrastructural conditions in black communities are a glaring reality. For example, the Commission on Budget and Financial Priorities of the District of Columbia reported in November 1990 that the 70 percent black District of Columbia has not kept pace with its infrastructural maintenance and investment needs for many years and that its backlog of infrastructural maintenance projects is $1.6 billion. Philadelphia, New Orleans, Oakland (California), Detroit, Baltimore, and Newark (New Jersey), which all have at least 50 percent black populations,

Table 10-1. Department of Defense Share of Spending for Goods, Services, and Research and Development in Selected Metropolitan Areas (Excluding Military Payroll), 1992

	Share of total spending	Share of R & D spending
Los Angeles,* Long Beach	7.2%	19.7%
Washington, D.C.*	4.2	5.4
Norfolk-Virginia Beach-Newport News	4.2	0.0
St. Louis, East St. Louis, Ill.*	3.8	1.1
Nassau and Suffolk, N.Y.	3.0	4.5
Boston	3.1	9.1
San Jose, Calif.	2.7	4.5
Fort Worth and Arlington, Tex.	2.1	2.4
Anaheim and Santa Ana, Calif.	2.1	3.7
Seattle*	1.7	3.9
Dallas	1.6	1.6
Denver*	1.5	7.8

*Cities with current or recent African American or Hispanic American mayors.
Source: U.S. Department of Defense.

report dangerously dilapidated and overutilized streets, tunnels, highways, water and sewer lines, wastewater treatment plants, landfills, gas mains, and other essential infrastructural resources.

A third observation about the generic level of fiscal policy is its frequent lack of racial sensitivity. For example, the Tax Reform Act of 1986 is income-based rather than racially based. The Earned Income Tax Credit (EITC) provides tax assistance to low-income working families to support their children. The assistance is provided without regard to family size, penalizing families, like those of blacks and Hispanics, that may be larger.[19] Gramm-Rudman-Hollings sequesters were not sensitive to their adverse impacts on predominantly black institutions like the District of Columbia government.[20] These institutions include populations with proportionately higher rates of participation in social services programs, higher rates of dependency on federal or local subsidies or grants, and African American–owned businesses dependent on government procurement because of their inability to penetrate private sector markets.

Consequently, an analysis of the generic level of fiscal dependency is essential for overall black economic and political development. It facilitates interface between black and other populations at the intersection of broad public use of public goods and services. Although the distributional effects on blacks of the generic level of fiscal dependency vary, its objectives may be found in broad statements about national, state, or local public needs.

In contrast to the generic level of dependency, the institutional level of black fiscal dependency more directly and specifically affects and targets African American–owned, –operated, or –influenced institutions. Black schools, hospitals, churches, fraternal organizations, professional and occupational organizations, and charitable and community-based organizations depend disproportionately on public finance. This level of dependency includes "targeted" or "earmarked" public programs aimed at black institutional development. Black institutions are supported in order to generate more black educational, career, employment, and business opportunities. Several examples of these programs illustrate the point. The Small Business Administration's (SBA's) Office of Minority and Small Business manages the minority set-aside program. Of more than four hundred thousand minority-owned firms, just over twenty-five hundred in 1990 (Table 10-2) participated in the sheltered

Table 10-2. Number of Minority Firms
Participating in SBA's 8(a) Program,
1985–1990

Year	Number of Participating Firms
1985	2,977
1986	3,188
1987	2,990
1988	2,946
1989	3,297
1990	2,500

Source: Small Business Administration, Office of
Minority and Small Business Files, 1989.

market reserved for them, which consists of working for various federal agencies. Through federal offices of "small and disadvantaged business utilization," the minority set-aside program has generated millions of dollars for minority firms that could not have been generated in the competitive marketplace.

Another example of a targeted federal program is reflected in the National Energy Act of 1978.[21] The Office of Minority Economic Initiative (OMEI), administratively housed within the Department of Energy (DOE), provides a comprehensive program of socioeconomic research on the impact of energy prices, supplies, and policies on minorities; assistance to minority institutions of higher learning on research and development opportunities; a Minority Energy Information Clearinghouse; and a Comprehensive Business and Community Development Program.[22] Moreover, OMEI (now the Office of Economic Impact and Diversity) collaborates with Argonne National Laboratory on the economics of household energy consumption and expenditures and with various black and Hispanic-oriented colleges and universities. Although small in both budget and staff (Table 10-3), OMEI is pivotal in both its monitoring of energy policies for minority impacts and bartering opportunities within DOE for nonwhite institutions. The monies reflected in these "minority programs" are minimal, but the impact on the financial well-being and development of the institutions they assist is substantial.

The last level of public financial dependency is quite direct. Black households are sensitive to minute changes in the financial disposition

Table 10-3. Budget of the Office of
Minority Economic Impact, U.S.
Department of Energy, 1985–1991

Year	Budget (millions of dollars)
1985	$2.4
1986	2.6
1987	2.8
1988	3.8
1989	4.1
1990	3.9*
1991	3.5

*Gramm-Rudman-Hollings sequester.
Source: U.S. Department of Energy, Office of
Minority Impact.

of either black institutions or generic fiscal policies. Taken together, Gramm-Rudman-Hollings, its 1987 amendments, the 1990 deficit reduction packages, and the Tax Reform Act of 1986 are fiscally regressive for black households. The minor benefits the Tax Reform Act provided to the poorest black households were eliminated by real-dollar budget-deficit reductions and changes in both generic and targeted federal programs.[23] Paradoxically, African Americans experience generic, institutional, and household dependency on public budgets while experiencing a perennial vulnerability to regressive taxation and revenue policies. Socioeconomic retrogression in inner-city and poor rural black communities are unfortunately correlated with declines in the levels of federal, state, and local spending in those communities.

The 1991 Budget Summit Agreement

The 1991 summit agreement had several key provisions. First, in contrast to the original summit proposals of September 1990, the final budget legislation adopted by Congress on October 27, 1990, was generally progressive. To reach a deficit reduction target of nearly five hundred billion dollars over the next five fiscal years, reductions in entitlement programs and defense spending were enacted together with increases in federal user fees for government services, various tax increases, and reductions of interest payments on the national debt.[24]

More than half the forty-one billion dollars in deficit reductions for fiscal year 1991 were to be generated by direct spending reductions. User fees for some federal services were to be increased by nearly a billion dollars, while entitlement programs were to be reduced by nearly ten billion dollars. These programs—mandated by a statute requiring the payment of benefits to any person or unit of government that meets the eligibility requirements established—are particularly significant to blacks.[25] Included among these entitlements are food stamps, AFDC, nutrition programs, housing programs, veteran's benefits, Social Security benefits, worker's compensation, and Medicare. Black participation in these programs ranges from 22.7 percent of Social Security beneficiaries to 53 percent of AFDC recipients.

Real dollar deficit reduction, while important to overall fiscal control, creates hardships for black beneficiaries in at least three ways: (1) the reductions occur during an economic recession and exacerbate existing crisis conditions, particularly in black urban neighborhoods and rural settlements; (2) reductions ignore accelerating needs in black communities, even when documented through means testing; and (3) reduction in net disposable income in the black community is a negative economic multiplier, that is, landlords, businesses, churches, local governments, and other institutions dependent on the purchasing power of blacks experience aggregate revenue reductions. These revenue reductions may significantly affect their continued capacity to provide goods and services to African Americans.[26]

However, President Clinton's fiscal plan seeks to balance the impact of spending reductions with some modicum of public investment, particularly in cities. In addition to reductions of eighty-eight billion dollars in defense spending over fiscal years 1994–98, freezes on civilian and military employee wages, controls on social entitlements, and health care cost reform, Clinton proposes increases in employment-generating public works programs, increases in Head Start, college assistance, and community infrastructure programs. Combined with his emphasis on small business support, the impact of these initiatives on African American households and institutions and, most importantly, on their dependency on fiscal policies remains to be seen.

Table 10-4. Percent Change in Federal Taxes, 1991

Income Level	Final Package	Summit Agreement	House	Senate
Less than $10,000	−2.0%*	7.6%	−1.3%	−0.0%*
$10,000–20,000	3.2	1.9	−1.6	−2.3
$20,000–30,000	1.8	3.3	1.0	2.7
$30,000–40,000	2.0	2.9	1.0	2.8
$40,000–50,000	2.0	2.9	0.8	2.8
$50,000–75,000	1.5	1.8	1.4	1.9
$75,000–100,000	2.1	2.1	1.5	2.5
$100,000–200,000	2.3	1.9	0.7	3.5
$200,000 and over	6.3	1.7	7.4	3.7

*Includes child care bill with approximately $12 billion in tax credits primarily for working families with children and incomes under $20,000.
Source: Center on Budget and Policy Priorities calculations, based on data from the Joint Committee on Taxation.

The Revenue Dimensions of Fiscal Policy

Almost eighteen billion dollars in deficit reduction in fiscal year 1991 was to be generated by revenue increases, principally tax increases. These provisions represented a reversal of the "no new taxes" pledge by candidate and then President George Bush. These tax provisions raised taxes for most income earners. Tax increases by income group are shown in Tables 10-4 and 10-5. Although those earning incomes of over two hundred thousand dollars experience a 6.3 percent increase in taxes and constitute 46 percent of the total of all income categories,

Table 10-5. Tax Increase Borne by Various Income Groups, 1991

Income Level	Final Package*	Summit Agreement	House	Senate
Under $50,000	19%	57%	11%	34%
$50,000–100,000	22	22	22	24
$100,000–200,000	13	10	5	18
$200,000 and over	46	11	63	24

*Includes effect of the tax provisions of the child care bill.
Source: Center on Budget and Policy Priorities calculations, based on data from the Joint Committee on Taxation.

tax increases are fairly well distributed among other income groups. Net increases in taxes over the next five years were projected to be $137 billion.

In addition, this tax program called for five major excise tax provisions, including a five cent a gallon rise in gasoline taxes; increases in cigarette taxes from sixteen cents a pack to twenty cents in 1991 and twenty-four cents in 1993; higher alcohol taxes; and greater airport and aviation excise taxes, including an increase from 8 percent to 10 percent in the tax on airline tickets. Moreover, the temporary 3 percent excise tax on telephone service now became permanent under the law.[27]

In contrast to the income tax provisions, these taxes are generally regressive. Given the documented tendency of poorer and larger African American families to use older, larger, less fuel-efficient vehicles, the gasoline tax will have a disproportionately higher impact on them and their Hispanic and white income counterparts.[28] "Sin taxes" on cigarettes and alcohol will also disproportionately and negatively affect blacks. Despite vigorous efforts to discourage smoking and drinking in black communities, smoking and drinking rates are still high. Health and moral issues aside, sales of cigarettes and alcohol support many small business establishments in those communities, such as liquor stores, small grocery stores, and franchises selling alcohol, cigarettes, and other commodities. Those businesses, and their customers, would be adversely affected by these taxes.

The positive structure of the revenue side of this enactment is best expressed in the Earned Income Tax Credit (EITC) (Table 10-6). The EITC is a tax credit available to working families with children that have incomes below twenty thousand dollars. For example, for the tax year 1990, the income cut-off is $20,264; for the tax year 1991, it was about $21,000. The credit is "refundable": If an eligible family earns too little income to owe federal income tax, or if the amount of the credit exceeded the income tax owed by the family, the Internal Revenue Service sends the family a refund.[29]

However, President Clinton's economic program included direct increases in income and corporate tax rates as part of this deficit reduction program. Families earning more than twenty thousand dollars a year are likely to feel the impact of the new tax program. The program includes a new tax on gasoline and home heating fuels and increases in the individual and corporate income tax rate from 31 to 36 percent as

Table 10-6. EITC Benefit Structure, 1993

Tax Year	Families with One Child		Families with Two or More Children		Supplemental Credit for Families with a Child under Age One	
	Credit Percentage	Maximum Benefit	Credit Percentage	Maximum Benefit	Credit Percentage	Maximum Benefit
1990	14% of first $6,810	$ 953	14% of first $6,810	$ 953	—	—
1991	16.7% of first $7,140	1,192	17.3% of first $7,140	1,235	5% of first $7,440	$357
1992	17.6% of first $7,440	1,309	18.4% of first $7,760	1,369	5% of first $7,760	372
1993	18.5% of first $7,760	1,436	19.5% of first $7,760	1,513	5% of first $7,760	388
1994	23% of first $8,090	1,861	25% of first $8,090	2,023	5% of first $8,090	405

Note: Dollar amounts for 1991 and beyond are based on current Congressional Budget Office estimates of inflation (using the consumer price index). Precise dollar amounts may vary when inflation estimates are revised.

Source: Center on Budget and Policy Priorities, 1990.

well as in various fees. Personal income taxes represent $126.3 billion of the $328.3 billion President Clinton hopes to raise between fiscal years 1994 and 2000. Consequently, the 43 African American members of Congress, the more than 500 African American state legislators, and more than 7,000 other elected officials will closely monitor the combined impacts of this revenue policy and the Clinton spending program on both African Americans and the nation as a whole.

Toward an Ethical Fiscal Strategy

Both the values implied in the struggle of African Americans seeking fiscal justice and the related criteria for good fiscal policies must be maintained. At a minimum, good fiscal policies include the principles of productivity, equity, and elasticity. A productive fiscal policy generates sufficient revenues to meet governmental needs on the tax side and makes investments in human needs, economic development, and defense on the spending side. If tax policies fail to generate adequate revenue, more public monies must be spent on borrowing, with a subsequent effect on interest rates and economic growth. An equitable fiscal policy is fair to both taxpayers and specific public constituencies benefiting from public expenditures. In tax policy, economists refer to two kinds of equity—horizontal and vertical. Horizontal equity means that taxpayers who have the same amount of income should be taxed at the same rate. Vertical equity implies that wealthier people should pay more taxes than poorer people. A related principle is that tax policies should be progressive: taxes increase in exact and direct proportion to increases in income. Regressive taxes impose greater burdens on taxpayers least able to pay.[30]

Although traditionally applied to taxes, notions of progressivity, proportionality, and regressivity also have a budgetary counterpart. Fiscal policies that cost the poor more and the rich less are inherently regressive. Generally, Gramm-Rudman-Hollins budget is regressive in its impacts on blacks and Hispanics because it uses budget bases that were already retrenched before 1985 as baselines of cuts mandated by their budget and because needs continue to rise as funding levels decline.

The principle of elasticity suggests that the fiscal system be flexible enough to address its revenue and spending needs regardless of changes in macroeconomic conditions. Taxes and spending help stabilize the economy as well as the society. As the Congressional Black Caucus, *The Quality of Life, Alternative 1991 Budget,* and the Center for Budget Priorities point out, when the Gramm-Rudman-Hollins budget and Tax Reform are considered together, they tend to be fiscally regressive for black and Hispanic households, individuals, and institutions. Strict enforcement of the 1990 deficit reduction provisions, particularly the EITC objectives, is generally progressive for low-income families and households.

Moreover, consideration of the ethics of good fiscal policy should include the reciprocal relationship between household and institutions. Institutions like charitable organizations; businesses; advocacy organizations; municipal, county, and state governments; trade unions; and others provide essential services to their members and constituencies. These institutions are profoundly affected by fiscal policies. If fiscal policies damage institutions, households suffer.

Thus, although President Clinton's original fiscal plan seriously attempted to address these ethical issues in the budget, congressional political priorities clearly restricted his efforts in this regard, particularly with respect to his urban investment strategy, his business investment tax credit program, and his proposed energy tax.[31] Neither African American institutions nor households will benefit directly from the program. Nor is it clear that they benefit from any generic short- or longer-term impacts of the program without targeted public investment, particularly in the human and physical infrastructure of inner cities. Wildavsky's reflections on the political implications of normative theories of budgeting are particularly appropriate to the analysis of the political implications of the federal budget to African Americans: "If a normative theory budgeting is to be more than an academic exercise, it must actually guide the making of governmental decisions."[32] Wildavsky indicates that the Congressional Black Caucus represents those who envisage "a high-tax, high service state geared to improving the lot of the worst off."[33] The key point is that a normative, ethical approach to budgetary politics is required not only in policy formulation and adoption but also in policy implementation.[34]

Summary and Conclusions

The disproportionately greater dependency on public sector funding by African Americans raises a key question for pluralist theory: Do the different experiences of political groups in the area of rights affect these groups' access to resources? This question raises two theoretical issues. First is the degree of institutionalized diversity of access maintained by various groups in the political system. If Group A historically influences public choices more than Group B, will government be biased or skewed in its policy-making orientations toward Group A? Will that policy bias institutionalize itself enough to require a greater effort by Group B to use its rights to influence resource allocation from government vis-à-vis Group A?

The second theoretical issue centers on the universe of resources available to government to satisfy the preferences of groups in the political system. Possible outcomes of competition between Groups A and B will be influenced by resources (taxes and other revenue sources) generated by Groups A and B into the political system and the total resources government has available, and is willing to allocate, to satisfy their preferences.

These two theoretical issues make the application of pluralist theory to African Americans and fiscal politics problematic. African Americans have been institutionalized into the political system at a different level than other groups. They begin and sustain competition with those groups for public resources at a much lower level. Specifically, blacks are substantially and uniquely dependent on government dollars for their most fundamental needs.

But other groups and institutions in the United States are becoming increasingly dependent on government budgets for their survival: groups such as farmers, the disabled, immigrants, the homeless, those who suffer from acquired immune deficiency syndrome (AIDS), and many others; institutions such as state and local governments, lending institutions, transitional foreign governments, and declining manufacturing industries. Consequently, African Americans are competing with an increasingly diverse constellation of budgetary needy while available budget dollars at all levels of government continue to shrink.

The anticipated availability of additional federal budget dollars through the peace dividend defense budget reductions was eclipsed by the country's participation in the Gulf War and longer-term uncertainty about the permanency of democratization in Eastern Europe and the former Soviet Union. An increasingly expensive banking and savings and loan crisis threatens to overwhelm other domestic budgetary and financial needs. Moreover, President Clinton struggles to address spiraling federal deficit and debt directly without further impeding the growth and vibrancy of the U.S. economy. Clearly, economic recession or slow economic growth signals greater demand for more beleaguered federal, state, and local dollars.

These developments combined to create clouded budgetary scenarios for blacks during the Reagan and Bush administrations. Equity issues raised by the controversy over President Bush's veto of civil rights legislation, an assistant secretary of education's thwarted efforts to prohibit the awarding of scholarships to nonwhite students, and exponential increases in the number of young black men killed and wounded in inner-city drug-related warfare generated serious political skepticism among African American politicians and political activists; this doubt was only recently and partially relieved by the guarded optimism associated with the presidency of Bill Clinton.

In response, the politics of federal deficit reduction made no effective response to any particular group or institutional need. In 1990, after a greatly flawed September budget summit, the final deficit reduction package combined eighteen billion dollars in new revenue generation and nearly twenty-three billion dollars in reductions in fiscal year 1991 to generate a forty-one billion dollar deficit reduction package. Major budgetary reductions were scheduled for social entitlement and defense programs as they are now in the Clinton fiscal plan. Blacks are inextricably intertwined in both spending areas. Reduced entitlements not only erode the value of food stamps, AFDC, Medicare, and other entitlement dollars but are nonresponsive to increases in need resulting from economic recession. Moreover, tax provisions, particularly the Earned Income Tax Credit, are generally progressive at the income tax level but generally regressive at the excise tax level. Consequently, the new fiscal package proposed by President Clinton, particularly the final compromise adopted in August 1993 (see Table 10-7), may be only partially responsive to the fiscal principles of productivity, equity, and elasticity.

The struggle to attain equity and financial choice for blacks, Hispanics, women, and the poor will escalate. Middle- and upper-income white Americans have as great, if not a greater, stake in the outcome of that struggle as do those who are needy. The ultimate financial beneficiaries of this struggle include white businesses, educational institutions, and public agencies, because those who are needy frequently patronize them.

Table 10-7. A Comparison of President Clinton's Original Budget Plan and the Final Congressional 1994 Compromise Budget

Clinton's Plan	Final Congressional Compromise
Income tax up to 36% for couples with incomes over $140,000 (individuals $115,000) and up to 39.6% for couples and individuals with incomes over $250,000	
Energy tax, including 7.5 cents a gallon on gasoline	No energy tax; 4.3 cents a gallon on gasoline
Tax to be levied on 85% of benefits paid to couples with incomes of over $32,000 and individuals with incomes of over $25,000	Same percentage of tax to be levied on benefits, but income thresholds raised to $44,000 and $34,000
Business investment tax credit	No business investment tax credit
$5.3 billion for enterprise zones	$3.5 billion for enterprise zones
$28.6 billion extra for earned income tax credit	$20.8 billion extra for earned income tax credit
Abolish honey subsidy	Keep honey subsidy
Reduce tax-deductible part of business meals from 85% to 50%	Same; plus a tax break for hotel and restaurant owners

Source: The Economist, August 7–13, 1993, p. 25.

Expanded use of formal policy and impact assessments should be used by black political and advocacy organizations to advance the needs of African Americans participating in legislative hearings, public rule-makings, regulatory processes, and judicial proceedings. All these points underscore the need for black policy advocates to acquire, utilize, and work carefully with their own and other experts. Policy expertise comes from many disciplines and is the major weapon of interests whose ethical preferences prevail in policy. The new fiscal imperatives are therefore best met by a new and more effective use of expertise.

Because of the budgetary constraints now faced by the federal, state, and local governments and the general malaise and morass of problems confronting lending institutions, blacks face, at best, an attitude of fiscal indifference from these governments despite the efforts of President

Clinton. Traditional policy approaches to the resolution of obstinate socioeconomic and institutional problems in black communities will be largely overlooked by fiscal decision-makers without linking those resolutions to visible financial and socioeconomic paybacks.

This analysis confirms the continuing dependency of many African American households and most African American institutions on public sector fiscal decisions. Moreover, the quality of life issues addressed by most African American politicians and political activists increasingly include an explicit reference to fiscal policy. As shown by the National Urban League's call for a fifty billion dollar urban Marshall Plan for cities with large, if not majority, African American populations, the Small and Minority Business Legal Defense and Education Fund demand for increases in government procurement opportunities for black business, and the demands of many civil rights groups for greater government investment in the education of African American children, African Americans are engaging the politics of fiscal policy more directly, more vigorously, and more explicitly. With four African American cabinet members presently serving in the new Clinton administration, forty-three African American members of Congress, and nearly eight thousand African American elected officials at all levels of government, how much impact the new black fiscal politics will actually exert on the context, content, and direction of national, state, and local fiscal policy remains to be seen. Indeed, pluralist theorists can measure the extent to which African Americans are a viable competing force in U.S. politics by their efficacy in achieving fiscal policy preferences in an increasingly complex public policy process.

Notes

1. Charles V. Hamilton, "The Welfare of Black Americans," *Political Science Quarterly* 101 (June 1968): 253.

2. John L. Mikesell, *Fiscal Administration: Analysis and Applications for the Public Sector*, 2nd ed. (Chicago: Dorsey Press, 1986), ix.

3. Frank Sacton, "Financing Public Programs under Fiscal Constraint," in *Managing Programs: Balancing Politics, Administration, and Public Needs*, ed. Robert E. Cleary and Nicholas Henry (San Francisco: Jossey-Bass Publishers, 1989), 147–166.

4. Lenneal J. Henderson, Jr., "Budget and Tax Strategy: Implications for

Blacks," in *The State of Black America 1990,* ed. Janet Dewart (New York: National Urban League, 1990), 53–54.

5. John W. Wright, ed., *The Universal Almanac 1991* (New York: Universal Press Syndicated Company, 1991), v–vi.

6. Charles H. Levine, ed., *Managing Fiscal Stress: The Crisis in the Public Sector* (Chatham, N.J.: Chatham House, 1980), 4. See also Georgia A. Persons, "Blacks in State and Local Government: Progress and Constraints," in *The State of Black America 1987,* ed. Janet Dewart (New York: National Urban League, 1987), 167–192; Persons, "Reflections on Mayoral Leadership: The Impact of Changing Issues and Changing Times," *Phylon* 41 (September 1985): 205–18; and Hanes Walton, *Black Politics: A Theoretical and Structural Analysis* (Philadelphia: J. B. Lippincott, 1972).

7. Henderson, "Budget and Tax Strategy," 55.

8. Congressional Black Caucus, *The Quality of Life, Fiscal 1991 Alternative Budget* (Washington, D.C.: Government Printing Office, 1989), 1.

9. Children's Defense Fund, *Children's Defense Fund Budget, Fiscal Year 1989* (Washington, D.C.: Government Printing Office, 1989), 12.

10. For example, see Congressional Task Force on Federal Excise Taxes, *Analyzing the Possible Impact of Federal Excise Taxes on the Poor, Including Blacks and Other Minorities* (Washington, D.C.: Voter Education and Registration Action, July 1987).

11. *State of Small Business, 1989* (Washington, D.C.: Government Printing Office, 1989).

12. Persons, "Blacks in State and Local Government," and "Reflections on Mayoral Leadership."

13. Hanes Walton, *When the Marching Stopped: The Politics of Civil Rights Regulatory Agencies* (Albany: State University of New York Press, 1988), 59.

14. 488 U.S. 469 (1989).

15. Lenneal J. Henderson, "The Impact of Military Base Shutdowns," *Black Scholar* (September 1974): 56–58.

16. "The Peach Economy: How Defense Cuts Will Fuel America's Long-Term Prosperity," *Business Week,* December 11, 1989, 51.

17. Ibid., 52.

18. Marshall Kaplan, "Infrastructure Policy: Repetitive Studies, Uneven Response, Next Steps," *Urban Affairs Quarterly* 25 (March 1990): 371–88.

19. Children's Defense Fund, *Children's Defense Fund Budget, Fiscal Year 1989,* 12.

20. District of Columbia, *Operating Budget, 1990 Fiscal Year.* Gramm-Rudman-Hollings is the informal title for the Balanced Budget and Emergency Deficit Control Act of 1985, which mandated steadily decreasing national government annual budget deficits through fiscal year (FY) 1991, when the deficit was supposed to reach zero. The legislation was amended in 1987 to (among other things) postpone the target date for a zero deficit to FY 1993. It was

amended further in 1990, in effect, by the five-year deficit reduction agreement reached by President Bush and the Congress.

21. 42 U.S.C. 7141, Section 641.

22. U.S. Department of Energy, *Functional Interrelationships of the Office of Minority Economic Impact* (Washington, D.C.: U.S. Government Printing Office, 1989).

23. William W. Ellis and Darlene Calbert, *Blacks and Tax Reform 1985–86* (Washington, D.C.: Congressional Research Service, 1986).

24. Paul Leonard and Robert Greenstein, *One Step Forward: The Deficit Reduction Package of 1990* (Washington, D.C.: Center on Budget Priorities, 1990), 5.

25. Mikesell, *Fiscal Administration,* 487.

26. Lenneal J. Henderson, Jr., "Fiscal Strategy, Public Policy and the Social Agenda," *Urban League Review* 13 (summer 1989–winter 1989–90): 9–22.

27. Ibid.

28. Leonard and Greenstein, *One Step Forward,* 12–14.

29. Ibid., 16–17.

30. Henderson, "Blacks, Budgets and Taxes," 84.

31. "Without Sacrifice," *Economist,* 328, no. 7823 (1993): 25–26.

32. Aaron Wildavsky, "Political Implications of Budget Reform," *Public Administration Review* 21 (January–February 1961).

33. Aaron Wildavsky, "Political Implications of Budget Reform: A Retrospective," *Public Administration Review* 52 (November–December 1992): 594–99.

34. Thomas Dye, *Understanding Public Policy* (Englewood Cliffs, N.J.: Prentice Hall, 1992), 241–67.

■ *Part V*

Summary and Conclusions

■ Chapter 11

The State of Black Politics in the United States and Implications for the Future

Huey L. Perry and Wayne Parent

The starting point for this book was the full-scale reemergence of southern blacks into the political process after the successful civil rights legislation by the federal government in the mid-1960s. This reemergence substantially affected not only southern politics but American politics as well. The addition of approximately four million new black voters to the political arena between 1965 and 1975 affected both the style and substance of southern politics, black politics, and American politics. Black political participation over the last three decades has increased not only in the South but also in other regions of the country where blacks reside in large numbers. This book takes stock of black politics in the United States in the wake of this substantially increased black political participation.

Many important conclusions are reached in this book. Paul Stekler and Wayne Parent, confirming the findings of a recent major work,[1] indicate that race remains one of the principal social cleavages in American society. They also conclude that while other groups that traditionally supported the Democratic party since the New Deal period have ceased to accord majority support to the party, blacks have remained steadfast in their strong support. This point is also made by Henry Sirgo in Chapter 5. Sirgo, like Stekler and Parent, finds that blacks' support of the Democratic party is based on rational self-interest as Democrats have been more supportive of black interests than have Republicans.

Stekler and Parent also point out that the overwhelming majority of black elected officials have been elected in majority black districts and jurisdictions and few such districts and jurisdictions remain without elected black representation; therefore if substantial numbers of additional blacks are to be elected in the future, they will be elected in nonmajority black districts and thus will have to appeal to racial coalitions as their support base. The election of L. Douglas Wilder as governor of Virginia in 1989, David Dinkins as mayor of New York in 1990, and Carol Moseley Braun as senator from Illinois in 1992, among others, are suggestive of the possibilities inherent in Stekler and Parent's observation.[2]

Michael Combs's analysis in Chapter 8 shows that during the 1950s and 1960s blacks received favorable rulings from the Supreme Court in education, voting rights, employment, and housing. Within this context, Combs further reveals that the Court provided blacks more benefits in policy areas that are regional in nature (education and voting) than in those that are national in scope (employment and housing). Before the 1960s, as several authors note, presidents and Congress seldom responded affirmatively to the requests of blacks and their supporters for racial advancement. This was especially true of Franklin Roosevelt and John Kennedy, who feared that a strong push to advance black civil rights interests would alienate southern whites who held powerful positions in Congress and would thus jeopardize their major policy initiatives. Despite their vaunted record as liberal presidents, Roosevelt never challenged the system of racial segregation in the South and Kennedy did so only during the last year of his presidency.

Because of the Supreme Court's support of blacks' interests during the 1950s and 1960s, studies examining racial attitudes on the performance of government show that blacks are much more positive in their evaluation of the Court than are whites.[3] A full appreciation of the Supreme Court's decisions vis-à-vis blacks' interests in the twentieth century, however, would have to counterbalance its supportive record during the 1950s and 1960s with the seeming hostility of the current Rehnquist Court. The overall trend of its rulings has been uneven regarding black interests: indifferent in the first third of the century, supportive in the middle third, and seemingly hostile in the last third.

Several chapters indicate the substantial increase in black political participation in the South since the 1950s and the pivotal role that the 1965 Voting Rights Act played in bringing about that increase. Significantly, the registration rates of blacks and whites in the South are approximately the same and have been so since 1986. In sum, substantial black political participation in the South has become routinized and has reached a stage of near equivalency with whites in the region.

Sirgo's analysis of the changing patterns of Democratic and Republican support of blacks' interests during the mid-twentieth century supports an argument effectively made by Edward Carmines and James Stimson about the racial transformation of American politics beginning with the presidential election of 1964.[4] Between 1944 and 1964, the two parties were fairly equal in their support of civil rights. However, after the presidential election of 1964, the two parties began to take opposite stances on civil rights issues and to reinforce racial differences rather than cross-cut on racial issues. Sirgo and Perry, Ambeau, and McBride indicate that presidential support of black issues generally has been most significant when black support provided the critical margin of victory, as in the presidential elections of 1948, 1976, and 1992. Sirgo further notes that in general these factors have resulted in blacks' being more supportive of the Democratic party than the Republican party in presidential elections and Democratic presidents more supportive of black issues than Republican presidents. However, this trend has not boded well for blacks, given the domination of the presidency by the Republican party since 1952.

One of the most important recent developments in the interface of black political participation, political parties, and presidential elections is the historic presidential candidacies of Jesse Jackson in 1984 and 1988. In Chapter 4, Mfanya D. Tryman's finding that Jackson's Democratic primary campaigns in 1984 and 1988 were beset by racial overtones in the Democratic party leadership's treatment of Jackson underscores the point made by Stekler and Parent about race as a major social cleavage in American society.

Richard Champagne and Leroy Rieselbach, in Chapter 7, posit that specific institutional arrangements in Congress are increasingly compelling the Congressional Black Caucus to resolve the question of how best to achieve racial advancement in favor of ordinary legislative politics rather than acting above the fray of normal legislative politics. Dianne Pinderhughes, in Chapter 9, applies these two approaches to racial advancement through the policy process to her analysis of interest group participation in the effort to renew and expand national voting rights legislation in 1982. The challenge for groups seeking racial reform, Pinderhughes writes, is whether to accept the existing institutional values, to bring the external norms from the social movement for change with them into the policy-making environment, or to challenge and seek to reform those existing values. Congressional norms require the acceptance of bargaining, in which the group does not necessarily attain all its goals, or does not take a hardened stand on issues, but attempts to win some portion of its values, even if compromised, from the legislative environment. In policy-making it makes sense to accept a compromise because by doing so the group achieves at least part of its objectives. That legislative compromise then becomes the floor on which the group can seek to increase the benefits it receives. Champagne and Rieselbach indicate that as Congressional Black Caucus members have risen in the seniority system to assume major positions of power, they have increasingly been drawn into the matrix of the bargaining, compromising, coalition-building politics that generally characterizes congressional behavior.

The increased influence of Congressional Black Caucus members in congressional politics is best represented by the meteoric rise of former Representative William Gray (D-Pa.) in the hierarchy in the House of Representatives. Gray's meteoric rise to the chairmanship of the Budget Committee and subsequently to the position of majority whip in the House Democratic leadership is one of the most amazing success stories in the postreform House. Perhaps the most important contribution of the Champagne and Rieselbach chapter is its demonstration of the importance of black elected officials and their full participation in the reward structure of the particular governmental body to which they are elected as a means of representing the interests of their constituents.

In Chapter 9, Pinderhughes provides an insightful analysis of how the constellation of interest groups comprising the civil rights coalition successfully lobbied for the 1982 renewal and expansion of the Civil Rights Acts of 1965 and how lobbying for the legislation exacerbated some of the tensions within the coalition. Pinderhughes concludes that the addition of a professional group of litigators—that is, lawyers who testify in voting rights cases—persuaded the traditional members of the civil rights coalition to seek to amend section 2 in order to overturn the intent standard imposed by *Mobile v. Bolden* [5] rather than seeking only a straightforward extension of the act. The specification of the effects standard to determine discrimination in voting rights cases by the 1982 legislation was a major victory for the civil rights community. Lenneal Henderson, in Chapter 10, concludes that in general major national fiscal policies have a largely negative macroeconomic impact on the black community. Marginal declines in income resulting from budget retrenchment, tax and expenditure limitations at the state and local level, and tax reform legislation during the Reagan-Bush years had unfavorable consequences for the development of social, economic, and political resources in the black political economy. However, the tax reform component of President Bill Clinton's 1993 budget package is likely to provide more favorable consequences for blacks. This is especially true of the black working poor who will benefit from the earned income tax credit that is part of the Clinton administration tax reform. The earned income tax credit will eliminate poverty among the working poor by guaranteeing them tax credits to increase their income to above the poverty level.

Black politics in the United States is at an important point in its development. The majority of the chapters in this volume portray a positive assessment of the growth of black political participation in the last three decades and of the impact of that increased participation. Of course, black politics face some major problems. One national problem is that the contemporary patterns of support for the two major parties has led both parties to take a cool attitude toward the black electorate in presidential elections. Reduced black support for the 1988 Democratic presidential nominee and efforts by the Republican party to recruit more blacks into the party might alter the relationship between black Americans and the two national political parties. However, Republicans struggled to keep those gains in 1992, and their defeat in the 1992 presidential election shows the need for dramatic gestures in 1994 and 1996 if they are to change that relationship.

Another problem is the uneasy relationship between black political leaders and President Clinton. Although Clinton appointed more blacks to his cabinet than has any other president in U.S. history, many black political leaders fear that Clinton may be too inclined to favor the interests of southern white conservatives at the expense of blacks. This concern came to the fore in Clinton's nomination of Lani Guinier, a veteran voting rights litigator, to be assistant attorney general for civil rights. Guinier's nomination drew vocal criticism from conservatives who believed Guinier would be too forceful in her advocacy of voting rights laws. Clinton withdrew her nomination in response to the extreme negative reaction—a decision that infuriated black political leaders and organizations, most vocally expressed by the Congressional Black Caucus. The forty members of the Congressional Black Caucus, whose membership had almost doubled as a result of redistricting and the very type of lawsuits that Guinier had filed as a voting rights litigator, had strongly supported Guinier's nomination and felt betrayed that Clinton had not consulted them before withdrawing the nomination. More fundamentally, the caucus members believed that Clinton should not have withdrawn the nomination, despite the increasing opposition to her confirmation in the Senate; rather, they thought that the president should have allowed Guinier to defend her views on voting rights as part of the confirmation process, just as President Ronald Reagan had allowed Robert Bork's confirmation hearings on his nomination to the Supreme Court to be held even after Reagan knew that the nomination was in trouble.

President Clinton's withdrawal of the Guinier nomination caused a further deterioration of the strained relationship between the president and the caucus, which was initially fueled by the caucus's perception that in his effort to reduce the deficit Clinton favored monied interests at the expense of entitlement programs benefiting the poor. The caucus felt that Clinton's actions in this regard violated their perception of his electoral mandate to operate government with a greater sense of fairness to low-income and disadvantaged groups than had been shown by the administrations of Reagan and George Bush. In clear defiance of the respect traditionally accorded a president, the Congressional Black Caucus refused an invitation to meet with President Clinton on June 10, 1993. This action was taken by the caucus to reflect disappointment in President Clinton with respect to his alleged caving in to conservative preferences on the budget deficit issue and on the withdrawal of the Guinier nomination. The caucus also refused the invitation because the organization believed that the invitation had been extended for symbolic reasons that benefit only President Clinton, not to discuss substantive policy issues beneficial to CBC constituents.

In general, the political process evinces significant black achievement over the last three decades. Present trends indicate that the future of black politics in the United States is positive and that the political process still presents the most realistic hope for black socioeconomic progress. Future black politics is likely to be characterized by a duality consisting of traditional black politics and deracialized black politics. Traditional black politicians will continue to be elected from majority black districts and jurisdictions, whereas deracialized black politicians will be elected from majority white districts. This duality in black politics may well present problems for black unity in the political process, as traditional black politicians and their supporters may cast aspersions on deracialized black politicians and their supporters. Another potential problem in this regard is whether deracialized black politicians will govern in a manner acceptable to their black constituents. These two burning concerns about the future of black politics suggest worthwhile topics for future research.

Notes

1. Edward G. Carmines and James Stimson, *Issue Evolution: The Racial Transformation of American Politics* (Princeton: Princeton University Press, 1989).

2. For a brief analysis of the major black electoral victories in 1989 and 1990 see Huey L. Perry, "Black Electoral Success in 1989," Symposium, *PS: Political Science and Politics* 23 (June 1990): 141–62. For a fuller analysis of the major black electoral victories in 1989 and 1990, see Huey L. Perry, "Exploring the Meaning and Implications of Deracialization in African-American Urban Politics," Mini-Symposium, *Urban Affairs Quarterly* 27, no. 2 (December 1991).

3. See, for example, Herbert Hirsch and Lewis Donohew, "A Note on Negro-White Differences in Attitudes Toward the Supreme Court," *Social Science Quarterly* 49 (December 1968): 562.

4. Carmines and Stimson, *The Racial Transformation of American Politics.*

5. 446 U.S. 55 (1980).

★ Bibliography

Abramson, Paul R., and William Claggett. "The Quality of Record Keeping and Racial Differences in Validated Turnout." *Journal of Politics* 54 (August 1992): 871–78.

Adams, Bruce, and Kathryn Kavanagh Baran. *Promise and Performance: Carter Builds a New Administration.* Lexington, Mass.: Lexington Books, 1979.

Amaker, Norman C. *Civil Rights and the Reagan Administration.* Washington, D.C.: Urban Institute Press, 1988.

American Civil Liberties Union. *Civil Liberties in Reagan's America.* New York: author, 1982.

Anderson, James E. "A Revised View of the Johnson Cabinet." *Journal of Politics* 48 (August 1986): 529–37.

Arieff, Irwin B. "House Continues Dispute on Committee Assignments." *Congressional Quarterly Weekly Report* 39 (1981): 197.

Arterton, F. Christopher. "Campaign '92: Strategies and Tactics of the Candidates." In *The Election of 1992*, edited by Gerald M. Pomper. Chatham, N.J.: Chatham House, 1993.

Atlanta Journal and Constitution, March 13, 1988, 2C.

Axelrod, Robert. *Conflict of Interest: A Theory of Divergent Goals with Applications to Politics.* Chicago: Markham Publishing Company, 1970.

———. "Where the Votes Come from: An Analysis of Electoral Coalitions, 1952–1968." *American Political Science Review* 66 (March 1970): 11–20.

Baker, Ross. "Sorting Out and Suiting Up: The Presidential Nomination," In *The Election of 1992*, edited by Gerald Pomper. Chatham, N.J.: Chatham House, 1993.

Barker, Lucius J. "Black Americans and the Burger Court: Implications for the Political System." *Washington University Law Quarterly* (fall 1973): 747.

———. "Ronald Reagan, Jesse Jackson, and the 1984 Presidential Election:

The Continuing American Dilemma of Race." In *The New Black Politics: The Search for Political Power,* 2nd ed., edited by Michael B. Preston, Lenneal J. Henderson, Jr., and Paul L. Puryear. New York: Longman, 1987.

———. *Our Time Has Come.* Urbana: University of Illinois Press, 1988.

Barker, Lucius J., and Mack H. Jones. *African Americans and the American Political System.* Englewood Cliffs, N.J.: Prentice Hall, 1994.

Barker, Lucius J., and Jesse McCorry. *Black Americans and the Political System.* Cambridge, Mass.: Winthrop Publishers, 1976.

Barker, Twiley W., and Michael W. Combs. "Civil Rights and Liberties in the First Term of the Rehnquist Court: The Quest for Doctrines and Votes." *National Political Science Review* 1 (1989): 31.

Barnett, Marguerite Ross. "The Congressional Black Caucus." In *Congress Against the President,* edited by Harvey C. Mansfield, 34–50. New York: Praeger, 1975.

———. "The Congressional Black Caucus: Illusions and Realities of Power." In *The New Black Politics: The Search For Political Power,* edited by Michael B. Preston, Lenneal J. Henderson, Jr. and Paul Puryear, 28–54. New York: Longman, 1982.

Barone, Michael, and Grant Ujifusa. *The Almanac of American Politics 1992.* Washington, D.C.: National Journal, 1991.

Bass, Jack, and Walter DeVries. *The Transformation of Southern Politics.* New York: New American Library, 1977.

Batt, William L., Jr., to Gael Sullivan. "Negro Vote." April 20, 1948. Box 20. Papers of Clark M. Clifford. Harry S. Truman Presidential Library, Independence, Missouri.

Berg, John C. "The Congressional Black Caucus Budget and the Representation of Black Americans." Paper presented to the annual meeting of the Midwest Political Science Association, Chicago, April 1987.

Boyd, Thomas, and Stephen J. Markman. "The 1982 Amendments to the Voting Rights Act: A Legislative History." *Washington and Lee Law Review* 40 (fall 1983): 1347–1428.

Broder, David S. ". . . and Healthy Signs of Change." *Louisville Courier Journal,* April 12, 1989, A11.

Brown, Michael K., and Steven P. Erie. "Blacks and the Legacy of the Great Society: The Economic and Political Impact of Federal Social Policy." *Public Policy* 29 (summer 1981): 299–330.

Brownell, Herbert. "Eisenhower's Civil Rights Program: A Personal Assessment." *Presidential Studies Quarterly* 21 (spring 1991): 235–42.

Browning, Graeme. "Strength in Numbers for Hill Group?" *National Journal* 24 (1992): 2732–33.

Brownstein, Ronald. "Kemp and Poverty." *National Journal* 42 (1986): 2531.

Thomas C. Buchanan to Philip Mathews. June 24, 1948. Box 1. Papers of

William Boyle, Jr. Harry S. Truman Presidential Library, Independence, Missouri.

Burbridge, Lynn. "Changes in Equal Employment Enforcement: What Enforcement Statistics Tell Us." *Review of Black Political Economy* (summer 1986): 76–77.

———. *The Impact of Changes in Policy on Federal Equal Employment Opportunity Effort*. Washington, D.C.: Urban Institute, Discussion Paper, 1984.

Burk, Robert Frederick. *The Eisenhower Administration and Black Civil Rights*. Knoxville: University of Tennessee Press, 1984.

Calmes, Jacqueline. "Aspin Makes Comeback at Armed Services." *Congressional Quarterly Weekly Report* 45 (1987): 139–42.

———. "Aspin Ousted as Armed Services Chairman." *Congressional Quarterly Weekly Report* 45 (1987): 83–85.

———. "Social Security Issue Splits Each Party . . . As House Opposes Senate on Budget." *Congressional Quarterly Weekly Report* 43 (1985): 1468–69.

Campbell, Angus, Philip E. Converse, Warren E. Miller, and Donald E. Stokes. *The American Voter*. New York: John Wiley, 1960.

Campbell, Bruce A. "Patterns of Change in the Partisan Loyalties of Native Southerners." *Journal of Politics* 39 (August 1977): 730–61.

Caplan, Lincoln. *The Tenth Justice*. New York: Alfred A. Knopf, 1987.

Carmines, Edward G., and James A. Stimson. "The Racial Reorientation of American Politics." In *The Electorate Reconsidered,* edited by John C. Pierce and John L. Sullivan. Beverly Hills: Sage Publications, 1980.

———. "Racial Issues and the Structure of Mass Belief Systems." *Journal of Politics* 44 (February 1982): 2–20.

———. *Issue Evolution: Race and the Transformation of American Politics*. Princeton: Princeton University Press, 1989.

Casper, Jonathan D. "The Supreme Court and National Policy Making." *American Political Science Review* 70 (March 1976): 50–63.

Casselman, Bill, to Bob Hartmann. August 8, 1974. Folder FG, Executive 90 (8/9/74–3/31/75). White House Central Files. Gerald R. Ford Library, Ann Arbor, Michigan.

Cavanaugh, Thomas, and Lorn Foster. *Jesse Jackson's Campaign: The Primaries and the Caucuses,* Number 2. Washington, D.C.: Joint Center of Political Studies, 1984.

Chertkoff, Jerome M. "Sociopsychological Theories and Research on Coalition Formation." In *The Study of Coalition Behavior, Theoretical Perspectives and Cases From Four Continents,* edited by Sven Groennings, E. W. Kelley, and Michael Leiserson. New York: Holt, Rinehart and Winston, 1970.

Children's Defense Fund. *Children's Defense Fund Budget, Fiscal Year 1989*. Washington, D.C.: U.S. Government Printing Office, 1989.

Clifford, Clark M., to the President (Harry S. Truman). November 17, 1948.

Box 21. Papers of Clark M. Clifford. Harry S. Truman Presidential Library, Independence, Missouri.

Cohen, Richard E. "What a Difference a Year—and an Election—Make in Producing a Budget." *National Journal* 15 (1983): 696–99.

———. "Moving to the Front." *National Journal* 18 (1986): 989–92.

———. "A New Breed for Black Caucus." *National Journal* 39 (1987): 2432–33.

———. "Moving Up the Ladder." *National Journal* 50 (1988): 3158.

———. "Getting Back to the Party's Business." *National Journal* 21 (1989): 1594.

———. "Gray's Game: Playing Democratic Ball." *National Journal* 22 (1990): 30.

Cohodas, Nadine. "Black House Members Striving for Influence." *Congressional Quarterly Weekly Report* 43 (1985): 675–81.

———. "By Wide Margin, House Impeaches Hastings," *Congressional Quarterly Weekly Report* 46 (1988): 2205.

———. "Judiciary Committee Votes to Impeach Hastings." *Congressional Quarterly Weekly Report* 46 (1988): 2100–2101.

Coleman, Milton. "Gains in the House Hailed as a 'Coming of Age' for Black Lawmakers." *Louisville Courier-Journal,* January 11, 1985, A15.

Combs, Michael W. "Courts, Minorities, and the Dominant Coalition: Racial Policies in Modern America." Ph.D. dissertation, Washington University, 1973.

———. "The Supreme Court as a National Policy Maker: A Historical-Legal Analysis of School Desegregation." *Southern University Law Review* 8 (spring 1982): 221–27.

———. "The Policy-Making Role of Courts of Appeals in Northern School Desegregation: Ambiguity and Judicial Policy-Making." *Western Political Quarterly* 35 (September 1982): 359.

Congressional Black Caucus. *The Quality of Life, Fiscal 1991 Alternative Budget.* Washington, D.C.: U.S. Government Printing Office, 1989.

Congressional Quarterly. *Congressional Districts in the 1980s.* Washington, D.C.: author, 1983.

Congressional Task Force on Federal Excise Taxes. *Analyzing the Possible Impact of Federal Excise Taxes on the Poor, Including Blacks and Other Minorities.* Washington, D.C.: Voter Education and Registration Action, July 1987.

Conover, Pamela Johnston, and Virginia Sapiro. "Gender, Feminist Consciousness and War." *American Journal of Political Science* 37 (November 1993): 1079–99.

Costain, W. Douglas, and Ann N. Costain. "Interest Groups as Policy Aggregators in the Legislative Process." *Polity* 14 (winter 1981): 249–72.

Curran, Tim. "Some Surprising Guests Turn Out on the Stump." *Roll Call* 36, no. 18 (1990): 1, 10.

Dahl, Robert A. "Decision-Making in a Democracy: The Supreme Court as a National PolicyMaker." *Journal of Public Law* 6 (fall 1957): 279.

———. *Who Governs? Democracy and Power in an American City.* New Haven: Yale University Press, 1961.

———. *Dilemmas of Pluralist Democracy.* New Haven: Yale University Press, 1982.

Daniels, Jonathan. *The Man of Independence.* Philadelphia: J. B. Lippincott, 1950.

Davidson, Chandler. *Biracial Politics.* Baton Rouge: Louisiana State University Press, 1972.

———. *Minority Vote Dilution.* Washington, D.C.: Howard University Press, 1984.

———. "Minority Vote Dilution: An Overview." In *Minority Vote Dilution*, edited by Chandler Davidson. Washington, D.C.: Howard University Press, 1984.

"Democratic Platform." 1953. Harry S. Truman Presidential Library.

"Despite Statehood Bill's Defeat, D.C. Advocates Claim Victory." *Congressional Quarterly Weekly Report* 15 (1993).

District of Columbia. *Operating Budget, 1990 Fiscal Year.*

Dodd, Lawrence C. "Coalition Building by Party Leaders: A Case Study of House Democrats." *Congress & the Presidency* 10 (1983): 147–68.

Donovan, Beth. "The Wilder-Dinkins 'Formula' Familiar to Blacks in House." *Congressional Quarterly Weekly Report* 47 (1989): 3099–101.

Dowd, Maureen. "Black Caucus, Back in the White House, Uses Straight Talk." *New York Times,* May 24, 1989, A29.

Duke, Lois Lovelace. "Racial Bias in Newsmaking." Paper presented at the annual meeting of the Southern Political Science Association, Memphis, 1989.

Duncan, Phil. "Quietly Assertive Freshmen Arrive for Orientation." *Congressional Quarterly Weekly Report* 50 (1992): 3746–47.

Dye, Thomas. *Understanding Public Policy,* 7th ed. Englewood Cliffs, N.J.: Prentice Hall, 1992.

Edelman, Murray. "Symbols and Political Quiescence." *American Political Science Review* 54 (September 1960): 695–704.

———. *The Symbolic Uses of Politics.* Urbana: University of Illinois Press, 1964.

Edsall, Thomas Byrne, and Mary D. Edsall. *Chain Reaction.* New York: W. W. Norton, 1992.

Edwards, George C., III, and Stephen J. Wayne. *Presidential Leadership.* New York: St. Martin's Press, 1990.

Ehrenhalt, Alan. "New Black Leaders Emerging in Congress." *Congressional Quarterly Weekly Report* 41 (1983): 1643.

Ellis, William W., and Darlene Calbert. *Blacks and Tax Reform 1985–86.* Washington, D.C.: Congressional Research Service, 1986.

Ely, John Hart. *Democracy and Distrust: A Theory of Judicial Review.* Cambridge: Harvard University Press, 1980.

Fears, D. D. "A Time of Testing for Black Caucus as Its Members Rise to Power in House." *National Journal* 17 (1985): 909–11.

Felton, John. "House Accepts Senate's Anti-Apartheid Bill." *Congressional Quarterly Weekly Report* 44 (1986): 2119–20.

———. "Savimbi: Selling Washington on Angola's War." *Congressional Quarterly Weekly Report* 44 (1986): 264–65.

———. "All But a Favored Few Feel Pain of Aid Cutbacks." *Congressional Quarterly Weekly Report* 46 (1988): 492–97.

———. "Funds for Panama, Nicaragua Move Down Hill Runway." *Congressional Quarterly Weekly Report* 48 (1990): 1007–10.

Fessler, Pamela. "New House Budget Chief Gray Weighs Local, National Claims." *Congressional Quarterly Weekly Report* 43 (1985): 185–87.

Frantzich, Stephen E. *Political Parties in the Technological Age.* New York: Longman, 1989.

Friedel, Frank. "The New Deal, Southern Agriculture, and Economic Change." In *New Deal and the South,* edited by James C. Cobb and Michael C. Namorato. Jackson: University Press of Mississippi, 1984.

Gamson, William A. "Experimental Studies of Coalition Formation." In *Advanced Experimental Social Psychology,* edited by Leonard Berkowitz. New York: Academic Press, 1964.

Garrow, David J. *Protest at Selma: Martin Luther King Jr. and the Voting Rights Act of 1965.* New Haven: Yale University Press, 1978.

———. *Bearing the Cross.* New York: Vintage Books, 1988.

Gettinger, Stephen. "Bill Gray Builds a Political Career on Paradox." *Congressional Quarterly Weekly Report* 44 (1986): 1739–43.

Gibson, James L., and Gregory A. Caldeira. "Blacks and the United States Supreme Court: Models of Diffuse Support. *Journal of Politics* 54 (November 1992): 1120–45.

Goldman, Sheldon. "Reagan's Judicial Appointments at Mid-Term: Shaping the Bench in His Own Image" *Judicature* 66 (March 1983): 339, 345.

Goldman, Sheldon, and Thomas P. Jahnige. *The Federal Courts as a Political System.* New York: Harper & Row, 1985.

"The G.O.P.: Wising Up About Race?" *New York Times,* January 23, 1994.

Graham, Otis L., Jr., and Maghan Robinson Wander, eds. *Franklin D. Roosevelt: His Life and Times.* Boston: G. K. Hall, 1985.

Granat, Diane. "Representative Gray: Junior Conferee at Center Stage." *Congressional Quarterly Weekly Report* 41 (April 1983): 1271.

Greenberg, Edward S. "Introduction: Models of the Political Process: Implications for the Black Community." In *Black Politics: The Inevitability of Con-*

flict, edited by Edward S. Greenberg, Neal Milner, and David J. Olson. New York: Oxford University Press, 1971.

Greenstein, Fred I. *The Hidden-Hand Presidency: Eisenhower as Leader.* New York: Basic Books, 1982.

Greenstone, J. David, and Paul E. Peterson. *Race and Authority in Urban Politics: Community Participation and the War on Poverty.* Chicago: University of Chicago Press, 1973.

Grubbs, Donald H. *Cry from the Cotton.* Chapel Hill: University of North Carolina Press, 1971.

Gurin, Patricia, Shirley Hatchett, and James S. Jackson. *Hope and Independence: Blacks' Response to Electoral and Party Politics.* New York: Russell Sage Foundation, 1989.

Haeberle, Steven H. "Regional Primary or Multiple Campaigns in a Region: Lessons from Super Tuesday 1988." Paper presented at the annual meeting of the Southern Political Science Association Meeting, Atlanta, November 3–5, 1988.

Hamilton, Charles V. "The Welfare of Black Americans." *Political Science Quarterly* 101 (June 1968): 253.

———. "Blacks and the Crisis in Political Participation." *Public Interest* 34 (1974): 188–210.

Hammond, Susan Webb, Daniel P. Mulhollan, and Arthur G. Stevens. "Informal Congressional Caucuses and Agenda Setting." *Western Political Quarterly* 38 (1985): 583–605.

"Health Plan Still Popular." *Lake Charles American Press,* January 23, 1994, 1–2.

Henderson, Lenneal J., Jr. "The Impact of Military Base Shutdowns." *Black Scholar* (September 1974): 56–58.

———. "Black Politics and American Presidential Elections." In *The New Black Politics,* 2nd ed., edited by Micheal B. Preston, Lenneal J. Henderson, Jr., and Paul L. Puryear. New York: Longman, 1987.

———. "Fiscal Strategy, Public Policy and the Social Agenda." *Urban League Review* 13 (summer–winter 1989–90): 9–22.

———. "Budget and Tax Strategy: Implications for Blacks." In *The State of Black America 1990,* edited by Janet Dewart. New York: National Urban League, 1990.

Henry, Charles. "Legitimizing Race in Congressional Politics." *American Politics Quarterly* 5 (1977): 149–76.

"Here Are the Final Tallies for President." *St. Petersburg Times,* November 8, 1992.

Hertzke, Allen D. *Echoes of Discontent.* Washington, D.C.: CQ Press, 1993.

Hill, David B., and Norman R. Luttbeg, *Trends in American Electoral Behavior,* 2nd ed. Itasca, Ill.: F. E. Peacock, 1983.

Hinckley, Barbara. *Coalitions and Politics.* New York: Harcourt, Brace, Jovanovich, 1981.

Hirsch, Herbert, and Lewis Donohew. "A Note on Negro-White Differences in Attitudes Toward the Supreme Court." *Social Science Quarterly* 49 (December 1968): 562.

Holmes, Steven A. "Senate Votes to Limit Debate on Provisions of Rights Bill." *New York Times,* July 18, 1990, A17.

———. "Veteran of Rights and Poverty Wars Tastes Bitter Fruit of Many Battles." *New York Times,* September 28, 1990, A10.

"House Backs Quick Passage of Rights Bill." Gerald R. Ford Scrapbooks, 1929–73. Reel 10, Scrapbook 24. Gerald R. Ford Library, Ann Arbor, Michigan.

Huntington, Samuel P. *Political Order in Changing Societies.* New Haven: Yale University Press, 1968.

Ifill, Gwen. "Clinton Appoints Two to Supervise Transition Group." *New York Times,* November 7, 1992.

"Jackson Heaps Praise." *Lake Charles American Press,* November 23, 1992.

"Jackson's Victories in Caucuses Display His Appeal to Whites." *Savannah Morning News,* March 12, 1988, 1A.

Jacobson, Gary C. *The Politics of Congressional Elections,* 3rd ed. Boston: Little, Brown, 1991.

Jacoby, Mary. "Battle Is On for Black Caucus Chair." *Roll Call* 38 (1992): 1, 12.

Joint Center for Political Studies. "An Administration That Looks Like America." *Political Trendletter,* in *Focus,* 21 (April 1993).

Juhnke, William E. "President Truman's Committee on Civil Rights." *Presidential Studies Quarterly* 19 (1989): 593–610.

Katz, Jeffrey L. "Growing Black Caucus May Have New Voice." *Congressional Quarterly Weekly Report* 21 (1993): 5–11.

Kean, Tom. *The Politics of Inclusion.* New York: Free Press, 1988.

Kaplan, Marshall. "Infrastructure Policy: Repetitive Studies, Uneven Response, Next Steps." *Urban Affairs Quarterly* 25 (March 1990): 371–88.

Karnig, Albert K., and Susan Welch. *Black Representation and Urban Policy.* Chicago: University of Chicago Press, 1980.

Kellogg, Charles Flint. *NAACP: A History of the National Association for the Advancement of Colored People, 1909–1920, Vol. 1.* Baltimore: Johns Hopkins University Press, 1967.

Key, V. O., Jr. *Southern Politics in State and Nation, A New Edition.* Knoxville: University of Tennessee Press, 1984.

Kluger, Richard. *Simple Justice.* New York: Alfred A. Knopf, 1976.

Koenig, Louis W. *The Truman Administration.* Westport, Conn.: Greenwood Press, 1979.

Kousser, J. Morgan. *The Shaping of Southern Politics: Suffrage Restriction and the Establishment of the One-Party South, 1880–1910*. New Haven: Yale University Press, 1974.

Krauss, Clifford. "The Old Order Changes in Congress—A Little." *New York Times,* November 8, 1992.

Krislov, Samuel. *The Negro in Federal Employment: The Quest for Equal Opportunity.* Minneapolis: University of Minnesota Press, 1967.

Lambert, Mark. "Texas Litigation Has Bearing on Louisiana Judgeships." *Baton Rouge Morning Advocate,* June 20, 1990.

Lawson, Steven F. *Black Ballots: Voting Rights in the South, 1944–1969.* New York: Columbia University Press, 1976.

Leonard, Paul and Robert Greenstein. *One Step Forward: The Deficit Reduction Package of 1990.* Washington, D.C.: Center on Budget Priorities, 1990.

Lewis, Neil A. "Solicitor General's Career Advances at Intersection of Law and Politics." *New York Times,* June 1, 1990.

———. "Jordan: A Capital Insider with Civil Rights Roots." *New York Times,* November 7, 1992.

Lewinson, Paul. *Race, Class and Party.* New York: Russell and Russell, 1963.

Linder, Robert D., to John Buggs. June 24, 1975. White House Central Files. Gerald R. Ford Library, Ann Arbor, Michigan.

Lipset, Seymour Martin, and Stein Rokkan. "Cleavage Structure, Party Systems, and Voter Alignments: An Introduction." In *Party Systems and Voter Alignments,* edited by Lipset and Rokkan. New York: Free Press, 1967.

Loomis, Burdett A. "Congressional Caucuses and the Politics of Representation." In *Congress Reconsidered,* 2nd ed., edited by Lawrence C. Dodd and Bruce I. Oppenheimer, 204–20. Washington, D.C.: CQ Press, 1981.

Manley, John F. "NeoPluralism: A Class Analysis of Pluralism I and Pluralism II." *American Political Science Review* 77 (1983): 368–83.

Mansbridge, Jane, and Katherine Tate, "Race Trumps Gender: The Thomas Nomination in the Black Community," *PS* 25 (September 1992): 488–91.

Matthews, Donald, and James C. Prothro. *Negroes and the New Southern Politics.* New York: Harcourt, Brace and World, 1966.

McAdam, Doug. *Political Process and the Development of Black Insurgency, 1930–1970.* Chicago: University of Chicago Press, 1982.

McNeil, Genna R. *Groundwork: Charles Hamilton Houston and the Struggle for Civil Rights.* Philadelphia: University of Pennsylvania Press, 1983.

McNutt, Paul V., to Jonathan Daniels. August 12, 1943. Box 10. Official File 4245g. War Manpower Commission. Franklin D. Roosevelt Library, Hyde Park, New York.

McQuaid, John. "Clinton Is Winning Support of La. Democrats." *New Orleans Times-Picayune,* January 27, 1992.

Meier, August, and Elliott Rudwick. "Attorneys Black and White: A Case Study of Race Relations Within the NAACP." *Journal of American History* 62 (March 1976): 913–46.

Mfume, Kweisi. *CSpan* (Broadcast), February 2, 1994.

"Michigan Just the Beginning, Jackson Vows." *Atlanta Constitution.* March 28, 1988, 1A.

Mikesell, John L. *Fiscal Administration: Analysis and Applications for the Public Sector,* 2nd ed. Chicago: Dorsey Press, 1986.

"Missouri Politics Post-Presidential." Box 4. Memoirs File. Harry S Truman Presidential Library, Independence, Missouri.

Moore, Frank, and Stu Eizenstat to the President (Jimmy Carter). September 6, 1977. Box 151. Papers of Stu Eizenstat. Jimmy Carter Library, Atlanta.

Morgan, Ruth P. *The President and Civil Rights.* Lanham, Md.: University Press of America, 1987.

Morris, Aldon. *The Origins of the Civil Rights Movement, Black Communities Organizing for Change.* New York: Free Press, 1984.

Morrison, K. C. Minion. *Black Political Mobilization: Leadership, Power and Mass Behavior.* Albany: State University of New York Press, 1987.

Morrow, E. Frederic. *Black Man in the White House.* New York: Coward-McCann, 1963.

————. Interview by Thomas Soapes, February 23, 1977. Dwight D. Eisenhower Library, Abilene, Kansas.

Mullins, Kerry, and Aaron Wildavsky. "The Procedural Presidency of George Bush." *Political Science Quarterly* 107 (spring 1992): 37.

Murphy, Walter, *Congress and the Court.* Chicago: University of Chicago Press, 1962.

Neely, Anthony. "Government Role in Rooting Out, Remedying Discrimination is Shifting." *National Journal 16,* September 22, 1984, 1772–75.

"New Budget Chairman An Unswerving Fighter." *New York Times,* January 5, 1985, 7.

Newman, Dorothy K., et al. *Protest, Politics and Prosperity: Black Americans and White Institutions, 1940–1975.* New York: Pantheon Books, 1978.

Nie, Norman H., Sidney Verba, and John R. Petrocik. *The Changing American Voter.* Cambridge: Harvard University Press, 1976.

"1948 Campaign." August 17, 1948. Box 21. Papers of Clark M. Clifford. Harry S. Truman Presidential Library, Independence, Missouri.

Olson, Mancur. *The Rise and Decline of Nations.* New Haven: Yale University Press, 1982.

————. *The Logic of Collective Action: Public Goods and the Theory of Groups.* New York: Schocken Books, 1988.

"Open-Housing Law Credited to Mitchell's Lobbying." *Congressional Quarterly Weekly Report 26,* April 26, 1968, 931–34.

"Oral History Interview with E. Frederic Morrow by Dr. Thomas Soapes." February 23, 1977. Dwight D. Eisenhower Library, Abilene, Kansas.

Orman, John. "The President and Interest Group Access." *Presidential Studies Quarterly* 18 (fall 1988): 787–91.

Ovington, Mary White. *The Walls Came Tumbling Down.* New York: Harcourt, Brace and World, 1947.

Palmer, John L., and Isabel V. Sawhill, eds. *The Reagan Record.* Cambridge, Mass.: Ballinger, 1984.

Parent, Wayne, and Paul Stekler, "The Political Implications of Economic Stratification in the Black Community," *Western Political Quarterly* 38 (winter 1985): 521–37.

Parenti, Michael. "Power and Pluralism: A View from the Bottom." *Journal of Politics* 32 (1970): 501–30.

Parmet, Herbert S. "Democratic Party." In *Franklin D. Roosevelt,* edited by Otis L. Graham, Jr., and Meghan Robinson Wander. Boston: G. K. Hall, 1985.

"The Peace Economy: How Defense Cuts Will Fuel America's Long-Term Prosperity." *Business Week,* December 11, 1989, 51.

Perry, Huey L. "Black Participation and Representation in National Energy Policy." In *Contemporary Public Policy Perspectives and Black Americans: Issues in an Era of Retrenchment Politics,* edited by Mitchell F. Rice and Woodrow Jones, Jr. Westport, Conn.: Greenwood Press, 1984.

———. *Democracy and Public Policy: Minority Input into the National Energy Policy of the Carter Administration.* Bristol, Ind.: Wyndham Hall Press, 1985.

———. "Recent Advances in Black Electoral Politics." *PS: Political Science and Politics* 23 (June 1990): 141.

———. "Black Electoral Success in 1989." Symposium. *PS: Political Science and Politics* 23 (June 1990): 141–62.

———. "Pluralist Theory & National Black Politics in the United States." *Polity* 23 (summer 1991): 549–65.

———. "Exploring the Meaning and Implications of Deracialization in African-American Urban Politics." Mini-Symposium, *Urban Affairs Quarterly* 27 (December 1991): 181–215.

Persons, Georgia A. "Reflections on Mayoral Leadership: The Impact of Changing Issues and Changing Times." *Phylon* 41 (September 1985): 205–18.

———. "Blacks in State and Local Government: Progress and Constraints." In *The State of Black America 1987,* edited by Janet Dewart, 167–92. New York: National Urban League, 1987.

———. "The Election of Gary Franks and the Ascendancy of the New Black Conservatives." In *Dilemmas of Black Politics,* edited by Georgia A. Persons. New York: Harper Collins College Publishers, 1993.

Petrocik, John R. "Realignment and the Nationalization of the South." *Journal of Politics* 49 (May 1987): 347–75.

Pickney, Alphonso. *The Myth of Black Progress.* New York: Oxford University Press, 1984.

Pinderhughes, Dianne M. "The President, the Congress, and the Black Community, or Logic and Collective Politics." Paper presented at the annual meeting of the Midwest Political Science Association, Chicago, 1979.

———. "Collective Goods and Black Interest Groups." *Review of Black Political Economy* 12 (winter 1983): 219–36.

———. *Race and Ethnicity in Chicago Politics.* Urbana: University of Illinois Press, 1986.

———. *Race and Ethnicity in Chicago Politics: A Reexamination of Pluralist Theory.* Urbana: University of Illinois Press, 1987.

Pohlmann, Marcus D. *Black Politics in Conservative America.* New York: Longman, 1990.

"Poll: Jackson's Run for Office Caused White Resentment." *Clarion-Ledger.* August 31, 1984, 3A.

Polsby, Nelson W., and Aaron Wildavsky. *Presidential Elections.* New York: Free Press, 1988.

Pomper, Gerald M. "The Presidential Election." In *The Election of 1980,* edited by Gerald M. Pomper. Chatham, N.J.: Chatham House, 1981.

———. "The Presidential Election." In *The Election of 1988,* edited by Gerald M. Pomper. Chatham, N. J.: Chatham House, 1989.

———. "The Presidential Nominations." In *The Election of 1988.* Chatham, N. J.: Chatham House, 1989.

Poole, Keith T. "Dimensions of Interest Group Evaluation of the U.S. Senate, 1969–1978." *American Journal of Political Science* 25 (1981): 49–67.

"Portrait of the Electorate." *New York Times,* November 5, 1992.

"The Power Broker." *Newsweek,* March 21, 1988.

President (Harry S. Truman) to Bill Boyle. "Democratic Presidential Campaign in Virginia." April 28, 1949. Box 1. Papers of William Boyle, Jr. Harry S. Truman Presidential Library, Independence, Missouri.

Preston, Michael B. "The Election of Harold Washington: An Examination of the SES Model in the 1983 Chicago Mayoral Election." In *The New Black Politics: The Search for Political Power,* 2nd ed., edited by Michael B. Preston, Lenneal J. Henderson, Jr., and Paul L. Puryear. New York: Longman, 1987.

Ranier, Drew, to Southwest Louisiana Steering Committee and Workers. Memorandum. 1992.

Reed, Adolph L. *The Jesse Jackson Phenomenon.* New Haven: Yale University Press, 1986.

Renka, Russell D. "Comparing Presidents Kennedy and Johnson as Legislative Leaders." *Presidential Studies Quarterly* 15 (1985): 806–25.

"Rights Bill Is Approved by House." *New Orleans Times-Picayune,* June 6, 1991.

Riker, William H. *The Theory of Political Coalitions.* New Haven: Yale University Press, 1962.

Rivlin, Benjamin, ed. *Ralph Bunche: The Man and His Times.* New York: Holmes and Meier, 1990.

Roberts, S. V. "Blacks in Congress Are Branching Out." *New York Times,* June 22, 1986, sect. 4, 4.

Robinson, Pearl T. "Whither the Future of Blacks in the Republican Party?" *Political Science Quarterly* 97 (summer 1982): 207–31.

Rockman, Bert A. Private correspondence, May 21,1991.

Rose, Doug, and Paul Stekler. "Validated Turnout and Jesse Jackson Primary Victory in Louisiana." Unpublished manuscript, 1989.

Rosenbaum, David E. "What Can Clinton Change and When?" *New York Times,* November 8, 1992.

Sabato, Larry J. *The Democratic Party Primary.* Charlottesville: University Press of Virginia, 1977.

Sacton, Frank. "Financing Public Programs Under Fiscal Constraint." In *Managing Programs: Balancing Politics, Administration, and Public Needs,* edited by Robert E. Cleary and Nicholas Henry. San Francisco: Jossey-Bass, 1989.

Salisbury, Robert H. "An Exchange Theory of Interest Groups." *Midwest Journal of Political Science* 13 (February 1969): 1–32.

Schattschneider, E. E. *The Semi-Sovereign People: A Realistic View of Democracy in America.* Hinsdale, Ill.: Dryden Press, 1975.

Schneider, William. "Bush, the GOP, and the Black Voter." *National Journal* 26 (May 1990).

Schuman, Howard, Charlotte Steeh, and Lawrence Bobo, *Racial Attitudes in America: Trends and Interpretations.* Cambridge: Harvard University Press, 1985.

Senate Judiciary Committee. *Voting Rights Extension, Report of the Committee on the Judiciary.* Washington, D.C.: Government Printing Office, 1982.

Shaffer, William R. "John F. Kennedy and the Liberal Establishment: Presidential Politics and Civil Rights Legislation in 1957." Paper presented at the Fourth Annual Presidential Conference, Hofstra University, Hempstead, New York, 1985.

Shapiro, Martin. *Freedom of Speech: The Supreme Court and Judicial Review.* Englewood Cliffs, N.J.: Prentice Hall, 1966.

Shingles, Richard D. "Black Consciousness and Political Participation: The Missing Link." *American Political Science Review* 75 (March 1981): 76–91.

Sifry, Micah L. "Jesse and the Jews: Palestine and the Struggle for the Democratic Party." *Middle East Report* 18 (November–December 1988).

Sinclair, Barbara. "Agenda and Alignment Change." In *Congress Reconsidered,* edited by Lawrence C. Dodd and Bruce Oppenheimer. Washington, D.C.: CQ Press, 1981.

———. *Congressional Realignment, 1925–1978.* Austin: University of Texas Press, 1982.

———. *Majority Leadership in the U.S. House.* Baltimore: Johns Hopkins University Press, 1983.

Sitkoff, Harvard. *The Struggle for Black Equality.* New York: Hill & Wang, 1981.

Smith, J. Owens. "Affirmative Action, Reverse Discrimination and the Court:

Implications for Blacks." In *Contemporary Public Policy Perspectives and Black Americans: Issues in an Era of Retrenchment Politics,* edited by Mitchell F. Rice and Woodrow Jones. Westport, Conn.: Greenwood Press, 1984.

Smith, J. Owens, Mitchell F. Rice, and Woodrow Jones, Jr. *Black and American Government.* Dubuque: Kendall Hunt, 1987.

Smith, Robert. "Black Power and the Transformation from Protest to Politics." *Political Science Quarterly* 96 (fall 1981): 431–43.

Smith, Steven S. *Call to Order: Floor Politics in the House and Senate.* Washington, D.C.: Brookings Institution, 1989.

Smith, Steven S., and Christopher J. Deering. *Committees in Congress,* 2nd ed. Washington, D.C.: CQ Press, 1990.

Smothers, Ronald. "A New Diversity for Congress's Black Caucus." *New York Times,* November 10, 1992, 9.

Sniderman, Paul. *Race and Inequality: A Study in American Values.* Chatham, N.J.: Chatham House, 1985.

Sniffen, Michael J. "Boston Lawyer Nominated for Civil Rights Job." *Baton Rouge Morning Advocate,* February 2, 1994.

Stanley, Harold W., and Richard G. Niemi. *Vital Statistics on American Politics.* Washington, D.C.: CQ Press, 1988.

State of Small Business, 1989. Washington, D.C.: U.S. Government Printing Office, 1989.

Stern, Mark. "Black Interest Group Pressure on the Executive: John F. Kennedy as Politician." Paper presented at the annual meeting of the American Political Science Association, Chicago, 1987.

———. *Calculating Visions: Kennedy, Johnson, and Civil Rights.* New Brunswick, N.J.: Rutgers University Press, 1992.

Strickland, Arvarh. *The History of the Chicago Urban League.* Urbana: University of Illinois Press, 1966.

Sundquist, James L. *Dynamics of the Party System.* Washington, D.C.: Brookings Institution, 1973.

"Super Tuesday." *Atlanta Constitution.* March 10, 1988, 13A.

Swain, Carol M. "Changing Patterns of African-American Representation in Congress." In *The Atomistic Congress: An Interpretation of Congressional Change,* edited by Alan D. Hertzke and Ronald M. Peters, 107–42. Armonk, N.Y.: M. E. Sharpe, 1992.

———. *Black Faces, Black Interests: The Representation of African Americans in Congress.* Cambridge: Harvard University Press, 1993.

Tate, Katherine. *From Protest to Politics: The New Black Voters in American Elections.* Cambridge: Harvard University Press, 1993.

Tryman, Mfanya Donald. "Race and Presidential Campaigns and Elections: The 1984 Democratic Primaries." In *Institutional Racism and Black America,* edited by Tryman. Lexington, Mass.: Ginn Press, 1985.

Trike, Laurence H. "The Curvatures of Constitutional Space: What Lawyers

Can Learn from Modern Physics." *Howard Law Review* 103 (November 1989): 1–39.

Tucker, Cynthia. "Race Is the Silent Issue in Presidential Campaign." *Atlanta Journal and Constitution,* March 12, 1988, 21A.

United States Commission on Civil Rights. *Fair Housing and the Law* 6 (1973).

U. S. Congress. House of Representatives. Committee on the Judiciary. "Voting Rights Hearings Before Subcommittee Number 5 on HR 6400." 89th Congress, 1st sess. March 18–April 1, 1956. Washington, D. C.: U.S. Government Printing Office, 1965.

U. S. Congress. House of Representatives. Committee on the Judiciary. "Voting Rights Act Extension: Hearing Before Subcommittee Number 5 on HR 4249, HR 5538, and similar proposals." 91st Congress, 1st sess. May 14–July 1, 1969. Serial no. 3. Washington, D.C.: U.S. Government Printing Office, 1969.

U. S. Congress. House of Representatives. Committee on the Judiciary. "Extension of the Voting Rights Act, Hearings Before the Subcommittee on Civil and Constitutional Rights on HR 939, HR 2148, HR 3247, HR 3501, and other extensions of the Voting Rights Act." 94th Congress, 1st sess. February 25–March 25, 1975. Serial no. 1, part 1. Washington, D.C.: U.S. Government Printing Office, 1975.

U. S. Congress. House of Representatives. Committee on the Judiciary. "Extension of the Voting Rights Act, Hearings Before the Subcommittee on Civil and Constitutional Rights." 97th Congress, 1st sess. May 6–July 13, 1981. Serial no. 24. Washington, D.C.: U.S. Government Printing Office, 1982.

United States Department of Energy. *Functional Interrelationships of the Office of Minority Economic Impact.* Washington, D.C.: U.S. Government Printing Office, 1989.

United States President. "Reaffirming Policy of Full Participation in the Defense Program by All Persons, Regardless of Race, Creed, Color or National Origin and Directing Certain Action in Furtherance of Said Policy." Executive Order 8802. June 25, 1941, 3 *Code of Federal Regulations* 956, 1938–43 compilation. Washington, D.C.: Government Printing Office, 1968.

Uzzell, Lawrence A. "The Unsung Hero of the Reagan Revolution." *National Review,* December 9, 1988.

Verba, Sidney. "Democratic Participation." *Annals* 373 (September 1967): 54.

Verba, Sidney, and Norman Nie. *Participation in America.* New York: Harper and Row, 1972.

"The Votes in the 1948 Election." In *History of American Presidential Elections Volume IV 1940–1968,* edited by Arthur M. Schlesinger, Jr. New York: Chelsea House, 1971.

Walters, Ronald W. "The Emergent Mobilization of the Black Community in the Jackson Campaign for President." In *Jesse Jackson's 1984 Presidential Campaign,* edited by Lucius J. Barker and Ronald W. Walters. Urbana and Chicago: University of Illinois Press, 1989.

Walton, Hanes, Jr. *Black Politics: A Theoretical and Structural Analysis.* Philadelphia: J. B. Lippincott, 1972.

———. *Invisible Politics.* Albany: State University of New York Press, 1985.

———. *When the Marching Stopped: The Politics of Civil Rights Regulatory Agencies.* Albany: State University of New York Press, 1988.

Ware, Gilbert. *William Hastie.* New York: Oxford University Press, 1984.

Wasby, Stephen L. "The NAACP and the NAACP Legal Defense Fund: Preliminary Observations on Conflict Between Allies." Unpublished manuscript, n.d.

Washington Post, March 15, 1968, A4.

Watson, Denton L. *Lion in the Lobby, Clarence Mitchell, Jr.'s Struggle for the Passage of Civil Rights.* New York: William Morrow, 1990.

Wayne, Stephen J. *The Road to the White House.* New York: St. Martin's Press, 1980.

Weaver, Robert C. to Jonathan Daniels. September 4 , 1943. Box 10, Official File 4245g. War Manpower Commission. Franklin D. Roosevelt Library, Hyde Park, New York.

Weekly Compilation of Presidential Documents. Administration of William J. Clinton, September 18, 1993.

Weiss, Nancy J. *Farewell to the Party of Lincoln.* Princeton: Princeton University Press, 1983.

Welch, Susan, and Michael Combs. "Intra-Racial Differences in Attitudes of Blacks: Class or Consensus." *Phylon* 2 (winter 1985): 91–97.

Welch, Susan, and Lorn Foster. "Class and Conservatism in the Black Community." *American Politics Quarterly* 15 (October 1987): 334–470.

Welch, Susan, and Lee Sigelman. "A Black Gender Gap?" *Social Science Quarterly* 70 (May 1989): 120–33.

Whalen, Charles, and Barbara Whalen. *The Longest Debate: A Legislative History of the 1964 Civil Rights Act.* New York: New American Library, 1985.

White House Central Files. Gerald R. Ford Library, Ann Arbor, Michigan.

Wildavsky, Aaron. "Political Implications of Budget Reform." *Public Administration Review* 21 (January–February 1961).

———. "Political Implications of Budget Reform: A Retrospective." *Public Administration Review* 52 (November–December 1992).

Wilson, James Q. *Negro Politics: The Search for Leadership.* New York: Free Press, 1960.

———. *Political Organizations.* New York: Basic Books, 1973.

Wilson, William J. *The Declining Significance of Race.* Chicago: University of Chicago Press, 1980.

"Without Sacrifice." *Economist* 328, no. 7823 (1993): 25.

Wolman, Harold L., and Norman C. Thomas. "Black Interests, Black Groups, and Black Influence in the Federal Policy Process: The Cases of Housing and Education." *Journal of Politics* 32 (November 1970): 875–97.

Woodward, C. Vann. *The Strange Career of Jim Crow,* 3rd rev. ed. New York: Oxford University Press, 1966.

Wright, Gerald, Jr. "Racism and Welfare Policy in America." *Social Science Quarterly* 57 (March 1977): 718–30.

Wright, John W., ed. *The Universal Almanac 1991.* Kansas City and New York: Universal Press Syndicate Company, 1990.

Zipp, John F. "Did Jesse Jackson Cause a White Blacklash Against the Democrats? A Look at the 1984 Presidential Election." In *Jesse Jackson's 1984 Presidential Campaign,* edited by Lucius J. Barker and Ronald W. Walters. Urbana and Chicago: University of Illinois Press, 1989.

Zuckman, Jill. "All the Right Moves." *Congressional Quarterly Weekly Report* 50 (1992): 3786.

★ Index